Stephen Armstrong writes for th.... ....Out, *Wallpaper** and *Men's Health*. He ....s to Radio 4's *Front Row* whenever they let him.... past he has, like all young men, wanted to be a pilot, played in a band and thought about building bridges in Third World villages. He has also promoted one or two genuinely disastrous club nights. This is his first book.

The White Island

TWO THOUSAND YEARS OF PLEASURE IN IBIZA

STEPHEN ARMSTRONG

CORGI BOOKS

THE WHITE ISLAND
A CORGI BOOK : 0 552 77189 9

Originally published in Great Britain by Bantam Press,
a division of Transworld Publishers

PRINTING HISTORY
Bantam Press edition published 2004
Corgi edition published 2005

1 3 5 7 9 10 8 6 4 2

Set in Berling by
Falcon Oast Graphic Art Ltd.

Corgi Books are published by Transworld Publishers,
61–63 Uxbridge Road, London W5 5SA,
a division of The Random House Group Ltd,
in Australia by Random House Australia (Pty) Ltd,
20 Alfred Street, Milsons Point, Sydney, NSW 2061, Australia,
in New Zealand by Random House New Zealand Ltd,
18 Poland Road, Glenfield, Auckland 10, New Zealand
and in South Africa by Random House (Pty) Ltd,
Endulini, 5a Jubilee Road, Parktown 2193, South Africa.

The Random House Group Limited supports The Forest Stewardship
Council (FSC®), the leading international forest certification organisation.
Our books carrying the FSC label are printed on FSC® certified paper.
FSC is the only forest certification scheme endorsed by the leading
environmental organisations, including Greenpeace. Our
paper procurement policy can be found at
www.randomhouse.co.uk/environment

MIX
Paper from
responsible sources
FSC® C018072

Printed and bound in Great Britain by Clays Ltd, St Ives PLC

For Georgia

Acknowledgements

Most authors start their lists of acknowledgements with thanks to agents and editors. I didn't understand why until I wrote this book. Entirely correctly, therefore, my first thank-yous are to the utterly brilliant Cat Ledger and Doug Young.

I would also like to thank all the people on Ibiza who gave up their time without thought of reward – Sue Bennison, Benjami Costa Ribas, Juan Lluis Ferrer, Marina Nixon, Sally Wilson, Pere Palau Torres, Juan Mari Serra, Rafael Costa Bonet, Danny Speigel, Jorge Alonso, Daniel Villedieu, Andy, Mike, Dawn and Claire at Manumission, Sandy Pratt, Colin Casbolt, Cushan Thomas, Danny Whittle, James Cooper, Tony Pike, Richard Lawson and especially Martin Davies and Emily Kaufman, whose books *Eivissa-Ibiza: A Hundred Years of Light and Shade* and *A History Buff's Guide to Ibiza* ought to be required reading for anyone interested in the White Island. Julie Savill at the Cowcross Street branch of Flight Centre got me there and back for a remarkably small sum.

Elsewhere, Gloria Mound, Director of the Institute for Marrano-Anusim Studies in Israel, supplied reams of information on Ibiza's Jewish population. In the UK, Jonathan Tubbs at the British Museum, Dr Michael Brett at the

School of Oriental and African Studies, Dr Ulrich Lehmann at the Victoria and Albert Museum, Peter Lyth at the Christel DeHaan Tourism and Travel Research Institute at Nottingham University Business School and Chris Hewlett at 5th Element all provided expert assistance. Anything factually inaccurate is my fault but I'd prefer it if you complained to them.

I'd also like to thank Richard Benson, Helen Hawkins, Alkarim Jivani, Richard Cook, John Ville, Tyler Brûlé, Britta Jaschinski, James Herring and Edward Waller.

My greatest debt, however, is owed to Georgia – for reading every word of every edit, making all the right suggestions and generally supporting me while she had more than enough on her own plate. Thank you is not enough.

Contents

Prologue   1

1. The Sea   11

2. The Goddess   30

3. The White Stuff   58

4. The Senator   89

5. The Poet   107

6. The Pirate   128

7. The Artist   152

8. The War   164

9. The Faker   197

10. The Hippies   227

11. The Host   251

12. The Hotel   275

13. The DJ   302

14. The End   327

Picture Credits   332

Index   333

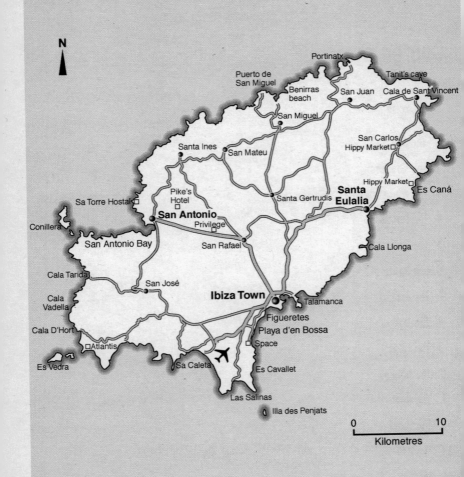

Prologue

It all started when the flames hit the water and floated out into the harbour, as if a dragon were breathing across the sea. I sat with James on the rickety chairs of a steak 'n' eggs and full English breakfast all-night café in Ibiza which was still packed with rollicking families at three in the morning. James was involved in composing a lager-fuelled haiku about the flames and his own family – 'I love these fireworks and I love my wife' – and, filled with the pleasure of the weekend, I had to agree. By any standards, these fireworks were pretty special.

They lit up the towering walls of the immense eighteenth-century fortress that looms over the harbour with an almost magical light. In the flash and bang of the display, you could imagine the castle was under sustained attack from a disorganized wizard whose conjured pyrotechnics bounced around the artificial bay in an absent-minded way while he leafed through his spell book to find the killer incantation.

And there must have been some sort of sorcery involved in this display. It was doing things that fireworks just didn't do. It was even doing things the laws of physics shouldn't allow. Fire fountained down the harbour wall onto the

Mediterranean, but it wasn't extinguished. Instead floating flames spread out across the water like a fleet of tiny Chinese junks. And that was just for starters.

Glowing embers flew into the air and danced in patterns around the night sky, as if a minor god were writing his name with multi-coloured sparklers. Devices that seemed to be Catherine wheels suddenly jumped up and flew off towards the castle walls. Tiny sparks blossomed into opulent flowers in the sky. Dancing, magical lights tripped across the harbour. Whoever was behind this display must have been some sort of practitioner in the dark arts, having swapped his immortal soul for control over the Devil's own elements. He was Gandalf, Willy Wonka and Faust all rolled into one, performing in front of us to the limits of his considerable ability for some nefarious purpose impossible to fathom.

Looking around me at the crowds gathered on the water-front to ooh and aah at the incandescence, I noticed a strange air of calm Spanish contentment spread across the assembled Anglo-Saxon throng. Being British, they were still cuffing their kids, belching and calling one another names, but there was a note of warm affection in the expletives that flew between strangers. It seemed to me that they were only one insult away from falling on one another's necks and weeping with joy. Although they might want to get their sunburn seen to first.

It made me think how happy the British would be if only we'd been able to shift our rock a few hundred miles south. Perhaps it wasn't too late? With a big saw and some oars? We could ask the Scots to build some sort of giant engine. I mean, they've always been a bit useful in the engineering department. Then we could park up next to Ibiza's tiny coastline and melt into the Balearic vortex of charm. And I don't mean charm as in 'nice smile and quite generous at getting the drinks in', I mean the arcane definition of faerie charm – to bewitch and fascinate as if by supernatural powers.

Take the old town, for instance, which was putting in such sterling service as a backdrop to the maelstrom of airborne explosions. To the ceaseless tide of tourists ebbing and flowing around the Marina it was only an elaborate stage set for the real show of whiz-bangs and sparkles. If they gave it a thought, they probably found it slightly confusing that the town was also called Ibiza, sharing its name with the island and leading to slightly panicky moments when first gazing on a road sign – IBIZA 10KM. 'But I thought we were already on Ibiza!' (Expats solve the problem by referring to Ibiza Town.)

These careless tourists are missing something. Deep in the foundations of Ibiza's towering cathedral – dedicated, in a curious piece of Ibicenco logic, to Santa María de las Neus, or Mary of the Snows, the patron saint of an island with over three hundred days of unbroken sunshine a year – a dark history lurks. The cathedral was imposed on the ruins of Ibiza's largest mosque by victorious Catalan Christians after they had forced through the citadel's supposedly impenetrable walls. Beneath the fragments of the mosque that remain lies the dust of a Roman temple to Mercury, the messenger of the gods. And beneath that ancient site lies a Carthaginian temple of unknown provenance that belonged to one of the gods beloved of the island's favourite Carthaginian deity, Tanit.

Tanit was the Carthaginian goddess of sexuality, a

voluptuous and sensual creature often portrayed sitting cross-legged as if meditating, lightly draped in folded, diaphanous garments that did little to cover her full, womanly figure. She was the first patron goddess of the island and an altogether more earthy protector than Mary of the Snows. The warmth of her tactile reputation, which encouraged a physical ritual of worship more recently imitated in the kind of orgiastic suburban parties that used to excite tabloid readers in the 1970s, was balanced by her other role as the goddess of death.

This sex-and-death duality provided a ready-made propaganda weapon for the Greeks, who hated the Carthaginians. They told stories of human sacrifices to Tanit including children and young virgins, and claimed that her priests practised prostitution from her temples. Tanit's worship is supposed to have died out when the Romans took Ibiza from the Carthaginians after Ibiza's first conquering son Hannibal failed to sack the eternal city. But in a way she has never left the island.

Guidebooks urge the casual visitor to keep an eye out for Ibiza's many village festivals where a curious local dance, the *ball pagés*, is something of a holiday treat. The dances take place near wells and streams and fountains – anywhere where water flows – and consist of strange, formalized, sexually charged steps that seem, ever so slightly, to resemble flamenco. In fact, these dances pre-date nineteenth-century flamenco by over two thousand years. Essentially they are fertility rites left over from Tanit's rituals of worship, and they hint at the kind of libidinous exchange between man and woman that must have made the weekly service slightly more exciting than the sip of wine and mouthful of wafer Mary's mass offers today.

But Tanit's legacy may be more potent than the tradition of a simple country dance. Cast your eyes back a paragraph or so and see that reference to the Christians storming the supposedly impregnable walls of Ibiza's citadel. Ibiza fell to the Catalans in 1235 after a sustained and brutal campaign that marked the tail end of the expulsion of the Moors. But the conquest of the powerful fortress surrounding the mosque was always going to be a tricky business.

The Catalan army, under Jaume I, had fought its way across the island's two hundred square miles and had left to last the capture of the citadel. The Moorish king who governed it had a reputation as a dogged warrior and, if he held out long enough, could have called in reinforcements from northern Africa. Jaume, not to put too fine a point on it, wasn't looking forward to the battle at all. The king, however, had problems of his own. His brother had fallen in love with a slave girl from the king's harem – a particular favourite for her sensual abilities in the highly specialized skills of the harem – and had fled with her.

The story has two endings, or perhaps it's better to describe them as the same ending with two different explanations. One version has it that the fleeing brother opened a secret entrance to the town and allowed the besieging Catalan forces to flood through undetected. The other has it that the king was so distressed at the loss of his slave girl that he failed to notice the approaching Spanish troops, as he was blinded by his streaming tears.

I prefer the second story, but the evidence supports the first. At least, there is an ancient secret entrance to the town in the Calle de San Ciriaco, now sadly fenced off to the public; and it is rather pushing it to suggest that the king didn't own a handkerchief. Whatever the reason, the Catalans took the town swiftly and the king didn't live long enough to regret falling under the power of this most beautiful sexual servant. Perhaps he thought – just briefly – of the goddess of sex and death as the Catalan steel bit home.

It's probably fair to say that most tourists don't give Tanit a thought when they arrive on the island. As James and I gazed up at the firework finale, however, they were preparing, in their own sweet way, to indulge in rituals of her worship all around us. Couples kissed and courted, either clamped to each other's faces like devouring aliens or just walking and holding hands along the walls of the marina. It felt right and proper that they should look so happy out here. The night was warm and the wind was soft. The music from the cafés was, admittedly, a little relentless with its pounding bass drum, but the mood of the harbour enveloped me slowly. I thought good thoughts about the world, feeling at one with beauty and truth and life and love, and it was in that mood that I heard the story of the Vanishing Boy drifting over from the next-door table.

James had fallen into conversation with a group of bronzed backpackers whose accents, like Ibiza, mixed influences from all over the world. Australia and South Yorkshire seemed to dominate as they debated how spiritual Ibiza used to be compared to its modern-day reputation for all-out, rampaging, no-prisoners hedonism. One girl in particular was taken with the idea that the island exerted a powerful magnetic force on those who strayed onto its shores. It was as if Ibiza were a kind of Bermuda Triangle of pleasure, and she felt that the legend of the boy who came and stayed illustrated this perfectly.

He was supposed to be a young lad, maybe from a northern town, maybe from Australia, and he'd come to the island with a group of friends. Perhaps it was his brother's stag night, or perhaps it was a summer holiday. Whatever it was, the boy didn't want to go home. He had supped so deeply from the cup of joy that he couldn't imagine returning to his miserable life in a high-rise concrete city with a job that slowly stole his life away. So when his friend went home, the boy, so the story goes, remained in Ibiza. In some accounts he actually lived in a nightclub; in others he headed out to the hills, joined a commune or lived on the beach. He slept during the day, stealing food and drinks and drugs when he came out in the evening. He washed in toilets, picked up discarded jumpers and jackets to dress himself and basically lived a feral existence in the heart of Ibizan clubland. Sometimes you could see him when you went about the town, the girl said, finishing her story. He was the young blond boy with the long, straggly hair who usually danced alone on the podium.

We sat there in silence, James and I, long after the back-packers had departed. We looked out to sea and sipped coffee, and I was in a sort of daze. For some reason the story had a profound effect on me. It seemed at once appealing and repellent. Coming at the end of a rare weekend of un-fettered misbehaviour, it forced me to stop and think. About the boy, about the island, but mainly about me.

I'd lived all my life doing the right thing. I'd carefully balanced responsibility with pleasure. However large I lived on Saturday night, I was always at work on Monday morning. Submitting yourself completely to a life of wild, hedonistic joy – it seemed so dangerously irresponsible. Devoting every waking moment to having fun, getting food when you needed it and drinks from the kindness of strangers ... well, how could you? Didn't you need discipline to function? Doesn't the human brain need pain as well as pleasure? Wouldn't you inevitably go mad?

Once, just before I embarked on my GCSEs, I brought home from school a particularly grim report card. My mum, who was a teacher, lost her temper with me. She took me around the house, pointing out all the consumer durables my parents had worked so hard to acquire – the television, the stereo, even the garbage-munching waste disposal unit. We ended our tour in the kitchen. 'How do you think we afforded them?' She was almost shouting. 'We worked for them! You can't sit about all your life and expect these things to just come to you. What do you want from your life, Stephen, eh? What do you want?' I knew she needed an answer that would reassure her, an answer that dripped with ambition or promise, but I couldn't think of one. I felt the pressure of exams and parental expectation sitting on my young shoulders and, miserably, sure that it would only inflame her anger, I told her the truth. 'I want to be happy,' I said. It was the wrong answer. 'Happy!' she screamed at me. 'Happy? Who's happy? No-one's happy. Life isn't about being happy.'

Sitting on Ibiza Town harbour, looking out into the still waters of the Mediterranean – the very waters that barely an hour ago had carried a display of magical fire that drifted across the ancient port like a flotilla of Elven adventurers – I thought, 'Well, Mum, you got me. I fought like the Devil, but in the end you got me. I work hard. I stay late. I've got a TV. I've got a house. And you know what? You were right. I'm not happy.'

But I felt happy tonight, albeit briefly. I could almost feel rocks being lifted from my shoulders. Ibiza does that to people. When the Carthaginians discovered the island, they knew there was something about the place. They felt it was holy, that it could regenerate damaged people, that it was a haven for the weary and the sick. But they also felt that it was a place of pleasure. They named the island after their god of dancing, Bes, and he sat beside Tanit in the island's esteem. Since then, everyone who has come to Ibiza has found joy and respite. The Romans, the Vandals, the Arabs, the Catalans, Jews fleeing both Spanish and Nazi persecution, Americans fleeing the draft and Brits fleeing, well, Britain – they've all come here and found a smile flitting across their tired, grim faces as their feet touch Ibiza's red soil. They landed as refugees and gradually vanished themselves, drifting into the island, living with the Ibicencos and forgetting the grim reality they left behind.

And the island has always welcomed them. When Spain's Jews fled the inquisitions of the fifteenth and sixteenth centuries, they found refuge on Ibiza though they were beaten and murdered on Mallorca, just eighty miles to the east. Even today the reckless hedonism of Ibiza's tourists takes place under the cool, considered eyes of the Ibicencos, who smile politely and treat us with great kindness and charm but seem to have their minds on higher things. It feels as if we are all of us, refugees and holidaymakers alike, fourteen-year-old schoolboys on an outward-bound adventure holiday chaperoned indulgently by sixth formers who know far more about life than we ever could. Or perhaps the UFO spotters have it right: perhaps they are kindly aliens who have returned to Earth to show us the error of our ways. Their wisdom is infinite and their patience a lot bigger than that.

Suddenly I knew what I had to do. I wanted to find all the Vanished Boys: the Vietnam vets, the last, defiant hippies, the clubbers who never went home, the actors who came to love and stayed to die and the celebrities who could find some sort of anonymity on an island that doesn't care who you are. I wanted to ask them how they had done it, how they found the life they were now living. Had the island delivered what it had promised? Had my mother been wrong? And, most importantly, was there time for *me* to change? So that's what I did. I went to find them.

CHAPTER 1

The Sea

Which is why, a few hours before midnight on a day towards the end of May 2003, I was slumped over the bar on a slightly rusty tramp ferry ploughing its way across the Mediterranean to Ibiza, talking to the barman about Noah.

Taking the ferry to Ibiza had been a matter of necessity. I hadn't been able to get a flight. Every single charter and scheduled flight seat to the island had been taken for the entire three days leading up to the bank holiday weekend. 'It's the war and SARS,' said Julie, the cheery Aussie who was sorting out my tickets. 'Everyone's going to Ibiza instead of Thailand or New York. You could try getting a ferry.'

A ferry . . . the thought wandered through my mind. A ferry – but of course! Almost everyone who mattered in the island's history had arrived by boat, from seafaring Phoenicians to 1950s jazzmen and artists. It would be a sort of ritual, a return – nay, a homage – to the island's seafaring past. I would stand on the windswept deck and watch as a dark smudge rose over the horizon, just as those early adventurers had done almost three thousand years ago. Is it a man-of-war? Some dark threat from the depths? No, sir, it's land, by God.

'Book it,' I told her.

'It's a nine-hour journey, overnight, and you dock at six a.m.,' she warned me, and for a moment my resolve wavered. Nine hours? On a boat? Overnight? Six a.m.? But then she told me I'd have to fly out to Barcelona the night before and my doubts vanished. Twenty-four hours in Barcelona, a city I'd never visited but had always felt would be my natural home. I even supported its football team in a half-hearted sort of way. I didn't check the results or anything, but I liked the fact that the club was owned by the fans and turned down commercial sponsors out of a fierce Catalan pride. My friend Al had once drunk so much absinthe on the Ramblas that he'd imagined a man was kissing his wife and punched him, only to find it was a mirror. That sounded like the kind of town I needed to experience. 'I can get you a hotel near the docks, but it's pretty cheap,' Julie went on, and I almost kissed her. A cheap dockside hotel – let's call it an inn – was something I'd read about in nineteenth-century adventure novels but never dreamed I'd actually stay in. The Ramblas, Barcelona's former red-light district and one of the few places in Europe (alongside Ibiza) you have always been able to buy absinthe, would be just a few hundred yards away. The inn was bound to have a low ceiling and to possess a bar stuffed with swarthy Lascars, if only I knew what they were. It would be the ideal send-off.

'The adventure begins,' I said as I boarded the flight.

Sadly, it was all a grave disappointment. The Ramblas was no densely packed, baroque-style narrow street lined with whores on balconies and gap-toothed anarchists. Instead it was a gallery of overpriced street cafés and the usual collection of portrait-while-you-wait scamsters who operate in the public spaces of every urban centre in the world. Not that Barcelona isn't a beautiful place; it's just that I'd steeled myself for the Limehouse of Sherlock Holmes and instead got a pretty Spanish city with a nice waterfront development. By the time my boat was due to leave, I was happy to climb aboard.

Here's a traveller's tip for you: if you plan to catch a ferry in Barcelona, get a taxi to the ferry terminal. It's difficult to see how much harder they could have made it to walk there. Fences, blocked streets and a complete absence of signposts meant I began to panic as I grappled my way along the industrial dockside. Short of having the entire staff of Trasmediterránea Ferries shower me with breezeblocks as I picked my way across the eight-lane motorway and building-site debris that surrounded the place, they seemed to have done everything possible to discourage me. When I finally arrived in the vast square concrete building where I was to check in, I was drenched in sweat and eager to get to my cabin to sluice off from my slightly pink flesh the thin layer of dust I'd picked up in the last five minutes.

I'd booked a cabin on Julie's advice. The other option was a seat and, although I'm as ready for cutlass-between-the-teeth adventure as the next man, nine hours tossing and turning on an orange plastic chair when a cabin to myself could be secured for a miserly sum made no sense to me. Thus I proudly stepped up to the cabin check-in and presented the man behind the counter with my ticket and a cheery grin. 'Good evening, my good man,' the grin clearly said, 'I am keen to board your fine vessel and take my place at the captain's table. Here's my paperwork. Let us dispense with the formalities and allow me to carry my dusty rucksack aboard.'

'Sí. Tú eres . . .' There was a pause as he read my ticket. 'Oh. Armstrong.' He sounded slightly disgusted. 'You want a cabin?' He looked hard at my ticket, which had seemed so legal and reassuring when I'd purchased it in London and had retained its official feel until roughly a minute earlier when it had suddenly begun to look like a strip of carbon paper with red biro marks scrawled on it. 'You have to pay the difference.'

'But I have paid,' I said, trying to convert sterling into euros and looking in my pack for any helpful bits of paper from Southern Ferries, who had issued the ticket in the UK. All I could find was a photocopied sheet offering to sell me Southern Ferries travel insurance. 'I've paid . . .' (Long pause.) 'A hundred and sixty euros . . .' (I hadn't, I'd paid a lot less, but maths was never my strong point.)

He looked doubtfully at me and at the ticket then went off and spoke in very rapid Spanish to a group of uniformed men at the back of the office. They all came forward and stood around a computer, typing different things into it and occasionally laughing in a way I found disconcerting. Then he came back and contemptuously wrote out a boarding pass for a cabin. 'Upstairs. Gate one,' he said, and looked over my shoulder at the Spanish Goths behind me.

The boat was a large tramp car ferry that ploughed daily between Barcelona and the Balearics. It was decorated in a functional, institutional white, with basic fittings and metal bulkheads. It was a long way from the *Titanic*. At some point, however, perhaps in the glory days of the 1960s when the route had been one of the most fashionable and glittering in Europe, the boat had taken on certain cruise-ship ambitions. Looking at the map of the craft pinned to the wall outside my cabin, for instance, I noticed that the bar was indicated by a martini glass complete with straw and olive, and that, insanely, there appeared to be a swimming pool on the upper rear deck. (I realize I may not be using the correct technical term for that part of the boat, but I am to sailing what Mikhail Gorbachev was to belly dancing – amusing to look at but you'd rather not get too closely involved.)

Having checked into my cabin – two bunks, warm sea-water shower, disinfected toilet; all in all far nicer than my hotel room – I hastened up the metallic, clanging staircase, eager to watch Spain's most fashionable gambolling in the swimming pool's balmy waters. I have to say, I was disappointed. I am, admittedly, a tall man, but had I stretched out inside that pool lengthways my head would have touched one end and my feet the other. Had I tried to swim a single stroke I would probably have knocked myself unconscious and drowned. Which might have been why the pool had long since been drained.

Expecting more disappointment, I then strolled into the bar and tried to order a martini. Not that I usually drink a triple measure of neat gin with a drop of aromatic fortified wine, but the cocktail glass on that map of the boat still danced in front of my eyes. The barman was a tired-looking Australian, his long, dark hair tied back in a pony tail; he wore a black T-shirt and a long, burgundy apron. He couldn't offer me a martini, he apologized, but he did have a Smirnoff Ice. I refused as politely as I could and opted for a beer.

The ferry was getting ready to cast off. There was some frantic activity on the dock as the last of the lorries chugged across the roll-on ramp. Most of the passengers were either settling in to their cabins or desperately marking out sleeping territory in the lounge using cases and bags in a slightly less gun-totin' version of America's Wild West land grab. The barman was cleaning glasses and, for want of anything better to do, asked me what I thought of Ibiza. Rather weakly, I said I thought it was an interesting place. He paused, looked at me with his head to one side, and smiled slightly. 'If you want my theory,' he said, with a conspiratorial air, 'I reckon Ibiza is where Noah's ark landed.' I must have looked disbelieving, because he began to gabble rapidly through the tenets of his faith.

'Look, the myth of the flood is all about the time when the rock wall at the end of the Mediterranean broke and the Atlantic flooded the huge valley that the Med had been.'

I blinked. This was certainly a favoured interpretation. The Mediterranean used to be a dry valley linking Africa and Europe. At some point, the land bridge connecting Morocco with Spain at the Straits of Gibraltar was breached and the valley became a sea. Cave paintings in Sicily showing the hunting of bulls and deer on an island too small to support wildlife larger than rabbits attest to the fact that this happened after humans began to paint, although no-one is entirely sure when. The enduring presence of the flood in human mythology – the Greek legend of Deucalion being one example – is thought to be a deep cultural memory of this event. So I felt on safe enough ground to agree.

'Well,' the barman continued, 'the Bible legends all start

in Canaan, which is where the Phoenicians came from. Now, the Phoenicians were the first people to discover Ibiza and they did so by following a strongly flowing current just off the coast of North Africa. So think about it. If Noah built his ark near Israel then logically the drift of the currents would mean the first landfall he would make would be Ibiza.'

I stared at him, unsure how to respond. My silence was clearly a common response, because he blushed deeply.

'It's not a widely accepted theory,' he admitted.

I instantly felt bad. 'No, no, it's a good theory,' I told him, 'really good. I mean, why not Ibiza?'

'Well, for one thing, it would help explain some of the weird shit about the place.' He laughed, as if including me in a joke we both knew.

'Weird shit?' I asked, but the lorry drivers must have finished securing their loads because twenty of them thundered up to the bar like a wall of irate bull elephants and started ordering inhuman quantities of beer.

With a cheery smile, I shouldered my way through them and found that all the chairs in the bar had been taken. Unwilling to lean against the wall while I finished my Estrella, I clanked back to my cabin, lay down on the bottom bunk and flicked through the handful of guidebooks I'd bought to see if there was any evidence to support the barman's claims.

It turned out that the Balearics had been part of a chain of mountains that stalked across mainland Spain just south of Valencia then strode out into what is now the Mediterranean. When the Atlantic forced its way in, these lime and sandstone peaks became jaunty little islands nosing above the waves. Thus isolated, they set about creating their own ecosystems. Ecologically, Ibiza and its small offshore sister isle Formentera are actually a sub-unit of the Balearics, known since ancient times as the Pitiuses. Although no-one is 100 per cent certain where the name comes from, it's probably because Ibiza has always been home to the Aleppo pine, and the ancient Greek for pine tree is *pitus*. I started to hunt for any mention of currents from the Levant, but the two strong anti-seasickness pills – 'Warning: may cause drowsiness; do not mix with alcohol' – seemed to be reacting with my beer and my eyes began to close. I rested the book on my chest for just a brief moment . . .

I'd wanted to watch the sunrise from the sea. Almost everyone who recorded their arrival on Ibiza by boat, from the American writer Elliot Paul through the Dutch artists and poets in the 1950s to the British actor Denholm Elliott, made sure they were up to observe this moment of romantic intensity. Sadly, the heady mix of cheap Spanish lager and powerful over-the-counter drugs combined to keep me snoring in my bunk until the cabin was filled with a soft golden glow that taunted my sluggardly failure.

After scrubbing down in the salty shower, I rushed up to the highest deck on the boat and watched as the coast of the island came into view. We were chugging slowly towards the old harbour and I could see the vast stone walls of Ibiza's oldest urban centre rising proudly above the docks. This oldest inhabited part of the island is Dalt Vila – the high town. Its walls surround a natural crenellated peak with the rest of the island sliding down and away, dotted with tree-covered hills and fringed with sandy beaches.

With the crisp early sunlight bathing Dalt Vila's golden walls and the boat throbbing and surging beneath me, the arrival felt strangely magical. It's a common sensation. The Dutch writer Cees Nooteboom spent the 1950s on the island and described arriving in Ibiza Town in his book *The Knight Has Died*:

> They drink absinthe and through the bar's portholes the shore draws nearer. Cyril points and points and spits out names: Cala Pada, Punta Arabi, Cap Roig, Cala d'en Serra, Platja de Talamanca. Close by now, a fortress high on a hill, the ship turns slowly round the mole and enters the sheltered harbour. He will never forget the vision of this arrival; caught in a renaissance painting, he gazes, and the bare skull of a town looks back at him, a lofty, triangular mass of white houses with open black eyes, the place of skulls topped by a medieval church, petrified sand.

Spanish teenagers gathered on the deck below me and held hands in awed silence, like children enraptured by a Christmas tree, as we passed the rocky outcrops that form Ibiza's original, natural harbour. Two girls dressed in crumpled black dresses kissed each other passionately. No-one even turned to look.

I looked down at the water surging around the prow. It's hard sometimes, when looking at the beauty of the Med, to imagine the blood that has been spilled in its depths and on its shores. Almost every empire the world has known has lost men to its shallow, warm water. The sea around Ibiza is no exception. Roman war galleys, Barbary corsairs and anarchist battleships had nosed through this very harbour mouth. But, as with the rest of the Mediterranean, it was the Phoenicians who sailed here first.

Ibiza owes the Phoenicians a great deal. They discovered the island, named it and transformed it from a semi-deserted rock into the home of one of the few true cities of Western European antiquity. The Phoenicians – the name means 'purple people' after the dye they extracted from shellfish and used to tint their clothes – were exceptional traders and sailors. They invented the modern alphabet and devised many of today's basic engineering techniques, digging canals where none had succeeded before and piping fresh water from undersea springs to supply their boats. It seems unfair that they don't figure in history's top ten civilizations, but then they didn't conquer and subdue, which seems to be the qualification for greatness. Instead, they were refined, cosmopolitan and peaceful. Peaceful and enormously wealthy. And in the blood-soaked Bronze Age, this made you an incredibly attractive target. The Phoenicians, wandering around the Mediterranean enthusiastically looking to trade with everyone, were like naive tourists carrying expensive video cameras in a violent city park.

They came to Ibiza for one simple reason – tin. Tin was the ancient world's oil. When smelted with copper it created bronze – essential in weaponry, jewellery and farming. Overstretched tin routes were the Achilles heel of any nation's economy and, just like oil today, bloody wars were fought to protect them. The Phoenicians created and controlled most of the tin trade, having found their way out of the Med thousands of years before anyone else and headed as far north as the UK, where they helped the Cornish develop tin mining.

Ibiza has no tin. But it played a vital role in maintaining the tin routes. If you were sailing from Lebanon to Cornwall in the small, square-sailed, oar-powered boats that ploughed the trade routes of the Bronze Age, you would skim the coast of North Africa until you fell south of Sicily and then, just as you came head to head with the cold, dark currents of water from the Atlantic – currents that could pull your small ship under – you would head north-west on a useful current that would bring you slap-bang into Ibiza. From there, you would hug the coast of Spain as you left the Med and head north to purchase metal from wild-eyed Celts with needlessly scruffy hair.

Until seafarers learned how to handle sails properly in the seventeenth century, all Mediterranean boats were galleys. The problem with a galley was that it was almost entirely filled with people, most of them rowing. There was little room for storage, and what space there was tended to be set aside for the goods the galley was trading. Adding extensive cupboards to store food massively reduced the profitability of the journey, so most galleys rarely went for more than a day without stopping to eat – much like heading out on a long car journey. The Phoenicians stumbled across Ibiza in roughly 700 BC when they were looking for a service station on a tough but necessary sea voyage. They landed and were delighted to find the island hospitable and with no indigenous poisonous snakes or insects. This was important to the Phoenicians, who felt that the unusually safe wildlife indicated something divine at work.

They paid Ibiza their greatest honour by naming it after Bes, their god of safety, protection and (Happy Mondays fans) dance. Ibiza, to the Phoenicians, was Ibosim – 'the

Island of Bes', I Bes A. The god himself is far, far older than the Phoenician civilization. Some think he began as the deity of pygmy tribes deep in the heart of the African continent. This may be down to his looks. He's short, bearded and jolly like a cheeky dancing dwarf, and often wears a leopard's skin wrapped around his shoulders and groin. The Phoenicians almost certainly picked him up from the Egyptians. He first appears in the Egyptian canon around 1500 BC and the Phoenicians start worshipping him some time after that. These purple-clad seafarers had a jackdaw culture; if they found something they liked – an art form, a way of working leather, or even a god – they would simply absorb it and make it their own. As they did with Bes.

The Egyptians placed the safety of the higher gods into Bes's care. By day, he was a court jester to the likes of Isis and Osiris; by night, he watched over their sleep, scaring away spirits and poisonous beasts by dancing, singing, shouting, clapping his hands and using powerful magic. Gradually, with the Phoenician influence, his role expanded. He began to protect humans as they slept, so by extension he became the god of the bed, then the god of love and sex, and then the god of childbirth. He looked after both mother and baby at this most dangerous of times, and this, coupled with his joyous appearance and beneficent mien, meant that his popularity grew and grew. Eventually, rather like the Hindu god Ganesh today, he became the favourite god of the majority of Egyptian and Phoenician people. His worship was one of the last to be crushed by the spread of Christianity, in AD 391 when the Byzantine emperor Theodosius I closed all pagan temples throughout the Roman Empire.

To some extent Bes's influence on Ibiza outlasted his worship elsewhere. Throughout Roman times, philosophers believed that the soil of Ibiza had strong magical properties against beasts that bit and stung. Greek writers said that snakes couldn't cross a line of the warm red dust from the island's hills. Scattering Ibiza soil around your house, the Roman historian Pliny the Elder wrote, would keep you safe from poisonous creatures. Perhaps when you name something, you give it power. Ibiza seems to have done its best to live up to Bes, whether through the chaotic hedonism of dancing or the eternal sanctuary the place has provided for the troubled and the wandering across the centuries. It's an island of escape and an island of the night.

For the Phoenicians in practical terms, however, it was an island of warehouses. They'd set up a small settlement on the south coast near Sa Caleta to supply their galleys, and this settlement scratched out a basic living until its inhabitants spotted the defensive value of the rock that now hosts Dalt Vila. Fifty years after first landing, the entire settlement moved north and founded a town which they also named Ibiza. The harbour, the port I was sailing into, was first carved out by their skilful hands.

For seven in the morning, this harbour was extremely busy. A lumbering cruise ship had just tied up, and a small flotilla of fishing boats was ploughing past it into the briny to get the day's work started. The ferry captain was acutely aware of the sailors on the cruise ship lining the side of their bridge to watch him bring his vessel alongside the dock. They were whispering and pointing like sarcastic schoolboys watching the fat kid run. Our captain, I'm afraid to say, reacted badly to this pressure and began screaming abuse at his helmsman almost before the docking process began. The poor man panicked and we lurched back and forth like a learner driver attempting a three-point turn while the crew tried to line everything up and dockers waiting with ropes laughed merrily at our feeble struggles.

Finally we disembarked, stepping off the gangplank and onto a wide dockside. This was a step steeped in more contemporary Ibicenco lore. Just down from the ferry dock the café Domino's used to squat, facing out over the harbour. Domino's was the focal point of Ibiza Town's bohemian expat scene in the 1950s and 1960s when artists, writers, actors and the flotsam and jetsam of post-war Europe washed up on the island's dusty shore. Most mornings found Domino's deserted after its fishing clientele had departed for the tuna beds, for the bohos were not early risers. Once a week, however, all Ibiza descended at dawn. Domino's provided a useful vantage point for the hungover artists who watched as the Barcelona boat docked and observed with watchful, predatory eyes as the bleary newcomers stumbled down the gangplank. These tenderfoot arrivals were like fresh-faced first-year students nervously peering into the union bar on their first night, unaware that their worth was being totted up by jaded third years ready to pounce. Like such freshers, they were usually stripped of their innocence within twenty-four hours.

Domino's has long closed, but its successors are legion. The entire seafront along the port's south wall, known as La Marina, is an endless collection of bars and restaurants: the Base Bar, the Rock Bar, Blues, the Mao Rooms, Mar Y Sol. When Domino's was at its peak, Ibiza harbour was a working dockside; today, the front is a tourist promenade, a clubber's early-evening mecca and a yachtsman's lunchtime hangout. The fishermen have moved across the harbour, so, at seven in the morning, the dockside I stood on was almost completely deserted.

Shouldering my pack, I started down the harbour wall towards the centre of town. For the first night, I'd decided to stay in a *hostal*, or small hotel, on the Plaza del Parque called, reasonably enough, Hostal Parque, but I had no idea where the place was. I was going to have to ask directions. And I was rather dreading this.

Like most middle-class Brits, I have a very low-grade smattering of French but my Spanish barely encompasses 'hello', 'beer', 'coffee', 'thank you' and 'the bill'. To help me around Ibiza, I'd brought a *Berlitz Spanish Phrase Book*. It offered only Castilian Spanish and not Ibiza's native Catalan, but it was better than nothing. Just.

In the section Making Friends, I was offered the following phrases, in the following order, under the pregnant title Encounters: 'Are you alone? Do you mind if I sit here? Do you mind if I smoke? Can I get you a drink? I'd love to have some company. You look great. Why are you laughing? Is my Spanish that bad? Shall we go somewhere quieter? Leave me alone, please! I'm afraid I have to go now. Thanks for the evening. Can I see you again tomorrow?' On the strength of this – the phrases Berlitz clearly thought were the most useful when Encountering someone – I was rather looking forward to my nights out. On Finding Your Way To Your Hotel, however, it had no suggestions.

I met my first local outside the Base Bar. He was running a lick of paint over a handful of high bar stools and seemed tanned and weather-beaten enough to be a native. I fumbled through my phrase book and began to ask the way, with as strong a Spanish accent as I could muster. He listened to me struggle for a few minutes and then, in a Brummie accent, asked politely, 'Do you speak English at all?' I almost fell on his neck.

Within minutes the landlord was leading me up the stairs of the Hostal Parque, past the TV lounge which bore a stern sign on the door warning people not to sleep in there, and letting me into my room. Despite having to pay in advance – usually the sign of a hotel that relies on the kind of patrons who are inclined to do a runner – the room was freshly painted, the beds were clean and the bathroom spotless and modern. After checking in, I opened my window, looked out on to the square and fell into a sort of daze.

The Plaza del Parque is a small, photogenic clearing squashed up against the towering walls of the Dalt Vila amid the cosy, tumbled buildings and narrow, winding streets of the old town. It's fewer than ten metres south of Ibiza Town's version of Barcelona's Ramblas – a semi-pedestrianized square known as Vara de Rey which is lined with Spanish colonial houses and boasts an art deco cinema – but the plaza feels more like a private garden than an adjunct to the main drag.

The square was kissed by Ibiza's hippies in the 1960s and 1970s, and it is still scrubbing off the scent of patchouli oil. Many of the cafés and most of the shops that surround its tiled centre have hippy trappings. Although these days the cafés serve coffee, beer, and pizza and *bocadillos* (sandwiches) rather than macrobiotic lentils and brown rice, a couple offer an organic menu and one messes about with sashimi. The denizens of Plaza del Parque are still fairly eclectic too. As I gazed down on them, still drowsy from my drugged sleep the night before, I saw dreadlocks and tattoos gathered around an acoustic guitar, black-clad grandmothers nattering contentedly, sharp urban Ibicenco twenty-somethings pushing smartly between the palm trees, and permatanned yacht-setters studiously dressed down as they lounged over their fruit juices.

The day passed in pleasant people-watching while drifting around the narrow streets that surround Dalt Vila and treating with suspicion the wider, modern boulevards of the New Town stretching off on either side of the Avenida Espagna. Built in the nineteenth century as shipbuilding, fishing and agriculture began to supplement the income from the salt pans, the streets around La Marina are as pretty a collection of boutique-stuffed thoroughfares as you could hope to find. Gucci, DKNY and Prada compete with record shops owned by Ibiza's oldest nightclub, Pacha, and, in one bizarre street, twenty chemist shops for the euros of the cosmopolitan consumers. I felt like poor white trash gatecrashing Fifth Avenue.

After the obligatory siesta, the shops reopened and seemed to trade all night. It was almost like shopping in a nightclub souk, with staff standing on the doorsteps enticing passers-by, chatting to friends and jigging up and down to the booming bass thundering from their speakers. The surging crowds looked tanned and young and rich. They must have spent all day on the beach, as well as all day in the gym, as well as all day earning money, as well as all day resting in preparation for their night-time adventures. They were so effortlessly fabulous, so filled with energy and enthusiasm, that I began to get quite grumpy.

Suddenly I was pushed to one side as a gaggle of incredibly sexy girls dressed only in white bikinis were chased down the street by musclemen in S&M gear. As they passed, they handed out club flyers for a night at Pacha to those who looked groovy enough to attend their bacchanal. I wasn't lucky enough to be selected. Behind them came a similar crowd of male and female lovelies, this time teetering on glittering stilts, and behind them came a bubbling collection of pecs and abs as the crew from the gay club Anfora exploded in a riot of leather and whistles.

These late-night processions – toned-down versions of the older club parades – grew from the promenading hippies of the early 1970s who'd line the dockside in colourful coats and suntanned flesh to smoke and chat and plan their evenings. Over the years, the posing became ever more flamboyant with summer residents, tourists and Ibicencos alike donning feathers and fun fur to start their evening. These days the punters dress down and mass parades are frowned on by the authorities, but almost every club on the island still sends a small troupe out towards midnight to plaster those who have yet to decide on their evening's entertainment with flyers and cheap offers. The idea is simple and seems to work – the more flesh you expose, the more likely you are to entice the waverers.

By one in the morning, all the promenaders had gathered in a small square that seemed suddenly filled with bass from a nearby bar, where they twisted and hollered and danced and sang like angels preparing to descend from heaven and celebrate baser instincts on the grateful bodies of the mortals below. Dizzy with alcohol and feeling slightly insulted that I hadn't been given any flyers,

I watched until the crowds began to disperse then made my way slowly back to my monk's cell at the Hostal Parque. That's the thing about angels. They prefer to celebrate the sinners than the faithful.

CHAPTER 2

The Goddess

The following morning, still faintly groggy, I went to work. The first thing to do was find somewhere nicer and cheaper to stay. To that end I went to meet Sue Bennison who runs an agency called Locomotives that books accommodation for the glitterati. If you want a villa in the hills with an eternity pool and a view of the sea, you call Sue. All her clients get guest-list entry to Ibiza's nightclubs. Record companies give her free CDs to put in her welcome bag. For the music, fashion and media industries, Sue Bennison is Ibiza. Which obviously terrified me. I'd thought about buying an extremely fashionable pair of trousers for my meeting with her, but had somehow let it slip my mind. I'd also meant to buy a new rucksack. As I sat and waited for her outside the café Mar Y Sol, I suddenly realized I was carrying the Clomper.

The Clomper is a large, red affair that dates from the innocent days when words such as Gore-Tex were still just a gleam in a marketing man's eye. The metal frame is on the outside, meaning that it looks rather like a medium-weight piece of scaffolding with some scraps of red handkerchief dangling from the bars. It was nicknamed the Clomper by my friend Richard who'd followed it down a European railway carriage corridor helpless with laughter as it clouted surly Italian after surly Italian while they tried to smoke a peaceful fag in a pose of sophisticated reflection.

Pale, skinny and hunched over my tatty Clomper, I felt about as ready to meet the queen of Ibiza's disco set as I was to flap my arms and fly to the moon. I'd only e-mailed her to ask advice and now she was going to meet me, presumably to have a bit of a laugh at the whitewashed Englishman before sending me over to the accommodation desk at the tourist information bureau.

Then I heard a cheerful 'Hiya, you Steve?' and a smiling, pretty woman in her thirties sat down in front of me and ordered a coffee. 'Sorry I'm a bit late, but I didn't get to bed 'til six last night.' I mumbled something that might have suggested similar debauchery on my part and we sat and watched men dressed as toga-clad statues try to persuade tourists to give them money while she handed me my car keys and hotel booking details.

As I leafed through the legal paperwork from the car hire company, I asked her how she'd come to live in Ibiza. She said she'd left Hartlepool at the age of twenty dreaming of adventure as a nanny in LA. The city had driven her crazy, so she'd decided to take a summer job with a holiday company while she worked out what to do with her life. Her outfit was the now-defunct Club Continental and they posted her to Ibiza as a rep. 'As soon as I stepped off the plane I thought I'd come home,' she told me, her voice still rich with a gentle, sub-Geordie twang. 'I felt more comfortable here than I did in Hartlepool. It was like I'd been born here.' She finished her first summer and booked straight back up as an airport greeter for Thompson's, supplementing her salary by 'propping' beaches – walking up and down the big tourist enclaves with discount offers at local discos to recruit punters planning big nights out. And that was the next couple of years of her life sorted out – summer in Ibiza, winter in Hartlepool.

Until 1986, when her dad died, and Sue decided to stay in the UK with her mum. She got a job on a local paper selling advertising space. She was good at it. She got promoted after three months and then again after six months. She had a bright future ahead of her. She had a boyfriend. There were plans for a mortgage. And then, one morning, she woke up and 'heard the island calling me'.

She handed in her notice that day, and within a month she was back in Ibiza thinking 'Shit, what have I done?' At which point InterSun, the UK package holiday company, collapsed and stranded hundreds of British holidaymakers as well as quite a few Ibicenco hoteliers. Two of Sue's friends had a set of twelve apartments and they asked her if she could get rid of them. She went up to the airport with a handmade sign and started touting for seat-only passengers coming off the charter flights at three a.m. with nowhere to sleep. These days, there's an official desk at the airport with that night's spare rooms ready to sell, but in those days there was only Sue.

She struggled along for weeks, returning home nine out of ten nights with nothing sold, until the holiday company reps realized she offered them a solution. The reps at the airport wanted to get their full-package clients onto the bus as quickly as possible. It was three in the morning. Everyone wanted to be in bed. The last thing they needed was the seat-only wasters hassling them for somewhere to kip. They started sending them over to Sue, and by the end of the summer she had queues of people forming in front of her every time a plane landed. Then, in the early 1990s, she had her epiphany on the dance floor at Amnesia.

The dance floor was packed, fuller than the week before, which had been fuller than the week before that. She'd just helped the DJ, Danny Rampling, find a villa on the island for the summer and she could suddenly see how things were going. By the end of the summer she'd set up Locomotives, and the following year she was booking accommodation for Boy George, Jamiroquai and Leftfield. And now me.

'I've booked you into a funky, cheap hotel over near San Antonio where I like to go and chill for a weekend when things get too much,' she said. 'It's called Sa Torre, and I think you'll like it. Follow me, I'll show you where.'

So I jumped into my Seat and hurtled across the island to the local radio soundtrack of desperate Euro-house.

Sa Torre was basic but elegant. It felt a little like a Foreign Legion fort, painted white with bedrooms built into the thick stone walls. The rooms looked out on to a dusty garden with hammocks swinging from the trees and dogs sleeping lazily in the sun. A path led down towards a large, white building that held a bar and the administration area where the hotel's owner, a youthful Ibicenco called Pedro, greeted Sue like a long-lost friend. He introduced me to his heavily pregnant wife and scuttled off to get some breakfast. Sue took me out onto a stone-flagged patio that overlooked the sharp, clear blue of the Mediterranean.

'Right,' she said, 'what's your plan?'

And I suddenly realized that I didn't have one.

'Well, look, if you've got nothing to do, my friend Marina's going to a party tomorrow night. Why don't you sort yourself out and go with her? I'll give you her number, give her a call. But before you go out, make sure you watch the sunset from here. It's the best place on the island.'

Sunset on Ibiza's west coast, although usually around 8.30 or nine p.m. during the summer, is the start of the evening. DJs play special sets to accompany the glowing orb as it dips below the horizon. Pedro himself liked to play just such a set at his hotel and was building quite a reputation, helped by the quality of the view from his patio. I stepped out of my room a little early and sat with a cold beer watching the people arrive and the sun glide down. I got to thinking thoughts of purity and wisdom, and my mind started reminiscing about a younger, more innocent version of myself.

I can barely remember what it was like being a student but I seem to recall that I could get out of bed when I actually wanted to. If that meant four p.m., well, so be it. In those days, I saw 7.30 a.m. only from the other side – coming to it out of the night. These days, 7.30 a.m. is a lie-in. So when the sun had set and I found, to my surprise, that I was master of my own destiny and completely sober, I decided to try a little experiment. I would start my labours tomorrow. For the first time in about five years I would go to bed without drinking any more alcohol and wake up when my body decided to.

Well, let me tell you, it was some kind of wonderful. I slept like a log for ten hours, with some rather vivid dreams set in a dark, wooden office about loss and loneliness, and woke into a sunny day with the sound of the sea in my ears.

For a moment I lay there peacefully with a light smile of contentment playing across my face. I decided I always wanted to wake up like this, drifting towards consciousness as the gentle crash and hiss of waves teased my fuzzy mind, rather than starting out of my sleep screaming as a smug radio DJ shouts the time at me.

After lying there for a good twenty minutes, I struggled out of bed and started packing the car for the day's questing. I planned on driving right up to the north-east corner of the island and trying to find some caves known as the Cova des Cuieram. This cave complex was used as a temple in Phoenician and Carthaginian times, and when it was re-discovered in 1907 it was filled with terracotta images of the goddess Tanit.

In many ways, Tanit is a mystery. She was probably the most important figure in the complex religious pantheon of the Carthaginians and she seems to have evolved from an ancient Phoenician goddess called Astarte, who may well have been as important as the Romans' Juno or the Greeks' Hera. The trouble is, it's very hard to be sure. When the Phoenicians invented the alphabet, they used it mainly to record financial transactions. They left very little literature, so it's hard to establish exactly what they believed. Records of Astarte and her worship are few and far between. Tanit's version of Astarte arrived on Ibiza with the Carthaginians as they gradually supplanted Phoenician rule, but the transfer of power was far from simple in historical terms because the Carthaginians were, fundamentally, Phoenicians themselves.

It's history as soap opera. The city of Carthage was founded around 814 BC when a group of Phoenicians left Tyre, the largest of the Phoenician cities, and moved westward along the North African coast. According to legend it was Dido, the daughter of a king of Tyre called Belus, who led the expedition. When Dido's brother Pygmalion ascended the throne, the legend goes, he went after Dido's husband Sichaeus's vast wealth and put the man to death in a bid to pocket his chattels. When Dido heard about her husband's murder, she rounded up a large body of friends and followers and fled, taking her husband's treasure with her. They sailed along the coast of North Africa until they reached a spot on the coast of modern-day Tunisia with a superb natural harbour and a position at the heart of the Med. Of course, the land was already occupied. The local Libyan king found Dido irresistibly attractive, but she spurned him for the memory of her dead beloved. Scornfully, he agreed to sell Dido only so much land as she could enclose with the hide of a bull. In one of those rather moot tricks in ancient history, she promptly sliced the hide up into tiny strips and enclosed an entire hill where – once the king had stopped complaining loudly about her inter-pretation of the word 'enclose' – she built a citadel called Byrsa. The city of Carthage grew up around this fortress.

As Assyrian attacks on the Phoenician city states became outright conquest, Carthage stepped neatly into the void left by the collapsing Phoenician infrastructure. Ibiza moved slowly from Phoenician to Carthaginian rule from about 550 BC. The island began to fill with settlers from Carthage – overspill from the crowded city – who spread out over the island building farms and kilns and scattered homesteads. They ended up in control of the island and developed it into the third most powerful centre in their empire, after Carthage and Cadiz.

Tanit arrived on the island at around this time, although once again the details are unclear. Archaeologists believe the Carthaginians might have kept a library, but the city's complete annihilation at the hands of the Romans in 147 BC meant that any record of beliefs and practices perished in the same flames that engulfed Tanit's buildings and her citizens. She was the chief deity of the city, but when it came to protecting her people from the iron swords of Rome's legions she melted back into the North African sands with her hands spread helpless before her. It is rare in history that an entire culture is utterly destroyed almost overnight – Rome even ploughed salt into the earth around the smoking ruins to make the ground infertile – and dead civilizations usually leave a clearer record. All we are really left with is accounts of the city and its people by Greek and Roman historians, writing for societies that had always hated the Carthaginians. So finding out about Tanit is tricky.

Exactly what Ibiza's relationship with Tanit was under the Carthaginians is also a matter for debate. Some argue that it was simple. Ibiza was the third city of the Carthaginian empire; Tanit was the chief goddess of that empire; therefore Tanit's patronage of the island was simply a reflection of those relationships. Others argue that Ibiza and Tanit were more fundamentally joined, that the place was special to her in the lore of the time. Whatever the truth, the twentieth century saw Ibiza fall for her all over again. If it ever forgot her.

Across the small rock there are countless roads, hotels, shops, bars, souvenir stands and T-shirts bearing her name. Her image appears in clubs and on street corners. She crops up in the conversation of muscled door staff and youthful hippy-chicks with equal fervour. One rather overwrought Ibiza website states 'Tanit was a sledgehammer. A strong Goddess. Goddess of fertility and sex. The island hasn't changed. She is always the island. Always the island.' An Ibicenco barman once told me that 'to understand Ibiza, you have to understand Tanit'. But that isn't so easy. How do you understand a long-dead goddess from a long-dead civilization that left no records apart from the propaganda of its enemies?

Some days before I caught my rusty ferry, I visited the British Museum to meet Jonathan Tubbs, the curator of the Ancient Near East Department. His office is deep in the heart of the museum in a magnificent room that used to house part of the British Library. Its walls are lined with two storeys of oak bookcases now filled with artefacts from Babylon, fragments of Egyptian tablets and endless learned tracts on obscure aspects of the kind of mysteries that play so well in spooky movies. I felt as if I were in an episode of *Buffy*.

He explained that the Phoenician deities were, in certain respects, the forerunners of today's Jewish, Christian and Islamic gods. The loose collection of Phoenician and Canaanite city states that occupied the Levant included Jerusalem, so when the semi-nomadic Hebrew tribes finally staggered into this relatively stable world after scratching out a living in the desert they began to piece together their own theology with a basic underpinning drawn almost entirely from their sophisticated Phoenician neighbours.

The supreme Phoenician spiritual ruler was El, a shadowy father figure who rarely got his hands dirty. He used two tiers of celestial beings to administer his wishes, chief among the top tier being Melqart, the chief god of the city of Tyre, and his consort Astarte as well as the storm god Baal and Eshmun, the god of healing. These are the gods with characters and personalities, the gods with stories and myths created for them as with better-known multi-deity pantheons such as those of the Greek, Roman, Egyptian, Norse and Hindu civilizations. Below these figureheads are the more practical day-to-day deities, the god of the harvest or the god of wine. What comes as a surprise for us, in a time when Muslim and Jew are at each other's throats and practising the wrong sort of Christianity can get you killed by other Christians, is how interchangeable these lower gods were with the vast range of similar deities sprawled around the shores of the Mediterranean. Faiths were far looser. Travellers arriving safely after a long voyage would look to give thanks to the god of the sea but wouldn't particularly mind what name that god went by in the town they'd reached. Poseidon or Neptune – it was all the same. This fluid attitude to religion allowed the Hebrew tribes to take on most of the Phoenician gods wholesale. Much later, they narrowed them down to El and Baal. It is El whose echoes can be found in the Jewish Elohim and the Islamic Allah. Indeed, El's description in the fragments of Phoenician literature that remain – 'the Kind, the Compassionate' – sets up Allah's epithets 'the Merciful' and 'the Kind'.

Of course, if you borrow your neighbour's lawnmower and intend to keep it, it's usually wise to give the thing a lick of paint to prevent discovery. It's the same with gods. As the Hebrew tribes began developing their own more settled ideas about culture and religion, they went about putting some clear water between their god and his Phoenician equivalent. In Exodus, El makes an elegant transition to Yahweh, the god of the Jews, telling Moses he appeared to Abraham, Isaac and Jacob as El Shaddy, or El of the Mountain, but is now revealed to them in his true form. Yahweh also inherits liberally from Baal. Both gods are called 'rider on the clouds' and both make significant appearances on a mountain – Sinai, in the case of Yahweh – with such a rage of fire and noise that 'the earth's high places shook'.

'It is significant that the revelation of the name of Yahweh, symbolising a dramatic change in Israel's under-standing of and relationship with her god, is set in the period of the Exodus and the Conquest,' wrote Michael David Coogan in *Stories from Ancient Canaan*, his rather academic account of the Phoenician gods drawn from ancient tablets discovered in the ruins of the city of Ugarit. 'It was when Israel made the transition from a semi-nomadic to a sedentary and eventually urban way of life that it passed from the milieu of the patriarchs who worshipped El, a patriarchal tent dweller, to the world of the Canaanite city-states and kingdoms, whose chief divinity was Baal, young, active and living in a house.'

The proof of this transfer lies in the Bible itself. There are passages on the Ugarit stone slabs that have survived almost intact all the way through to the Old Testament, where they appear as psalms with little alteration from the original. In one of Baal's epics, for instance, the following exchange appears:

> Behold, your enemy, Baal,
>> behold, you will kill your enemy,
>> behold, you will annihilate your foes,
> You will take your eternal kingship,
>> Your dominion forever and ever.

Fast forward to the book of Psalms, and you find Psalm 92:9 reading,

> Behold, your enemies, Yahweh,
>> behold, your enemies have perished,
>> all evildoers have been scattered.

Then, in Psalm 145:13,

> Your kingdom is an eternal kingdom,
>> your rule is forever and ever.

As the two faiths separate once the Old Testament is up and running, the Bible leaves behind a rather messy victim of the schism – Tanit's precursor, the goddess Astarte. She does appear in the Bible under the name Ashtoreth but she is mentioned with particular loathing. The name itself is a deliberate fusion of the Greek name Astarte and the Hebrew word *boshet*, meaning 'shame'. Ashtaroth, the plural form, became a general term denoting goddesses and paganism. King Solomon 'went after Ashtoreth the goddess of the Sidonians'. Later the high places that were sacred to her were destroyed by Josiah.

Astarte's main problem in surviving the transfer from Phoenician to Hebrew was that she was such a potent, sensual and lustful figure. Today she'd probably be labelled feisty. She was one of the oldest forms of the Great Goddess, the Mother, who was worshipped across Mediterranean lands from the Stone Age. 'Her groves were the high places and her worship was the worship of life itself,' says Ernle Bradford in *The Mediterranean*. Where Astarte differs from the conventionally peaceful, fecund Mother goddess is that she embraced lust and love, and – in her own sweet way – extreme violence. A lot of the Astarte stories are to do with rebirth and regeneration. They are linked with the rising of the sun, the cycles of days and months and the agricultural seasons. At one point, however, she is raped by her brother, so she goes on the warpath and cuts off the heads of almost everyone she meets. It's terribly bloody and makes *Kill Bill* look like a fairy story. Astarte was a curious mixture, the goddess of both love and war: a kick-ass good-time girl with a gun.

In the end, the Greeks and Romans smoothed and shaped her into the passive love goddess Aphrodite or Venus. For the Phoenicians, however, she was as earthy as . . . well, as the earth. She was usually depicted naked, holding her breasts, nursing a baby or wielding an axe in a war chariot. Rituals associated with her worship included wild orgies, and her priests and priestesses had regular sex with her enthusiastic followers in an act of devotion known to archaeologists as sacred prostitution.

Although initially worshipped by the Hebrew tribes alongside El and Baal, her exotic ways proved too much for their increasingly dour culture, and she was expunged from the Jewish pantheon to make the Old Testament mono-theistic. It seems to me, if you'll forgive an immense generalization, that this is where we all stopped having fun. With Astarte's plucking went the worship of sexual pleasure and the joy of fertility, removed at a stroke from the roots of Western culture. The three great monotheistic faiths – Judaism, Christianity and Islam – spend so much time browbeating us with our responsibilities and the fact that our reward will come in heaven rather than on this earth – indeed, that getting any reward on this earth is somehow to be frowned upon – that we have ingrained into our souls guilt and servility instead of high jinks, hot love and good times. Plus, we stopped having orgies in church, which may account for the falling attendance figures.

Once you start to turn your gaze away from the world around you and focus it instead on rewards to come in the afterlife, rewards you can earn by penitence and self-sacrifice, you stop worrying about how grim your lot is down here and start waiting for the glory of Judgement Day. This is the kind of attitude priests and rulers simply love. Blessed are the meek, my child, for they shall inherit the earth. If you die in battle for Islam, my son, you will find seventy-two virgins waiting for you in paradise. Now, just strap on these explosives.

I have to say that if I was going into battle, I'd far rather be led by the warrior priests of a naked goddess who held her breasts in one hand and a battle axe in the other than the devotees of a god who promises that things will be better once I'm dead. This was probably why the Phoenicians found Astarte so appealing. What's not to like?

In Tanit, traces of Astarte's power and glory lived on. Her rise is probably linked with social change in the city, when the monarchy was replaced with a form of democracy. Tanit added the skies and the moon to Astarte's love and war, but how many of Astarte's ritual acts she embraced is unclear. If her worship did include orgies and priestly love – and it's a reasonable punt to assume it did in some form – then a curious possibility opens up.

One of Ibiza's most successful club nights is Manumission, a huge bacchanalian romp that takes place every Monday night during the summer at the world's largest venue – the eight-thousand-capacity Privilege. In the 1990s, one of the two couples who ran Manumission, Mike and Claire, became famous for having sex on stage as dawn broke outside the club. Known as the Manumission Sex Shows, they began as spontaneous acts of daring that grew into a weekly feature until Claire became pregnant in 1998.

These shows developed until they achieved the size and spectacle of vast pagan rites. In 1996, for instance, Manumission's show had the theme of Milkmaids. Every Monday night over the summer, Claire led the club's evening procession through town in a corset and a very short skirt. As she strode along the waterfront she was trailed by an adoring entourage of girls dressed in similar fashion, with Mike in close attendance. The team handed out flyers and special offers and returned to base only in the early hours of the morning. They always proved successful and the club was always packed.

About six or seven in the morning, without fanfare or announcement, Claire would take to the stage, a large platform above and behind a huge swimming pool in the centre of the dance floor. Mike would join her, followed by a gaggle of girls and guys, and the performance just started happening. People slowly realized and stopped dancing, turning to look until the dance floor was filled with rank after rank of curious clubbers, craning their necks to watch the frolics.

They saw a stage full of semi-naked people, mainly girls, stroking one another in a vague and dreamy way. Touching, kissing and writhing, they would work towards the peak of the show. A girl lay naked on her back with her legs splayed in the air while Claire poured milk all over her thighs and into her vagina. The girl then rose and, Thai style, squirted the milk across the stage and into the audience.

At this signal, the performers, now drenched in milk, began the final undressing. They went down on one another, with boys on boys, girls on boys and girls on girls until you couldn't really tell who was doing what with which to whom. Then Claire lay down on a bench, Mike lowered himself gently into her – it may be worth pointing out that he was generously endowed – and they made love slowly until finally Mike came. After he climaxed, they rose, faced the audience and held their arms aloft in triumph. The crowd cheered wildly and the performers melted away.

It doesn't take much of an intellectual leap to see a reflection of the goddess in those Manumission shows. And it's a nice idea, that two and a half thousand years after Tanit worship began on Ibiza the hedonistic excess of the island's club culture was a re-creation of those rituals. In these times of religious strife, the idea of a faith that demanded actual physical proof that we loved each other has a certain appeal.

Tanit as a proto-feminist deity has also taken good care of her sisters on the island. Under traditional Ibicenco inheritance rules, a father divided his assets in a very particular way. He gave the house and half his land to his eldest son.

He then took the rest of his land and divided it equally between all of his children, including the favoured eldest son. The boys got the best land – the agricultural land at the heart of the island where the soil was fertile and the crops grew well. The daughters, on the other hand, received the low-grade coastal land – sandy, salty, hard to farm and tough to live on. As the tourists began to arrive on the island in the 1950s and 1960s, the value of this land was turned on its head. No-one wanted to build vast hotel complexes in the middle of the island. They went searching for the women to buy up their barren expanses of beachside ground and they were willing to pay top, top dollar. One thing the Ibicenco fathers passed on to all their children, male or female, was a canny eye for a deal, so Ibiza now has a huge number of enormously wealthy women with large property interests. A good percentage of them, it is worth pointing out, opted to remain unmarried. Perhaps Tanit's continued presence in hotel names and concession stands is their little vote of thanks.

When I tried to reach Tanit's cave, however, she didn't seem that keen to receive visitors. Finding the site was difficult, and there was no parking nearby. A path led off to the north, but it was badly signposted and its poorly kept route was largely overgrown by a pine forest. Branches whipped my face, the sun baked my back and odd rockslides meant I lost my footing every few hundred yards. To my right, the hill sloped steeply away to the waves below. A fall would have been fatal. Just how much did this deity want to be worshipped? I imagined lines of Phoenician priests toppling off the edge of the cliff and plummeting into the sea like lemmings, and it slightly cheered me, until the path got even tougher and I had to think about clinging on with both hands in order not to die.

Finally I scrambled, breathless, onto a concrete ledge that jutted out of the hillside. A formal metal sign told me I'd reached the temple, but looking up the slope all I could see were a few black steel bars peeping out of a sheer rock wall about seventy feet above my head. I looked down into the valley where waves broke against some jagged rocks and back up again at the black grilles cemented firmly into the rock. It looked forbidding. This was her cave, the steel bars seemed to say, but she is long gone. You're too late. Move along. There's nothing for you here.

Standing nearby was a large purple sign provided by Ibiza's regional assembly, called – in Catalan – the Consell d'Eivissa i Formentera, with a sketched map of the caves within. It looked as if there were four chambers, all opening out on to the cliff face, but I couldn't make out the words that explained what each of them was for. I decided to scramble up the rock face and peer into the grilles to see if any trace of altar or fragment of statue remained. The rock was pitted and rough and the short climb was easy, even under the dry glare of the afternoon sun, but by the time I reached the first grating I was sweating so hard I had to remove my T-shirt.

The first hole was disappointing. It was a small cave, nothing I hadn't seen when I was a boy, eager to climb or crawl into anything that might lead me to sleeping knights and magical adventures. The second cave was more promising, offering stalagmites and stalactites and a dark passage at the back leading off into the earth. The third was barely a cave at all, but at the fourth, behind a low grille furthest to the right, I found something curious. This grille wasn't a grille at all. It was a gate. And it wasn't locked.

I struggled with the catch for a while with little success, then realized that if I pulled the gates towards me they should open. It wasn't easy, because the catch that held them together was so long that I had to step back and slide awkwardly down the sandy slope in order to get the gates far enough out, but in the end I managed it. Tanit's cave was open to me.

Unaccountably, I felt a little nervous, but I ducked down below the overhanging rock and crouched inside. Feeling rather vulnerable, I put my T-shirt back on, like someone who hears a noise downstairs at night and prefers to face the burglar in jeans than pyjamas. Then I crawled off to my right to see what was what.

The first cave was shallow and dry and rapidly became too small to crawl down. Right at the back there was a dark opening, but I couldn't reach it, which I have to say relieved me. Clambering back to the entrance, I went left and found what seemed to be a rudimentary stairway cut into the rippling walls. The stalactites and stalagmites had clearly been growing for many, many years and had mostly joined together, giving the walls of the cave a faintly eerie organic effect, like the Swiss surrealist H. R. Geiger's twisted alien forms that inspired Ridley Scott's stomach-churning beast.

I started down the stairs, into the darkness, then stepped on something that crunched beneath my shoe. I picked it up. It was a shallow tin case for the kind of small candle people put around their gardens or in lanterns. The last traces of wax and a burnt-out wick were inside. And it was new – no dust or rust or earth. It must have been here less than a week.

Cautiously I peered into the darkness, allowing my eyes to get used to the gloom, and caught sight of something that jolted adrenalin right through me. There was a shape down there, a sort of altar. It had flowers on it, fresh flowers in a white porcelain vase with a note leaning against the side. I looked again. It was definitely there, on a rock standing in the middle of the cave floor. There were other things on it too, things I couldn't make out from where I was standing. Feeling like a character in a bad made-for-TV horror film, I stepped slowly down the rock stairs into the chamber.

The altar – it was clearly an altar, even though the rock was just a rock and hadn't been carved into any shape – was packed with offerings. There were the flowers, and two freshish apples that could only have been there a couple of days, lying on a couple of leafy olive branches. There was also a transparent ribbon all around the rock and, just behind the vase, a small white cushion with a fake pearl tiara resting on it. In the middle of the tiara stood a tiny bust of Tanit. The pillow and the bust were covered in faded petals, there were burnt-out candles all over the rock, and coins had been scattered. Some had been there for so long that they were covered in wax and their metal surfaces were scorched; others had been added more recently and still looked shiny and clean. The cave roof was blackened with smoke and, as I looked around the entire cave, I could see burnt-out candles on every available surface. Someone was still using this cave to worship Tanit.

I leaned forward and delicately picked up the note by the vase. It was in Spanish but the words were similar enough to

English for me to make out the meaning: 'Please respect the sanctity of this sanctuary – and do not touch.' I walked around the altar stone for about five minutes, examining all the little bits and pieces, trying not to touch anything. Then, I'm still not sure why, I took out a coin and added it to the collection.

Suddenly I felt fearful. I turned and scrambled out of the cave, irrationally worried that stepping on that candle would earn me some sort of lightning bolt from the outraged divinity. If you count scraping the skin off your back on the rocks as a bolt of sorts, then I suppose I did get slapped with something. Then I walked back to the car through the woods, smiling with delighted amazement. There was still Tanit worship on the island. The old gods may dwindle and fade but one or two of them never die. It warmed my heart to think that, on her island, they still remembered her in the old ways.

Certainly, Tanit had been good for the wealth of the island. Under Carthaginian rule Ibiza flourished. The Greek commentator Diodorus wrote, in the third century BC, that the island was a cosmopolitan place 'inhabited by people of all countries'. He was impressed by its 'memorable ports, the ample construction of its walls' and by the honest toil of its farmers. Ibiza's produce compared favourably with the best of Greece and Rome, he opined.

Ibiza Town itself remained the only urban centre, and it was quite the boom town. Outside the city walls, the Carthaginian burial grounds – dug deep into today's Puig des Molins ('hill of the windmills') – were accounted the largest in the empire. Ibiza was the preferred burial spot for the wealthy, a sort of Miami of the ancient world, because its patronage by Bes and his success in keeping poisonous animals away meant the path to the afterlife was unusually smooth.

On the other side of the town, commercial warehouses ran along what is now the edge of the Marina, stuffed with African gold, Spanish silver, British tin, Greek pottery, elephant tusks and hides, perfumes from the East, marble from the Aegean islands, and linen from Egypt. The goods came in from all over the world and Ibiza acted as a kind of trade centre cum giant commercial post office depot. Deals were done and goods traded or simply stored in transit, waiting to be shipped to other parts of the Mediterranean.

In front of these warehouses the harbour waters would have been packed with long merchant ships sporting a square sail and a single bank of long oars on each side. Perhaps there might have been one or two Carthaginian trireme warships, with three rows of oars on three separate decks and a vast, bronzed ram poking out in front, just below the waterline. The dockside would have been packed 24/7 with merchants, dockers, officials and soldiers, working, dealing, drinking, whoring and fighting. It would have been noisy and colourful with sailors and merchants of all races. Outside the port area, the Greek chronicler Diodorus Siculus described an imposing capital with a temple to the god of healing, Eshmun, at the top of the hill where Dalt Vila now squats. The hill was protected by great walls and surrounded by 'a considerable number of admirably built houses'.

As a point of comparison, around this time London was a collection of temporary huts made from mud and sticks that would be abandoned in the winter by its nomadic inhabitants as the Thames Valley flooded and became too marshy to support the community. Resting comfortably on their wealth and influence, Ibicencos would have had no idea the place existed.

The good times weren't to last. The island's downfall was swift and followed that of its mother city. Between 264 BC and 146 BC, Carthage fought three great wars with Rome and lost the lot. The mastermind behind the greatest of these wars, the Second Punic War, was Hannibal, the general who is still avidly studied at military colleges across the world over two thousand years after his audacious campaign on the Italian mainland. And Hannibal, it turns out, may have been born just off the coast of Ibiza on a small island called Conillera, a long, low-lying rock, now uninhabited but dotted with shrubs and topped by a lighthouse.

There is some doubt about Ibiza's claim on Hannibal, to put it mildly. Malta has also put in a bid to be the great man's birthplace, and then, of course, there is the more than significant chance that he popped out in Carthage itself. Ibiza's claim chiefly rests on a passage in Pliny the Elder which seems to credit Conillera, although many historians argue that this is the result of a mistranslation by a less than diligent monk in the Middle Ages.

Hannibal, whose name means 'Favourite of Baal', was born the son of Hamilcar Barca, a Carthaginian general in the First Punic War (264–241 BC). Daddy was a military man through and through and held a deep grudge against Rome for the loss of Sicily and Malta in the first war. When his son was nine years old, Hamilcar took him to the altar of Melqart, the principal god of Tyre, in Carthage and had Hannibal swear that he would never be a friend to Rome.

Hamilcar then whipped his boy off to conquer Spain, where he hoped to make up for the losses Carthage had suffered during the first war, secure control of the western Mediterranean and maintain the supply of Spanish and Cornish tin. Ibiza was a key part of his plan. In a bid to keep Greek traders out of markets in Spain, Carthage built up Ibiza Town into a significant naval base. With the other Iberian colony of Cadiz and Carthage itself, the three formed a triangle that entirely closed the Straits of Gibraltar to rival navies.

In 221 BC, after his father and his father's successor were killed, the army voted for Hannibal as its new leader. Once he had taken command, Hannibal consolidated the Punic hold on Spain. He married a Spanish princess, Imilce, then began to conquer various Spanish tribes. In two years he had subjugated all of Spain between the Tagus and Ebro rivers, with the exception of the Roman dependency of Saguntum – modern-day Sagunto. And this is where his trouble started.

Despite their agreements with Hasdrubal, Hannibal's brother, that Roman influence stopped at the Ebro, Rome increased her involvement with Saguntum. At the same time, Hannibal was seeking to bring it into line with Carthage. In 219 BC, he attacked the city, finally conquering it after an eight-month siege. The Romans exploded, sending envoys to Carthage to demand that Hannibal be handed over. Carthage refused and Rome declared war. Hannibal rapidly recruited a new army and began his legendary march on Rome.

In recruiting this army, Hannibal turned to Ibiza. The island was to become one of the key sources of revenue during his campaign, minting its own silver coins to pay for his battles. There is a story that he stood in what is now the Vara de Rey and spoke to a gathering of Balearic slingers – highly skilled Talayotic slingshot hunters from Mallorca, Menorca and parts of Ibiza's hinterland – persuading them to join him. If so, he spoke persuasively. Balearic slingers were a key part of his artillery right up to his final defeat at the hands of Scipio. They would be at the front in the opening stages of any conflict, hurling round stones or lead bullets before retiring as the major engagement took place. So devastating was the effect of these slingers that the Romans incorporated them into their own armies after the war was over. Given the hardships these slingers suffered to remain at Hannibal's side to the bitter end, they must have been an intensely loyal band. Contemporary accounts describe Hannibal as charismatic, but it takes a special kind of charisma to inspire devotion in a mercenary army that speaks up to twenty different languages.

Hannibal's journey over the Alps with his elephants has been told and retold so many times that it hardly needs another outing. By the spring of 216 BC he had crossed the mountains, lured a Roman army into an ambush where they were picked off by Balearic slingers, moved south and defeated another army at Lake Trasimene, near the modern-day Italian city of Perugia. Rome panicked, electing a stern general of the old school, Quintus Fabius Maximus, to take charge of defeating Hannibal. He opted simply to follow the Carthaginian, harassing him but refusing to meet him in battle in a bid to wear him out. Eventually Fabius bottled Hannibal's troops up tightly and prepared to attack the following day. That night Hannibal sent oxen towards Fabius's army with burning sticks tied to their horns. While the Romans investigated what they considered an attack, he escaped with his army over wooded hills.

In the meantime, a Roman army had begun to attack Carthaginian possessions in Spain. They reached Ibiza in 217 BC and fought a pitched battle that lasted three days. The walls of Ibiza Town and the doughty defence of the locals proved too much for the legions and they gave up the siege, turning their attention to Ibiza's lush countryside, which they ravaged mercilessly. Ibiza's resistance is an impressive achievement when you consider that, on the mainland, both Cartagena and Cadiz fell to Rome. The Roman historian Livy claimed that the booty snatched from Ibiza's country-side was greater than the rest of the swag from the entire campaign on mainland Spain, which gives some idea of the richness and importance of Punic Ibiza.

Meanwhile, in Italy, Hannibal was beating anything the Romans threw at him in the field. The one thing he couldn't do was attack the city of Rome. He hadn't brought any siege equipment with him, so her towering walls were im-pregnable. Hannibal roamed freely across southern Italy for fifteen years, but without taking the game to Rome he was doomed. The Romans sat tight behind the walls of their city and waged a long, slow war of attrition. They harassed him constantly, defeated a reinforcing army that his brother had also led over the Alps, and, finally, in 204 BC, landed an army in Africa under Publius Cornelius Scipio. Carthage panicked and sued for peace.

Ibiza had one last part to play in the war. When Cadiz surrendered in 205 BC, the admiral of the Carthaginian fleet, Magon, put to sea with his fleet and made for Ibiza. He was supplied and reinforced by the island before heading off to

Menorca to recruit fresh troops. This last, brave flourish was too late, however. The war was over. Hannibal, returning to Africa to save his beloved city, was defeated for the first time in open battle by Scipio. Carthage was in no position to dictate terms. Surrender was absolute.

Back in Carthage, Hannibal moved into Civvy Street and played a major part in rebuilding the city. He was so successful that Carthage grew even faster than before. The excessive war reparations Rome had imposed were met. The Romans were furious. They accused Hannibal of conspiring with an enemy of Rome – King Antiochus the Great of Syria – and sent envoys to have him arrested. Hannibal fled Carthage and became the Che Guevara of the ancient world, helping Rome's enemies wherever he could find them.

He was run to ground in Bithynia, part of modern Turkey. As the Romans took up positions around his house, Hannibal's servants spotted them. When warned that legionaries were outside, his reply was sardonic: 'It is now time to end the anxiety of the Romans. Clearly they are no longer able to wait for the death of an old man who has caused them so much concern.' He then took out a phial of poison and swallowed it. When the legionaries finally burst through the door, swords at the ready, they found him dead. He was sixty-four.

With Hannibal out of the way, the Romans set about dismantling his city. They needled Carthage into breaking the terms of their peace treaty, screamed in moral indignation and attacked with the full force of their war machine. They trapped a large part of the population in a temple at the heart of Carthage's citadel and burned them to death, then flattened the city and ploughed salt into the ground so that it would never rise again. After that, they helped themselves to her empire, which is how Ibiza passed into Roman hands in 146 BC.

Tanit's relationship with Ibiza survived the destruction of Carthage, but the city's defeat presaged hers. The process of Romanization on the island was gradual. Initially the Romans collected cash from their new dominion and allowed the locals to worship their old gods and speak their own language. Tanit's caves were enlarged and Ibiza's economy blossomed. In AD 74, however, Vespasian re-organized the empire, eradicating local differences to produce a vast, globalized trading block. Tanit's temples became Juno's temples and the Romans assumed they'd stamped her worship out for good. But, as the altar at Cova des Cuieram proves, they didn't quite succeed. I guess the lesson of Tanit is, you can't keep a good girl down.

CHAPTER 3

The White Stuff

I'd arrived on Ibiza in the middle of an extremely heated election campaign. All the seats at the island *consell* and the Mallorca-based Balearic *consell* were being contested, and fundamental decisions on the island's economy and ecology were at the heart of the political debate. The whole shape of Ibiza hung in the balance, and – it transpired – I had a way into the heart of the campaign. Now that European rules allowed any EU citizen to take part in elections anywhere in the community, one of Sue Bennison's friends, the British expat called Marina she had mentioned on my first night at Sa Torre, was standing for office. Sue wangled me an invitation for her political party's pre-election hoedown.

I drove over to Ibiza Town to pick Marina up just outside her flat. She turned out to be a tall, blonde woman in her fifties who slid elegantly into the Seat's low-budget interior exuding the kind of hard glamour that made me want to be her friend rather than her enemy. Although she'd been on Ibiza for years, she still had a strong Midlands accent. When I asked her which part of the country she came from, how-ever, she just smiled and changed the subject.

As we drove, she filled me in a little. The party we were

on our way to was hosted by the PREF, a Balearic Islands splinter group from Spain's national conservative party, the PP or Partido Popular. The PREF was founded four years ago by a paediatrician called Manuel Alsonso after a series of disagreements within the local PP and this was the first election they'd fought. In between giving me directions, Marina sketched out the issues surrounding the election as she saw it: a row over enlarging the airport, plans to introduce golf courses, debates over late licences and arguments about conservation. 'This place needs to sort itself out,' she sniffed. 'We've got the Red/Green alliance in power now and they're running the island into the ground.' The PREF's campaign seemed to be going fairly well, she added, but it had been long and hard and, now that the election was almost here, everyone was getting tired. In a bid to inject some energy into their weary footsoldiers, PREF had decided to throw a party. 'Don't expect an all-night rave,' she told me. 'It's a political party hosting it after all.'

I felt fairly sure I knew what to expect. As teenagers, my friends and I had gatecrashed various political bashes at a hotel on Widmore Road that doubled as Bromley's most fashionable function room. We showed no political bias in our party favours, although someone had informed us that Young Conservative girls were better-looking than young socialists. In Bromley, there didn't seem to be much difference. The discos were exactly the same as well – truly dreadful music played by a deeply moronic DJ, some sort of raffle to win a bottle of Pomagne, and a couple of inaudible speeches made through a crackly mike at the end of the evening saying how much fun it had been. Which was not only patently untrue, but also taught me that it really doesn't matter what colour they sport, the political class are a different species who wouldn't know a good time if it came up and biffed them over the head with a bottle of Smirnoff Ice.

So it was with a slight sense of dread that I walked through the doors of the Garbi Disco in Figueretes, across the other side of Ibiza Town. The Garbi was a vast tourist nightclub picked by the PREF for their hoedown because it rarely opened its doors to punters before midnight. It was a concrete cavern of a place, decorated throughout with enormous palm trees and towering plastic theme-park rocks built into podiums, which at two a.m. would be filled with gyrating disco bunnies at the peak of their excitement. Right now, however, it was filled with an equally bouncy mob of children jumping around with gay abandon while their parents chatted and downed the complimentary sangria. Yep, I'd seen all this before.

I was just about to plead heavy commitments the following day when, with a flash of light and a roll of drums, the dance floor cleared and a well-built drag queen in a thigh-split lacy dress strode out to the centre of the room. All around me, conservative politicos whooped and cheered and their children started bouncing so high I feared they'd get their heads stuck in the plastic rock roof. Pouting camply, the singer worked through some hi-energy cross-dresser classics, striding back and forth along the rows of thirty- and fortysomething Ibicenco businessmen who grinned awkwardly every time their faces were stroked. After a sterling rendition of 'It's Raining Men', the singer led the packed nightclub of party workers in choruses of popular Spanish diva classics. He was like a camp Mary Poppins.

My brain struggled to connect this display of professional-level hedonism with the facts – namely, that I was watching a hard-right splinter party at its pre-election shindig. As merrymakers of all ages danced delightedly with the burly cross-dresser – and this was a full-scale drag act, not some bumbling rugby player in a dress – I tried to imagine a British political party of any hue letting its hair down with such unselfconscious abandon. I just couldn't conceive it. The rank and file would either walk out or start debating the issues of transgender oppression in late-stage capitalism. The idea of any of them simply taking a drag act at face value and enjoying the fun of it, without taking offence or placing it in some elaborate context, would be beyond them.

Meanwhile, back at the Garbi, the camp factor was suddenly increased by the introduction of two male and three female dancers in full salsa costumes, performing elaborate fruit-based dance routines to the jovial Latin classic 'Cuban Pete', who, in case you've forgotten, is the king of the rumba beat. And, when he plays his maracas, they go chick-chicky-boom. For the final, percussion-heavy bars of the song, the drag queen led a conga line around the dance floor. The children leapt into place enthusiastically, beckoning their parents and friends until almost the entire membership of the PREF was snaking between the plastic palm trees. At the back, the professional dancers whooped and gyrated, and I couldn't help but notice that the male dancers were energetically simulating intercourse with the women in front of them.

'Cuban Pete' ended with a flourish and, before anyone could applaud, the DJ crashed into a pounding Latin house track. With shrieks of delight, the party faithful of all ages raised their hands in the air and twisted like writhing snakes to the beat. Gradually, the older members slipped away to the side of the club, but 70 per cent of the crowd were still on the dance floor twenty minutes later when an earnest-looking man in his mid-forties took the DJ's microphone and began to make a speech. I couldn't understand the words, but I knew exactly what he was saying: 'We've all had a lovely time, and I'd like to thank Mrs Jenkins and the rest of her committee for her lovely decorations and the wonderful finger buffet. I for one won't be able to eat for a week. Now, let's all keep the energy levels up for the last stage of the campaign. We've got a real momentum here and we don't want to let it slip away just because we're all getting tired.' Thank-you speeches at functions are the one great unifying factor across cultures, classes and nations. Admittedly your typical British equivalent is unlikely to include 'and wasn't the he/she dance routine and high-camp singalong splendid? Three cheers for Dave/Davina', but the principle is the same.

Now that the party was back on familiar territory, I joined Marina at the bar, where she introduced me to the PREF's local leader, Rafael Costa Bonet. Rafael was running the party's Ibiza election campaign and standing as a candidate himself in nearby San Jordi. As a result, he looked about as exhausted as it's possible for a man to look under a luxurious tan.

I bought him a beer and we talked about the election, while all the time I was desperate to ask him who'd booked the drag act and why. As the island's political landscape unfolded in front of me, however, I found myself increasingly fascinated. Rafael's arm of the PREF seemed to be a group of small businessmen who'd done pretty well out of the tourism industry – Rafael himself owned a bar and a car hire company that had been in the family for twenty-three years – and who were now scared that Ibiza's ruling party, a Red/Green alliance known as the PACTE Progresista, were in the process of dismantling their living. Swept into office on a wave of popular concern about the environment, the PACTE had tapped into people's fears about the future of the island. But, Rafael grumbled, they'd gone too far. They'd already stopped issuing licences for new hotels, and if you wanted to create new beds you had to get rid of an equal number of old beds first. 'If they get in again they'll stop all building across the island completely!' he groaned. And then he got stuck into his biggest bugbear: that the PACTE had changed the name of the island.

This, it turned out, was a long-running sore on the Pitiuses' fair skin. In theory Ibiza's first language isn't Spanish, it's a dialect of Catalan. Catalan is the language of Barcelona and Girona. It was banned by Franco after the Spanish Civil War as the Generalissimo sought to weld his disparate regions into one uniform, fervently nationalistic whole. For years after the civil war, a small-scale guerrilla graffiti war had raged on the island's road signs as Catalan nationalists protested at the destruction of their culture. Spanish names were crossed out and Catalan names inked in, usually in red paint, but the issue seemed of minor concern until the PACTE Red/Green coalition formed. This loose political grouping included a couple of small but troublesome Catalan nationalist parties, and as a quid pro quo for their support the coalition changed Ibiza's official language to Catalan in 1999.

Every town had its name returned to the pre-war original.

Thus, San Antonio became Sant Antoni and San Juan became Sant Joan. But it was the renaming of Eivissa that really bothered Rafael, because in Catalan, Ibiza is Eivissa. As he wound himself up to full throttle on the issue, his voice rose to a high, adrenalin-fuelled pitch and his eyes kept darting about the room. 'Why would you do that?' he pleaded with me, rhetorically. 'The name Ibiza, it's like a brand all over the world – cars, records, T-shirts, everything. No-one knows what Eivissa is, no-one's heard of Eivissa. They go to the travel fairs under the banner Eivissa and no-one knows where they're coming from. It's going to ruin us all.'

I could understand his point about Ibiza – although Eivissa does have a certain ring, don't you think? – but I couldn't really work out why they'd split from the PP. Both parties, from what he was saying, opposed the renaming. Both opposed the restrictions on building. Why didn't he stay with the big boys? Rafael made vague noises about the PP being a group of old men, with the same faces staying in the same posts for twenty years. 'We think they need a new, younger team,' he added, which sounded a little like a job application.

Around us, the party was grinding to a halt. The lights flickered on and the bar staff flirted with one another as they changed shift, newcomers polishing up fresh glasses for the queue of hardened clubbers gathering outside. Marina said it was time to leave and we stepped out into the night where we found a young, hard-faced, flyer-pushing girl dragging deep on the nub of a faltering cigarette. She turned towards us, ready to offer up her cheap drinks and reduced price admission, then paused, focused on Marina and split her face into a cheese-eating grin. They gabbled away at each other so fast that it took me a few minutes to realize they were actually speaking English. It transpired the girl had propped for Marina when she'd owned an Irish bar called Baileys. They hugged like old friends before Marina lowered herself gracefully into my grimy car.

'I didn't know you used to own bars,' I said, letting the statement hang like a question in the air.

It took her a long time to answer. 'I had Baileys and then an after-club club called Conga,' she said, after such a long pause that I had begun to prepare a new subject for conversation. 'It was the kind of place the Spanish went, the locals. It was quiet in the summer, but it did well.' She paused again. 'It burned down last year.' She looked over at me then back out at the road. 'It was arson. I know who did it. That's partly why I'm standing. I want to see his face if I win.'

There didn't seem to be a great deal to add to that so we drove on in silence for a bit, the gaudy neon of the tourist strip flashing across the windscreen like a movie. Eventually the silence became a little uncomfortable so, to fill the hole, I asked her when she'd moved out here.

'Nineteen seventy-two,' she said.

'Why did you decide to come?'

She seemed slightly evasive and stared out of the window at the crowds drifting past the bars, cafés and arcades in the warm night. 'I might tell you one day, but not now,' she said, finally.

As we neared her flat, she suggested I pull over next to a coffee shop called Mana, a small concrete affair lit by painfully white fluorescent lights. Mana had been built into the ground floor of a modern housing development on a roundabout beside Ibiza's flashy yacht club but, despite the flats above and the boats nearby, it was completely empty.

We went in and found a young English girl mopping the floor disconsolately. Mana's owner walked out from a darkened storeroom when he heard us clatter in. Marina, who was clearly an old friend, introduced us. His name was Michael and he was a tall black Londoner in his thirties. We shook hands and I asked how long he'd been out here. I hadn't met enough of the island's refugees to know that this was a rude question. He took it well, though, and told me he'd been here since the mid-1980s working the VIP lounge at El Divino, the upmarket Eurotrash club that squats on the side of the harbour. This café, his café, was built with some financial help from the family who ran El Divino. 'I couldn't keep working those nightclub hours,' he confided. 'I needed to slow down.'

I looked at my watch. It was two a.m. Feeling rather feeble, I asked him if two a.m. wasn't nightclub hours.

He snorted and turned to Marina to discuss a minor earthquake that had hit the coast of Ibiza a few days earlier. 'Apparently the seafront at San Antonio was covered in fish,' he said gravely.

Marina nodded but didn't seem terribly interested. Her voice became immensely casual and she asked him about a new nightclub called Penelope's. Initially, it was as if she had some deep, hidden reason for bringing up the subject, but by the end of her question she seemed to be asking about its prospects in much the same way football fans would discuss the forthcoming season. Michael paused and frowned, slightly irritated that he couldn't discuss the San Antonio apocalypse. 'They're backed by a lot of money from

Georgio,' he said, 'and they've been stealing people from Pacha. That isn't going to go down well. There's Italian money in there and they're looking to make some cash. It won't last if they go on like this. The ten families, the ones who run the island, who were here before the tourists came, don't like it if the money leaves the island. Things will start to change. Suddenly their licence will be altered and they'll have to close at four a.m., then there'll be no more free parking outside. I've seen it happen before. You had all these British promoters coming over in the 1990s thinking they could just rent somewhere out for the summer, employ all their mates and piss off at the end of the season with the money. That's not how it works here. You've got to give something back to the island if you want to stay in business.'

I found my attention wandering. The two of them looked pretty settled, gossiping away like two old generals, veterans of a thousand all-night battles, debating the outcome of wars they no longer had to fight. As they talked on, it occurred to me that I had no idea what Marina did for a living now that her club had burned down. And just then, Michael asked the same question.

'So, what are you up to these days?'

'I've got an art gallery,' she told him. 'It sells fakes.'

I did a double take, but Michael surfed the moment with equanimity, as if a gallery selling fake art were an everyday thing for him. 'Oh yeah?' he said. 'Can you do me a deal?'

'Of course!' She grinned.

I was intrigued, but my eyes were heavy and I had a lot to do the following day. I offered Marina a lift home, but she said she could walk. 'Come and see me in the gallery when you've got a minute,' she added. 'I've got some names of some people you might want to meet.' Thanking her and wishing her luck with the election canvassing, I made for the door and the darkened road to San Antonio.

I wanted to check out Rafael's account of the election, which seemed a little too simplistic to me, but I wasn't sure who to ask. I thought of trawling around all the political parties or asking one of the Brits on the island for a more neutral account. But the Brits I'd met so far didn't seem the kind of people to be gripped by town-hall politics and I couldn't face wading through mountains of propaganda from the politicos in search of hints of truth. And then I dimly remembered my two weeks' work experience on the mighty *Pontypridd Observer* in the South Wales valleys. I'd been forced to sit through endless council meetings trying to get a grip on proceedings with my hopeless shorthand and I'd had to file daily reports on the minutest goings-on in the chamber. Of course! The local press! If you want to get a deeply cynical view of anything, ask a journalist.

I rang the offices of Ibiza's local newspaper, the *Diario de Ibiza*, in the full expectation of a polite but firm rejection along the lines of 'our reporters are far too busy to take an hour out of their day to explain local politics to a curious Englishman'. Instead, I found myself making an appointment to meet the paper's political editor, Juan Lluis Ferrer. I was impressed. The *Pontypridd Observer*'s political reporter would have preferred to gnaw off his own legs before he explained the comings and goings of the town hall to some Spaniard who'd rung up on the off-chance.

Ferrer turned out to be an affable young man with thick, dark hair and an extremely cheerful grin. He led me past reception and into an empty office with scruffy furniture and old, faded posters on the wall, then called in his colleague, Marga. 'She's going to help me with my English,' he said, before getting me a cup of vending-machine coffee that turned out to be surprisingly palatable. We smiled at each other, and he began a story of such scandal, passion, intrigue and tension that I quite envied him his job.

'You have to understand this is an island.' Ferrer spoke slowly and threw sentences over to Marga when he got stuck. 'It's a closed community. The politics here are not like the politics on the mainland. In many ways, they are turned on their head. The Partido Popular, for instance, is nothing like the PP in Madrid. Over here, it is a social entity and it really represents the people born on the island. The people vote PP not because they are a conservative party but because everyone knows someone who's standing. The main left-wing party, the Partido Socialista Obrero Español, really represents the people from mainland Spain.'

This, he went on, was very Ibicenco. The PSOE is the people's party. It represents the trade unions, the workers and, usually, Catalan speakers. Voting PSOE and supporting Barcelona football club are the badges of the left, while voting PP and supporting Madrid are the badges of the right. On Ibiza, however, the Catalan speakers make up the ruling class. They'd made buckets of cash from the tourist boom and employed mainland labour from poor parts of Andalucía to do the dirty work. On Ibiza, supporting Barcelona means you are part of the establishment; supporting Madrid means you are an outsider, struggling for your rights. In a neat reversal, the Catalan speakers vote PP and the Spanish speakers vote PSOE. This twist, coupled with the curious

Ibicenco blend of fiscal conservatism and social tolerance, meant the PP had won every single election ever held on Ibiza.

Until 1999. That year, Ibiza had its equivalent of the storming of the Winter Palace. The PSOE-led PACTE alliance swept to power, putting left-wing candidates in charge for the very first time. But it was a murky business. 'The PACTE didn't win,' said Ferrer, and his tone was cynical. 'The PP lost.'

The PP, it turned out, were caught up in the kind of internal feuds and political scandals that wouldn't seem out of place in a dubious banana republic. For a start, there were three powerful families within the party jockeying for dominance just as a huge vote-rigging scandal broke in Formentera. The PP were caught using the votes of seventy-four Formenterencs, people who had left the island years ago and moved to South America to make their fortunes. These absentee voters, who had no idea their names were on the ballot papers, shored up the PP vote on an island that usually voted to the left. 'Formentera is a very small island,' Ferrer explained, 'so even one vote is important.'

At the same time, the left were better organized than before, had created a popular front in the PACTE and benefited from a wave of completely unfamiliar protest marches that swept the island. These stemmed from alarm over the rampant building that had raged unchecked since the 1960s. When two tourist developments were announced in the last areas of natural wilderness – the unspoiled hills overlooking the beach at Cala D'Hort and the salt flats out by the airport – Ibicencos rose like lions, taking everybody completely by surprise. 'The Cala D'Hort development made for the biggest protest the islands have ever seen.' Ferrer's journalist's eyes sparkled with joy at the memory of the conflict. 'In January 1999, we had eleven thousand people marching through the streets of Ibiza Town over Cala D'Hort. But the movement really began with the fuss over the salt flats.'

'The salt flats?' I couldn't see why something with such a dreary name could be so politically important. So Ferrer told me the story of the salt flats.

Out by the airport, standing like paddyfields between the runway and the sea, stretch over a thousand acres of low-lying land that has kept Ibiza alive for the past two thousand years. Each football-pitch-sized field, known as a pan, is flooded with sea water at the start of the summer, which then evaporates in the blazing Mediterranean sun to leave crusts of salt that can be harvested and sold like any other cash crop. From the ground the pans look like a strange, wintry scene with piles of salt dotted around as if a classroom of children were about to embark on a snowman-building competition. Most visitors' first glimpse of them is from the air. The glare of the sun on the water and the salt collecting beneath the surface gives a dirty white glow that can look, from above, like corn on a hot summer's day.

Perhaps because they are, essentially, large square pools of sea water, guidebooks tend to gloss over the salt pans, mentioning them merely as something of a visual curiosity. History books concentrate on Ibiza's port and its agriculture when tracing the island's economy. It is true that a wander across the pans on a hot afternoon isn't exactly top of any sensible tourist agenda, but these crusts of sodium chloride almost certainly kept the island going as a viable economic entity after the fall of Carthage. The pale gleam of these acres gave Ibiza its nickname – the White Island. And then, in the twentieth century, the pans awoke Ibiza's latent social conscience.

It's hard to see how mere salt could do all this. But then, from the luxurious position of our twenty-first-century dining table, it is difficult to comprehend the enormous rarity and high historical value salt used to possess. So expensive was this mineral that revenues from the Chinese state's monopoly on the salt trade largely funded the construction of the Great Wall of China. In fact, it's only in the last hundred years that we've been able to see it as commonplace. In his book on the white powder, appropriately called *Salt*, Mark Kurlansky quotes the Welsh Jungian psychologist Ernest Jones in his essay on human obsession, describing how salt has been invested with significance throughout the ages. 'Homer calls it divine,' Jones wrote with some bemusement, 'the Romans described a lover as being in a "salted state" and celibate Egyptian priests abstained from it because it excited desire.'

It was the Phoenicians who left Ibiza this legacy of wealth and power. As the Mediterranean's foremost seagoing people, they invented the salting of fish, using it as a staple food source on long voyages. After setting up the pans, they founded a sizeable fish-salting factory in Santa Eulalia which produced the foodstuff and an even more valuable by-product, a delicate purple dye extracted from a tiny vein in a local whelk-like mollusc called *Murex brandaris*. This dye gave the Phoenicians their name – the purple people – and the salt pans were a vital part of its manufacture.

Legend attributes the discovery of this dye to Hercules

who, while getting a little R&R in the Phoenician city of Tyre, took his dog for a walk along the beach. Rover snaffled a couple of murex shellfish and, after scoffing the lot, Hercules noticed that his saliva had turned purple. In a move of astounding generosity, Hercules opted not to keep the information to himself but instead passed it on to the local citizens.

The process of extracting the dye was tortuous. The Phoenicians removed the tiny vein, ideally from a live murex, salted it and placed it in litres of extremely salty water. They warmed this mixture for days then filtered it repeatedly until, about fifteen days later, the purple liquid was concentrated enough to colour a fleece. This dye was so rare and valuable – something like a thousand murex were needed for a small drop of the stuff – that Julius Caesar decreed only he and his household could dip their togas in it, giving rise to purple as the colour for emperors.

When Carthage fell and Rome occupied Ibiza, the export of salt and dye continued, but the Romans also invested heavily in the production of a highly prized luxury sauce called garum. This was a by-product of the fish-salting process and it would further boost Ibiza's coffers. In effect, garum was the culinary equivalent of the valuable purple dye. The Romans created it from leftover scraps cut out of the salted fish – the guts, gills and fins – which they placed in jars with salt and weighted down until fermentation produced a thick, dark liquid that they drew out and separated. They boiled this intensely flavoured pickle with herbs then filtered it to produce the sauce.

The Roman elite used garum as we would use a relish, scattering it on food in tiny drops in much the same way as soy sauce is used today. Indeed, it probably tasted fairly similar. Soy began its culinary life as a Chinese version of garum, with the Chinese eventually replacing fish innards with the soy bean. Soy's flavour is probably gentler than garum, just as garum's recipe found popularity in Britain under the empire but gradually evolved into tomato ketchup as most British cooks found the taste too domineering. Garum features heavily in the oldest cookbook we know of, Apicius's first-century *De Re Coquinaria*, written exclusively for the Roman aristocracy. The sauce was also prescribed as a medicine, mixed with other ingredients for digestive disorders, applied to sores and taken neat for sciatica, tuberculosis and migraines. With this sort of product to sell, someone on the island had to be making a lot of money.

After the fall of Rome, Ibiza struggled to survive. The island fell into disrepair; wandering bands of itinerant sea-faring plunderers passed through, liberally dispensing fire and the sword, and the inhabitants scratched out a living as a simple, poverty-stricken agrarian people. All was desolate and bleak. The salt flats were Ibiza's only life support during these dark times, giving ships a reason to stop on its blighted shore.

The Muslim emirs who ruled Ibiza at the end of the first millennium effected a sweeping plan to modernize the salt business. They developed complex networks of sluice gates and channels, most of which are still in use today. These controlled and pumped the sea water using a chain of windmills and stone aqueducts along the coast. So well designed was this Moorish set-up that the only significant modification has been the gradual mechanization of the pumps and the arrival of conveyor belts to collect the dried salt at harvest time.

In 1235 the Catalans forced the Moors out of Ibiza, and initially the conquering King of Aragon shared the revenue from the salt industry with his noble supporters. Then, in 1267, with stunning munificence, they handed over all the rights of extraction from the salt pans to the people of Ibiza, retaining only their ownership of the land.

At this time, city states such as Genoa and Venice were expanding. They needed salt fish to feed their sailors. At the same time, new curing techniques in Spain and Italy were creating luxury salted foods such as Parma ham. The Genoans, who had been part of an earlier anti-Moorish crusade in 1114, made contact with Ibiza and found the quality of its salt very much to their liking. Gradually, the salt trade rebuilt Ibiza's former international links.

By 1290, salt trading with the Genoese had become Ibiza's largest source of revenue, and the Italian city's investment in the salt pan infrastructure had built Ibiza into the largest salt producer in the entire Mediterranean. In a number of thirteenth-century deals between the Genoese and the salt-cod-obsessed Basques, the Basques were happy to swap fully built ships for access to Ibiza's crisp white crystalline flats. Ships from Spain and as far north as the North Sea and the Baltic docked to load great sacks of the stuff. Profits soared. And then soared again.

In the sixteenth century the Basque people hit on fecund, cod-filled waters off the coast of Nova Scotia and there was a new explosion in the demand for salt, needed to preserve the fish on the long transatlantic voyages. At the same time the European powers were building their overseas empires, and the switch in trading emphasis from the Mediterranean to the Atlantic meant that ships were setting out on longer and longer voyages. Feeding the sailors became a strategic business for navies across Europe, and salted food was the answer.

So successful were Ibiza's salt pans that they almost entirely financed the extensive Renaissance walls that still surround Ibiza's old town. Designed and built by the Italian architect Giovanni Battista Calvi and completed in 1585, they stretch for two kilometres with seven bastions and a road atop. Unfortunately, this brought the profitability of the salt pans to the attention of the Spanish mainland.

In 1702, the War of the Spanish Succession broke out, with France and Castile attempting to put Philip V on the Spanish throne while Austria, England and the Netherlands backed his rival, Charles III. The Catalans, fearing Castile's burgeoning power, went with the Austrian-led Grand Alliance. Halfway through the war, the English switched sides – gaining Gibraltar and Menorca for their favours – and tossed their Catalan allies to the wolves of Castile. A victorious Philip V stripped the Catalans of all their ancient rights and merged them into the Spanish nation state. For Ibiza, this meant the loss of considerable freedoms and, more importantly, the loss of their only visible means of support. Philip punished Ibiza for its support of Charles by claiming the salt flats for the government, and he diverted the salt-pan profits directly to the Spanish Crown. With revenue from the island's main industry now heading to the mainland, a deep economic slump set in which lasted roughly two hundred years.

Towards the end of the eighteenth century, salt's value

and importance began to wane. Perhaps the Ibicencos permitted themselves a wry smile when, in 1803, a Parisian chef named Nicolas Appert came up with the idea of sealing food in a jar to preserve it. In 1809, the first canning plant in Britain opened, in London. By 1830 most European navies had replaced salted food with tinned food. The demand for salt plummeted. In 1871, the state sold the pans to a private company for 1,160,000 pesetas.

The Ibicencos remained in the salt-pan business but it was always a tough job. Mules couldn't work the flats because the salt ate into their hooves, so the 100,000 tons of salt extracted every year had to be dug out with axes and carried to the port on men's shoulders before the first rains at the end of September – right in the heat of the summer, in other words. A steam engine took over the long haul to port in the late nineteenth century, then twentieth-century improvements saw conveyor belts, trucks and tractors handling the bulk of the work.

With the men no longer attending to the pans every day, leggy marsh birds such as the egret, heron and European flamingo flocked to the delicately balanced environment, feeding on the brine shrimp alongside waders such as the black-winged stilt. The birds have always loved this gentle, warm breeding ground – the Romans used to trap them here, and Apicius offers a recipe for a delicately flavoured casserole of flamingo – but with the pans so quiet most of the year, they flourished. The area became a rare and complex ecosystem.

Then, in a 1972 plan to develop the Balearic Islands, the salt flats were offered up as a potential location for sea-view apartments. In 1977, a proposal to develop luxury housing in the soft, untarnished hills that surround the pans lit the first spark of Ibiza's Green movement. This proposal was stopped at Ibiza's planning commission after public protests and, crucially, opposition from the island's College of Architects. In 1990, however, the developers came back with a plan to build over six hundred tourist villas – a move that would have covered the entire hillside with houses and permanently destroyed the delicate salt-water habitat.

Conservationists who went digging into the paperwork found out exactly who would be the current beneficiaries of the potential riches locked up in the pans – members of Ibiza's wealthiest and most politically connected families. These environmentalists spread the word. Two local Green organizations, Friends of the Earth and the highly vociferous Grupo de Estudios de la Naturaleza (GEN), launched the 'Save the Salinas' campaign and set about agitating to build popular opposition. GEN protesters locked themselves in Ibiza Town's cathedral, organized marches and protests, leafleted and planted stickers all over the island. They began a push for the salt pans to be protected under a new environmental law on natural spaces that was before the Balearic government in Mallorca. They also reported the development to the European Commission as an infringement of the law on protected species, the pans being home to several threatened plants and birds.

The political establishment initially counterattacked, accusing the Greens of acting like communists. Then they changed their tune, offering concessions on the number of villas and the amount of land they'd use. In the meantime they'd been lobbying over in Palma, and the Salinas were excluded from the draft list of protected natural spaces. The

GEN had to spend considerable sums counter-lobbying, and the battle went right to the wire.

Finally, in January 1991, the Balearic government included the Salinas in the list of natural spaces by a tiny majority. The salt flats were awarded the status of Area Natural de Especial Interés, which secured them the highest protection under the law. Since then they have been designated a National Park and received recognition from both the EU and UNESCO.

Bolstered by this initial success, the Green movement went on to oppose a plan to build a luxury hotel, golf course and desalination plant on the hills behind Cala D'Hort. With the area home to rare orchids and Eleanor's Falcon, a highly endangered species, victory seemed certain. The campaign started in 1992 and initially looked like a short-term shoe-in, but it didn't quite work out like that. After years of legal wrangles, the development snuck past all the Green movement's objections and got the go-ahead in 1998. The bulldozers moved into position, ready to set to work on the golf course once the pesky Greens stopped chaining themselves to their tracks. The GEN decided to take the matter to the people, and in January 1999 organized their protest, described by Ferrer as the biggest demonstration in Ibiza's history. Eleven thousand people took to the streets of Ibiza Town – over 14 per cent of the island's population.

The wave of popular opposition to the Cala D'Hort golf course helped sweep the PP from power. By August 1999 the PACTE government had put a stop to development, creating the Cala D'Hort National Park in February 2002 and slapping down protection orders on the salt pans. The imminent election of 2003 was the islanders' first chance to vote on the PACTE's environmental policies – they had also vetoed plans to enlarge the airport so that it could handle jumbo jets – with the Partido Popular eager to license building in the area again. The salt was on the table.

'What about PREF?' I asked Ferrer.

He smiled. 'You remember I said there was a power struggle within the PP between three families? One of the ones that lost set up PREF,' he said. 'They are more conservative than the PP, and most of the founders are people from the mainland originally. The PP has Ibicenco people who speak Ibicenco, born and bred here. In PREF they only speak Spanish, and they disapprove of Catalan.'

Still, I pointed out, they had a drag queen at their party.

He laughed. 'You should go and see the salt pans,' he told me. 'They're quite unusual.'

And so I did.

Sometimes it's good to go against the flow just for the sheer joy of it – taking the path less travelled, ploughing a lonely furrow, standing out from the crowd. It gives you a sense of independence and of mission. For many people it reassures them of the rightness of their path. Isolation breeds conviction.

At three o'clock on any sweltering afternoon, the Ibicenco section of the island's population will sensibly be partaking of a siesta. The international section will be lying on sandy beaches, swimming in cool turquoise sea water, splashing in sparkling swimming pools or, in certain cases, still sleeping off the excesses of the night before. After leaving the *Diario*'s offices I, on the other hand, found myself standing in the middle of a vast, heat-hazed plain trying to wipe sweat drips off my nose and wishing I'd brought a hat. Sometimes it is good to go against the flow, but sometimes it isn't. The sun was beating down on my rapidly reddening head and I'd just finished my last drop of unpleasantly warm mineral water. The car offered air-conditioned comfort – as the handbook gleefully pointed out – but I was having none of it. I had come to look at the salt pans, so look at the salt pans I would.

Ferrer was right when he described them as unusual. They looked like an endless collection of flat fields on the receiving end of a heavy fall of snow. Each shallow pan was filled with sea water, but the stone floor was covered in dirty pink layers of fresh salt, forming strange patterned crusts beneath the surface. In places, the water formed its own white scum, although I couldn't tell whether this was a by-product of the salt or some seaborne detergent pollution. In between each pan I spotted narrow footpaths, some laced with weeds, others with drying flakes of saline deposits. The extreme heat created a haze that seemed to beat and throb, adding a curious, twisted slant to the surreal vision. Every few minutes an Airbus roared over my head on its way in to land, making me duck even though I knew its wheels wouldn't hit me. It felt as though I'd landed on a Mars space station. In a Seat.

I'd had vague hopes of finding a gleaming headquarters building, perhaps called Casa Salinas, housing the local salt company. I'd thought I might step into their air-conditioned foyer where a graceful receptionist would hand me a plastic cup filled with ice-cold water then direct me to a keen PR executive sitting behind a large wooden desk who could talk me through the supply-and-demand-level economics behind scraping it up and sending it out. In fact, all I found was a walled compound with a rusty iron gate enclosing three or four mountains of salt, each one the size of a small castle keep, watched over by a bored-looking man in a dusty shirt. He watched me without a flicker of interest as I picked my way along the narrow paths between the pans until I made my way up to the gate and smiled as cheerfully as my sweating, exhausted frame would allow.

'Hi,' I gasped.

He nodded behind me at the route I'd taken to reach him. In the distance I could see my white Seat, looking absurdly out of place in a timeless landscape. 'Those paths are private property,' he said, in almost perfect English. 'You can't walk on them unless you are an employee of the company. There are signs.'

'I didn't see them,' I said. 'Sorry.'

He didn't seem all that bothered by my trespassing, and we gazed at each other in silence for a few seconds. I'd brought a notebook to record interviews with salt company staff, but it didn't seem appropriate to wield its sweat-damp pages just yet. Still, I'd come all the way out here, so I'd better ask him something.

'Where does all the salt go?' I blurted out, mainly to fill the increasingly embarrassing pause in our budding conversation.

He shrugged. 'Norway.' Slight pause. 'And Scotland.' Longer pause. A drop of sweat began to trickle down the bridge of my nose. 'They salt herring with it in Norway and pour it on the roads in Scotland.' He seemed to find this slightly amusing. There was another pause.

I turned to follow his gaze out across the acres of shallow, lapping water. Another jet thundered towards the runway. 'Must be quite a lot of water out there,' I ventured.

He sniffed.

I pulled out my guidebook and flicked to the relevant page. 'It says two and a half thousand litres here.' My voice sounded slightly shrill as my confidence faded. I had intended to ask if the salt company had a phone number I could call, but somehow my courage failed me. I wanted to be somewhere else, preferably somewhere else with air-con, San Miguel and comfortable chairs, and I wanted to be there now. 'Well, *adios, señor.*' I attempted a lame grin.

'Goodbye,' he said.

And I picked my way back to my car, slipping on some loose earth about halfway back and feeling the power of his gaze on my back, out-scorching the sun in the heat of its scorn.

Election day dawned, the day the island decided. I drove Marina to San Jordi where she was standing for her seat. San Jordi is a small, concrete village on the road from Ibiza Town to the airport, and it's fair to say that it is not the most attractive place on the island. It takes a certain amount of dedication to realize that you aren't just driving through an industrial estate. There is, I am told, a fine church in the heart of the village – strongly fortified against pirate attacks with full battlements – but actually walking around San Jordi requires such an act of grim determination that few people have the will power to go looking.

The polling station was in a primary school, just like polling stations everywhere in the world. The voting took place in the main hall although, unlike the rundown Victorian gyms that had hosted my London ballots, this hall boasted a high, white, concrete ceiling that arched above a small stage like a miniature concert arena. The local worthies in charge of the vast Perspex boxes into which people posted their votes were perched uncomfortably on primary-school chairs behind primary-school tables and the whole thing reeked of the delightful amateurism that surrounds most immensely profound experiences.

I know this sounds pathetic, but I honestly find myself on the verge of tears every time I exercise my franchise. As people line up to have a say in the way their country is run, patiently dealing with the bizarre, ritualistic bureaucracy, marking their boxes and going on about their business, I feel so strongly moved that I think there must be something wrong with me. It's such a simple thing, but when you think of the people who fought and marched and wrote and dreamed of the chance to have some control over their lives, and who were exiled, imprisoned, beaten or killed by those who wanted to keep that tiny moment of power out of their hands . . . well, it gets to me, anyway. It got to me in Ibiza too, although the Ibicencos eschewed the silent dignity of the British electorate and opted, instead, for an extended party.

The room itself was packed. Voting in Ibiza seemed to be a social occasion. People arrived with their families and friends; there were couples pushing babies, parents trying to control their kids, bewildered-looking teenagers casting their first votes in expensive clothes. People strolled in, saw old friends, stopped for a chat, said hello to the mayor, went to the table to register, saw another friend, had another chat, picked up their voting forms, broke off for a brief political row with their partners, caught their kids, sent them outside, saw someone else they knew, told a funny story, finally got round to voting then bumped into their parents on the way out. In the name of scientific enquiry I timed a family from the moment they walked in through the door to the moment they left. The whole process took over an hour and a half. As a result, the hall was seething with people the entire day, talking, laughing, shouting greetings. The actual voting part seemed just an excuse for a village square get-together.

By seven p.m., with an hour to go before the polls closed, the pace of the punters was showing no signs of slowing down but the candidates were beginning to relax. The PACTE cracked open a bottle of Johnny Walker and sipped it out of paper Coca-Cola cups while Marina's PREF opened cans of lager. They exchanged friendly banter and put their feet up on the concert stage. I fell into conversation with one of the socialists, Juan Mari Serra, the economics and tourism secretary for the party. He was feeling pessimistic about the result. Rafael walked past looking tense and worried, trying to get his footsoldiers out to knock a few more people up and make sure they voted, but he seemed philosophical when they waved beer cans at him in mock-indignant refusal.

After the polling stations closed, everyone piled into a collection of cars and drove up the road to a lino-tiled tapas bar for more beer, bread, sardines, chicken and olives. They were stuffing it down, Marina told me, because the count was about to start and everyone wanted to get to the town hall. I asked her how long it would be until the votes were tallied. She reckoned it would be about three a.m. 'And what do you do while you're waiting?' I asked. She shrugged. Now, I may be moved by the actual casting of the vote, but sitting on plastic seats for eight hours watching people count slips of paper lacks appeal. It was time to sneak off. I told Marina I'd phone her in the morning.

While I slept, Ibiza changed hands. I woke up to find the Partido Popular back in power. Marina, when I called, was gloomy. The PREF had failed to win a single seat on Ibiza, but held the balance of power on Formentera. I wondered what this meant. Fumbling through my pockets, I pulled out the business card of the man from the PSOE I had met the day before, Juan Mari Serra. He agreed to meet me a few days later in a small café opposite the party's offices on the Avenida Espagna.

Serra turned up five minutes late. He had a friendly, bearded face and looked like a Californian baby boomer with slightly greying hair and the hint of a tan. As we waited to be served, he told me that he had worked for the PSOE for years. 'I have cousins on the council all over the island, but they all stand for the Partido Popular.' He grinned. 'I am the black sheep of the family.' He went into politics as a young man because Franco outlawed his language, Catalan. When he was growing up, had he spoken the tongue he'd been born into in a bar or a public place, he could have been arrested. Now, some of his anger had dissipated, but as we spoke it seemed to be rising up again.

'In the end, it was the money.' He sighed. 'They played a nasty game, the right wing. A lot of the building companies, who are owned by people with links to the PP, refused to extend their employees' contracts until after the election. They told them that they weren't sure there was going to be any more building if we got in, so they didn't want to tie themselves to contracts. Some of the hotels were opening very late. People began to get scared. If people think they are going to lose their jobs, they vote the way their bosses tell them.' We sat in silence for a moment, and his kind, Californian face began to darken. 'I don't think they will do all the things they say, the PP.' He spoke quietly, a little unsure. 'They want to build golf courses, but think of all the water that it takes to supply a golf course. We don't have very much water on the island. Already some of the farmers drilling down have started to strike salt water. There is no coast left. All the beaches that were so beautiful have apartment blocks and hotels just thrown up without care, without planning. Now there is no coast, where will we go? Into the interior? I cannot believe they want to destroy everything.'

We talked for a little bit longer about growing up as a black sheep, about his children, about life in San Antonio before the tourists, and then he had to go. He refused to let me pay the bill, slapping down his money in a way that brooked no discussion. We stepped outside the café where I shook his hand, turned and wandered back down the Avenida Espagna to the Marina. On the way I passed through the Vara de Rey and nipped into Llibreria, the international bookshop, to buy a copy of the English-language magazine *Ibiza Now*. On page eleven there was a story headlined NEW HOTEL BEDS:

The Island Council has given the green light for the development of a tourism complex in the municipality of San Josep. The Vistabella, in the area of Benimussa, will have 11 bungalows and a total capacity of 33 beds. According to current law, which has been in effect for several years now, no new tourism beds can be built on the Balearic Islands unless others are closed down, a zero-sum game. Vice President Enrique Fajarnes, during the presentation of the project, could not give any information about when and where the appropriate number of old hotel beds will be eliminated.

It seemed that Serra had been wrong. The PP were getting ready to do everything they said they were going to do. One of their policies was to amend the environmental protection law Ley de Espacios Naturales, passed in 1991 to protect the salt pans. The PP was especially keen on relaxing building restrictions in protected areas. The hotels would finally be coming to Salinas.

CHAPTER 4

The Senator

Turning up at a new hotel is always fun. It's like a blind date, and even the questions are the same. What will they look like? Will you enjoy sleeping with them? Have they left a poo in your toilet? My new lover was the Hotel Ses Figueres, up the coast from Ibiza Town in a sandy bay called Talamanca. The hotel was basic, but clean. My small single room boasted a balcony that looked out over the Mediterranean with a distant glimpse of the walls of Dalt Vila. Below me, German teenagers lounged on the harsh stone surface of a solarium, their gangling, adolescent bodies slowly turning pink.

I'd arrived towards dusk, checked in, unpacked and gone to sit outside the hotel with a beer as night fell. I was watching the waves lick the shore and wondering what to do that night when Pablo, the tall, slim young man who'd checked me in, wandered out. We got chatting about the hotel, which belonged to his family. He'd been working there since he was fifteen – from standing behind the reception desk to cleaning the rooms to working in the family shop over the road, and he seemed unusually dedicated. Because they had a large number of German guests, he'd taken jobs in Munich and Cologne in order to learn the language. He had wanted to become a pilot, but it hadn't worked out.

'There isn't really any option but to go into tourism.' He sounded slightly pessimistic as he sipped his dark coffee and stared at the solarium jutting into the sea. There was a pause. 'My father and his father built that solarium with their hands. They had to carry the stones themselves and mix and pour the concrete. We have a saying in Spain: a man builds a business with his blood and his sweat. His son makes it work. Then his grandson runs it into the ground.' He laughed.

As it turned out, Pablo owed his life to that hotel. His grandfather opened the place in the 1950s as a nine-room *pensión* on a deserted beach. In those days the tourists – usually wealthy adventurers – would be picked up at the port by his grandfather in a horse and cart and taken as near to the guesthouse as the roads would allow. Then they'd heft up their cases and stride across fields dotted with thousand-year-old Moorish water gates to reach the low white building. Pablo's grandfather would be behind them, shouting directions and carrying a huge slab of ice on his shoulders that he'd picked up from the same boat.

By the time Pablo's mother, Patricia Brown, sitting in her London office, spun a globe, stabbed her finger down at random and found herself pointing at Ibiza, the island had an airport. Patricia was working as a secretary, and she spent the next year saving like mad to stack up enough cash to get there. She flew out to the island, landed on a gravel runway, passed through immigration in a wooden terminal building and caught a bus that was so high off the ground she had to jump up to board it. When the bus pulled up outside the

Hotel Ses Figueres, she was so excited she stood right at the front and was the first to get off. The owner's son had come to meet them, and as the doors opened he reached up and offered her his hand. She saw a boyish, tousled man with a cheeky grin smiling up at her. Two years later they were married. Two years after that, Pablo was born.

I looked back at the hotel's five storeys of gleaming white modernity. 'So did you knock the original *pensión* down?'

'No,' he replied with a smile, 'it's still there. We just built around it. You know, it's hard to build things in Ibiza. In most small towns in Europe they have street lights and drains. Here, if you build something, you have to provide the drains and the lights and even the pavements yourself. We pay taxes, which go to Madrid, and then the money comes back, but somehow Mallorca always gets a bigger share. And the money that does come here – well, Ibiza Town has lights and pavements and new roads that we paid for out of our taxes, but we have to pay again for our own roads. Over the last forty years we have earned a lot of money from the tourists, but it isn't shared out very fairly.'

Another silence fell. In order to fill its gaping maw, I told Pablo I didn't know what to do that night.

'But you must go to the Festival of San Juan tonight – it starts in a couple of hours,' he exclaimed, sounding slightly horrified that I wasn't already there. I excused myself on the grounds that Ibiza had so many festivals it was impossible to keep track of all of them.

It doesn't take much to persuade the Ibicencos to throw a festival. There's pretty much one a month. Boats parade through the streets to celebrate seagoing saints at the drop of a hat, and there are fireworks almost every week. In February, there's the El Gato satirical religious festival that involves *Spitting Image*-style mockery of political figures. There's a football match between bachelors and married men in San Augusti over the summer, but no-one quite knows what that's for. And then there's my favourite – the watermelon fight. This takes place every August to celebrate the victorious arrival of the Catalans. It starts with a small ceremony at the Capella Sant Ciriac followed by a procession through the town, and then there's basically a mass watermelon fight beneath the walls of Dalt Vila. The association between conquering Christians and watermelons is sadly lost to the cupboard of time, but it doesn't really matter. It's hard to conceive of anything more fun than diving into a mass of people who are hurling armfuls of watermelons at one another. I, for one, would be far keener to celebrate historic victories if the anniversary were accompanied by a vast food fight.

It shouldn't be too hard to arrange. London already has Trafalgar Square, a large, open space that seems almost built for the purpose. Perhaps we could select a few ancient skirmishes that went our way – usually against the French – and head down to Admiralty Arch with a vast collection of foodstuffs, ready to chuck them about with gay abandon. Watermelons, of course, are fine for Ibiza, but for colder climes perhaps the traditional Hollywood custard pie would be more fitting. We could invite the French president to participate to show there was no ill will, that we were all European brothers now. Chirac could start proceedings by hurling a flan at the Queen – who would then, of course, be required to administer the ceremonial Oliver Hardy Wipe of Her Mouth and Eyes before we all fell to with a will. Trust me, it'd work.

Pablo, however, waved the watermelon fight away with a casual hand. In his view, the Nuit de San Juan was the most important. On Ibiza, it signalled a cleansing and a rebirth of such significance that it might as well be the Ibicenco New Year. Pre-Franco, all legal contracts came into force and terminated on the Nuit de San Juan. For me, Pablo said, it would be a night of bonfires and hedonism in honour of St John the Evangelist; for Ibicencos, he implied, it meant something I could never grasp. 'You must go to the town of San Juan itself,' he commanded, sounding like a youthful Obi Wan Kenobi. He grabbed my empty beer bottle. 'Go now.' So I hit the old Roman road heading up from Ibiza Town towards the tiny northern town of San Juan.

Of course, the Romans left Ibiza the roads. They left roads everywhere. From a modern-day perspective it's arguably the defining feature of their civilization. Apart from the roads, however, the Romans treated the White Island very badly. They arrived to take control over one of the great cities in Europe, a powerful trading force and minor military power in its own right; five hundred years later they departed leaving a small, scrappy, ill-defended island with a dormant economy that was struggling for survival in a hostile world.

The archaeological record after the Romans arrived in 146 BC is deceptive. Initially, the occupation seems to have led to a golden age. The city grew larger, the production of pottery increased, agriculture took off and garum production developed. Roman technology – specifically, enormous stones to squeeze more oil out of the fruit – helped boost Ibiza's olive oil production. Similar milling techniques helped grind flour, and complex irrigation systems fuelled greater crop yield. The Romans introduced the contemporary equivalent of factory fishing: tuna were guided through mazes of nets to waiting fishing boats and a bloody death at the hands of fishermen wielding machetes. This technique, most recently known as *almadraba*, was used in Ibiza until the 1950s when tuna finally disappeared from the area.

Although this seems generous, local historians such as Benjami Costa, curator of Ibiza's archaeological museum, have begun to see the signs of economic prosperity as the result of the Roman demand for war reparations. He believes that the Romans were milking Ibiza as hard as they could, treating it as a sort of vassal state and allowing the Ibicencos to keep their currency, temples and traditions pretty much as they would with a conquered people. This is why Tanit worship survived for so long. The same language and the same gods ruled the occupied Punic population. Out in the countryside, it's doubtful the farmers even knew the island had changed hands.

For the urban elite, who well knew of their precarious relationship with the world's largest military force, forgiveness finally came in 80 BC. Ibiza submitted to Rome, and its social and economic structures were broken up and remodelled along Roman lines in the process of federation. It was a sudden and hasty step, and it probably came about because the Romans realized Ibiza's incredible strategic value for controlling the eastern Mediterranean. This became important because a bout of insurrection was troubling the mother city.

On the mainland, a Roman general called Quintus

Sertorius was leading the Iberian tribes in open revolt. He had taken part in a previous civil war under his mentor, Gaius Marius, in 87 BC, lost, fled to Spain and then sailed for North Africa with a small band of three thousand soldiers. It seems likely that he passed through Ibiza on the way there, and possibly again on his return to lead the Iberian rebellion. With Sertorius fighting to get control of Spain, the Roman navy desperately needed strategic offshore bases, and Ibiza's worth was revalued. Ibiza became federated to bring it into the fold. Everyone was friends again and the Romans could prevent Sertorius receiving supplies and reinforcements from the sea.

In 72 BC, Sertorius was murdered and his revolt failed. Ibiza settled back to enjoy the fruits of its new-found status, but the empire had big plans, and Ibiza was just a small island. Within fifty years Rome had reorganized the empire into a single economic entity. Through the *latifundia* system, agriculture was centralized with entire regions providing enormous quantities of a single crop. Olive oil, for instance, was produced in southern Spain and North Africa, especially Tunisia, from vast olive groves stretching away to the horizon, tended by thousands of slaves. These regions produced in such huge quantities that Ibiza and Formentera couldn't begin to compete in terms of quality or cost.

Before the Romans arrived, the world was a world of city states. They may have been related to one another, as Ibiza was related to Carthage, but Ibiza always kept its own government and its own rules. Under Rome's unified empire, the town became just an administrative unit in an enormous territory centralized under the authority of the Eternal City. Ibiza lost all value except as a base for navigation and began to sink into decline under the effects of the first great globalization experiment.

I must admit that Rome's relationship with Ibiza came as something of a shock. For most of my life I had basically bought into the view that the Romans were the best thing that could have happened to the world. They were my favourite people from history. I loved the blend of order, decadence and practical beauty that made up their world. Given the choice, I would do projects on them, buy books on them or read historical novels set in their ancient empire. I was a chariot spotter.

Perhaps this is because I went to a fairly rough all-boys south London comprehensive. It wasn't one of those guns 'n' crack sink schools – this was in the nice middle-class London Borough of Bromley after all – but random violence was the currency of the playground. Our peer group induction as first years was a sustained programme of a rite known as 'bog washing', where our tender young heads were forced into the porcelain bowl of a WC and the cistern emptied repeatedly. The Sandwich Patrol stole packed lunches. The Snorkel Patrol picked up small boys wearing snorkel parkas and swung them round by the hood. The Soul Patrol beat up kids wearing pleated trousers. Until the fourth year, you could never be sure whether you were going to end up in a fight at lunchtime or not – usually for reasons that remained unclear even when the fight was over.

Against such a wall of random uproar, the Romans stood out as models of order. Their power was based on justice and intelligence, and that appealed immensely to me as a skinny, bookish and shy adolescent. I had to dodge blows twice a day, but the Romans had triumphed over mindless tribes of primitive thugs with reason, planning and organization. They'd formed rigid defensive lines and crushed the bullies beneath their shields. And then there was sex. The tough kids from the estate were getting laid every night. I could only dream. In the darkness of my early adolescence, the Romans proved it was possible to have wild orgies and still maintain a sensible attitude towards morality and footwear.

In my school playground, I had stood shoulder to shoulder with the legions at the outskirts of the empire, facing down barbarian hordes in the driving rain while dreaming of marble columns and intellectual debate. I knew their suffering and loved them for it. So finding out that they were the ancient equivalent of the World Bank was a little tough.

Ibiza didn't do as badly as some parts of the empire. The salt pans were a valuable commodity, allowing the island to punch slightly above its weight. Take the case of the senator's money. In AD 112, the wealthy Roman magistrate Caius Julius Tiron Gaetulicus died and left a considerable sum of cash to an up-and-coming Ibicenco called Lucius Sempronius Senecio. The denarii would have come in very useful to Senecio, who was on his way up the political ladder, and in Rome this was an expensive business. But Senecio held a low-level office in a branch of the legal system that might have allowed him access to Gaetulicus's will, so the praetor's family cried foul, arguing that Senecio had faked the will to further his own ambition.

After some legal rough and tumble, the case was finally heard by the Emperor Trajan himself. That summer the trial was the talking point of all Rome. Over in Ibiza the Cornelius family, a wealthy and powerful clique who had privately funded the construction of Ibiza Town's aqueduct, received a detailed report on the case from Pliny the Younger – which today would be roughly like being sent a personal report by John Simpson. Few Roman families could boast their own court reporter, particularly one of such status. The top Ibicencos were no rock-bound hicks. Ultimately Trajan found for Senecio, who returned to Ibiza Town and raised a tablet of thanks to his friend Gaetulicus. Senecio rose to govern Judaea, a high-profile but turbulent province that might have proved an ill wind but at least got him away from the unfashionable backwater he had grown up in.

Before they were finally forced out, their legions returning to defend the Eternal City from rampaging Germanic tribes, the Romans did at least give Ibiza Roman Catholicism, the faith it has tussled affectionately with ever since. Admittedly, Ibicencos allowed Catholicism to sit on top of their pagan traditions rather than to replace them root and branch. Artists fleeing to Ibiza from fascist persecution in the 1930s found rural songs, dances and ceremonies with roots in the Carthaginian era still being performed in houses, village squares and around wells in the countryside. Some were fertility rites, others worshipped the water spirits to ensure a healthy harvest. The tourist industry has since lapped these up with glee, and water-worshipping ceremonies that are a few thousand years old are now part of the calendar of entertainment offered by the tourist board.

The Nuit de San Juan also has some distinctly unchristian

elements to it, as I found out. The entire evening felt rooted in rituals far, far older than the preaching of the gospel. When I arrived, though, everything seemed ordinary enough. I parked my car some distance from the town so it took me some time to pick my way through the mass of slow-moving vehicles blocking the roads and arrive in San Juan's main street.

Most of the houses I passed seemed to be hosting some sort of party. A block of modern flats to my right had so many people dancing – and dancing extremely flamboyantly – on their various balconies that I wondered if someone was shooting a music video nearby. About a hundred yards up from the flats the police had barricaded the road, closing it off to traffic, so the crowds spilled past and into a little slice of pedestrianized alternative-culture heaven.

As I stepped beyond the barricade, I might have travelled a thousand miles and wound up in Camden. Stalls lined the street offering every possible item a New Ager could require to complete himself. Tie-dye. Joss sticks. Clothes, towels and posters with, variously, Bob Marley, the Buddha, Che Guevara, the cannabis leaf and obscure mystical symbols picked out in ultra-violet. The crowd pushed past them all, heading for two bars on the left towards the top of the hill.

I couldn't help but notice how many children were running around the place. Most were under ten. They were doing the things kids usually do at garden parties, school fêtes and family weddings – playing tag, skidding, shouting and screaming with laughter – but it was around 10.30 at night and almost everyone else was drunk. Initially, with my British sensibilities, I assumed these kids had sneaked out or were being callously ignored by their parents who, like all true Brits, preferred to get pissed in the pub and forget about their progeny. As I watched, however, it became clear that the families were actually all out together. Mum, Dad and the kids in town for the party. Teenagers who should have been sulking with the rest of their surly mates were messing about with kid brothers and sisters. Little three-year-old girls were dancing with their dads to deep house. Granny was having a beer and jigging up and down at the edge. It was like a mythically perfect rural community fused with a Hollywood vision of Woodstock, mixed to a heavy dance soundtrack.

Still a little baffled, I reached the small square opposite the town's church. Beneath it and to my right stretched a street that had been decorated to resemble a long, open-air nightclub. The DJ was running through his soundcheck with the usual deep trance house – Ibiza's catch-all blend of throbbing basslines and squeaky electronic noodling. Luminous shapes hung from netting above him, creating an effect that was designed to be Warlock's Cave but actually looked like a church hall Hallowe'en party.

Clearly the main fun was going to wind up there at some point, but in the meantime the opposite side of the square grabbed the crowd's attention. A low stage filled one end, supporting one of the largest musical ensembles I'd seen anywhere since the decline in popularity of the village brass band. In the case of this collective, the bongo drum had replaced the cornet as the backbone of the community sound. Of the eleven musicians, one played the guitar, one owned a keyboard and the rest flailed away at drums with varying degrees of enthusiasm and skill. The resulting noise was energetic but a little confusing. Fortunately, as I eased through the square, the sound man decided to whack up the actual instruments and switched off all amplification to the massed ranks of drummers, despite their increasingly frantic signs for more volume. At a stroke, the sound mix achieved an almost holistic balance and the rattle of percussion blended successfully with the sub-Hendrix ambitions of Mr Guitar.

Despite the rather haphazard nature of the performance, people were gradually congregating around the stage, carefully leaving a small space out in front that had curious papier mâché shapes dotted around it. There was a sense of anticipation. Something was clearly about to happen, so I shouldered my way into the scruffiest of the nearby cafés – which was packed to the rafters with yelling Ibicenco families – grabbed a couple of beers and weaved slowly out.

By the time I got back to the stage, the square was almost full and the band had slimmed down to a T. Rex-style guitar, bongos, Indian tabla and curiously amplified tambourine that somehow sounded like a full drum kit. All around me were people dressed just anyhow, from Sunday best to barely a bikini. There were couples, families, teenagers, clubbers, hippies and even the odd pensioner. It felt like a big village fête being held at midnight with a freaky psychedelic band. Like, say, the village fête from *The Wicker Man*.

Given my height, I am rarely popular at any outside event where there isn't a sharp hill rising under the audience, so I thought it best to squat down. Just as I'd levered myself into position, however, the crowd behind me surged forward and stumbled over my hunched form. Wrong choice again. I turned to see who was pushing from behind and saw, rising above the crowd like vengeful dominatrices, two stiltwalking angels driving all before them with cracking whips. Dressed like angels from a Renaissance artist's erotic nightmare, these girls wore gold bras and gold codpieces over tight white trousers. They crowned this excessively saucy ensemble with flamboyant white afro wigs and had large gold wings proudly strapped across their impressive bosoms. This was heaven as conceived by Hugh Hefner.

As they cavorted joyfully, like cherubs at the dawn of time (with whips and stilts), the band suddenly pounded into a dark musical crescendo. From behind the stage a Marc Bolan lookalike appeared, dressed as the Devil in scarlet trousers and demonic make-up, his powerfully muscled body oiled up and gleaming in the moonlight. Behind him stalked two equally well-toned male assistants. The powerful erotic overtones startled me slightly, given that this was, after all, in the church square don't you know, and there were kiddies about. A quick glance at the crowd revealed most parents giving their children a shoulder lift so that they could better view the spectacle, so I kept my prudish Victorian reservations to myself.

The devils and the angels fell to fighting with a vigour that decried their elaborate costumes. Although the angels had the advantage of height and whips, the dark lord won the day, reappearing on stage walking on two vast oil drums packed with fireworks. The devils cavorted around him, letting off crackers and bangers with the enormous cascading Roman candles they had rammed into the ends of their staffs. Finally, they touched their streams of liquid fire to the oil drums, which exploded in a glare of white light, flames pouring out as the lord of the underworld strode about laughing with glee and occasionally looking a little alarmed as a particularly big explosion threatened to topple him.

The music stopped for a second and the angels wafted back on, this time carrying with them two black-clad puritans who were protecting a pretty blonde woman dressed in virginal white. The devils fell upon them and, after yet another battle, the puritans fell. The devils stripped the girl in white to her knickers and tied her, topless, to a steel scaffold covered in fireworks. As they writhed orgiastically around her struggling body, the fireworks cascaded sheets of flame down towards the ground until the poor ravished virgin and her hellspawn tormentors vanished from view.

Finally, the fireworks sputtered, faltered and went out. Behind them was a black curtain. The music died away and a hush fell over the crowd. There was a pause, long enough to allow me to see if the kids were still watching and to register that they most certainly were, and then, kablam! Another burst of fire, another musical sting from the band and the curtain fell to reveal our mistreated innocent clad in body-hugging red leather, with straps and porno boots and an evil gleam in her merciless eye.

And then it was over. The cast ran forward, took a brief bow, and carried on running out of the top of the square. The crowd rippled, applauded and began to follow. I sat for a moment trying to fathom the message behind this lewd mummers play. I couldn't exactly identify the part of the saint's life that this performance was illustrating. And the Devil had clearly won, converting our young blonde from virginal heroine to lustful sex queen. Were they saying that it's more fun to be bad than good? And then, as the whole crowd cavorted up the hill behind the dancers and bonfires blazed into life at the summit and people passed one another bottles of beer and laughed and talked and sang, I realized the meaning behind the whole enterprise. The essential message appeared to be, 'Let's party!'

Following the crowd up the hill, I briefly felt like Edward Woodward in *The Wicker Man* again. A long, empty field lay before me and a line of ten blazing bonfires had been drawn down its centre. It all looked very mysterious and pagan. I could see a crowd of teenage boys milling around behind the flames while crowds surrounded the fires, clearly waiting for something to happen. Suddenly, a boy ran forward and seemed to leap into the first bonfire, stumbling as he fell through the flames onto the ground on the other side. Another followed, and then another, as the first boy hopped and stepped his way through all ten blazing beacons. Within minutes, young men were hurtling through the flames in huge numbers, occasionally emerging with wisps of fire playing through their hair. Fresh volunteers queued up behind them, jumping each fire in sequence and rejoining a growing queue to take another turn.

I couldn't work out the reason for this, but it seemed a waste not to take part. I stood at the back of the queue and moved forward as slowly as I could, hoping that the flames would die down a bit by the time I got to the front. They didn't, but I couldn't wimp out in front of such a crowd, which seemed to take great delight in cheering each jumper as he cleared each of the fires. I took a deep breath, half closed my eyes and ran as fast as I could, leaping like a crippled antelope through the blaze as sparks flew around me.

The final fire was the biggest and I'd mistimed my

approach to its neighbour, slipping and almost twisting my ankle before preparing myself for the boldest leap. As a result my jump wasn't quite right and I came down early, my left foot catching on a fiery log that rolled and almost tipped me into the flames. At the last minute I righted myself and tried not to break my stride as I jogged away with as much grace as I could muster, keeping my eyes firmly on the ground to check for stray branches that might yet unseat my fragile pride.

I pulled away to the left, saw the ground was clear and raised my eyes, only to look right into the face of a woman who seemed slightly familiar. I stopped, panting, with my hands on my knees, then looked back up to confirm my first suspicion. I was sure I was two feet away from Jade Jagger, daughter of Mick, star of gossip columns the world over and the island's reigning celebrity queen. She was dressed down and scruffy, with two kids playing about her ankles. Our eyes met again, and for a second I thought I was actually going to have the guts to speak to her. The mood of the evening seemed so friendly and she looked so unguarded and approachable, with hints of her daddy in her face but without his stage-show arrogance. Just as I opened my mouth, however, I lost my bottle and ventured a timid smile instead. She smiled back and turned away.

When I got back to the hotel, Pablo was in reception. I told him about jumping the fires and he smiled. 'Jumping over the fire is a ritual cleansing process,' he said. 'In jumping through fire, you are laughing at the Devil and cleaning yourself of your sins for another year, allowing you to emerge from the flames new and ready for the next twelve months. Having jumped the flames, you should head straight for the sea, take three steps into the water and make a wish which will come true in the next year.'

I looked at the door leading out to the beach.

'But it doesn't work,' he added with a sniff. 'Take it from me, I've done it three times.'

CHAPTER 5

The Poet

The resort of Figueretes is a bit like a post-war matinée idol who's spent the last ten years playing the patsy in Christmas pantos. Back in the 1950s, the tiny hamlet's wide, sandy beaches were the heart of Ibiza's all-night jazz scene. Since then it has mutated into a grim blend of yellow neon and unruly concrete that also plays host to the island's only lap-dancing bar, the Blue Rose. Right by the shoreline, though, there's a quiet strip of bars and restaurants where hipsters who now have families and older gay couples mix, united in their desire to keep some distance between themselves and the throb of Ibiza Town. Figueretes is a kind of halfway house. You could walk to the Marina from here if you had a strong pair of legs, but if you opted for an early night, no-one would be any the wiser.

I was in Figueretes to have dinner with Martin Davies and Emily Kaufman, the Robert Benchley and Dorothy Parker of Ibiza's expat set. Martin came out in 1993 after falling for a local boy he met while working as an art historian at the V&A in London. Emily, originally from Pennsylvania, fell in love with Spain as a visiting student, then fell in love with a Spaniard and shifted to the White Island when her former husband Pepe was headhunted by a local hotel. Both teach English, but use the wages to fund their other pre-occupations. Emily spends hours researching the island's history while Martin digs out any references he can find to Ibiza in the work of the many artists who passed through. They've both published books. Emily's tome, *The History Buff's Guide to Ibiza*, has both English- and German-language editions, although the German version sports an extremely saucy cover while the English version offers only a Phoenician galley, suggesting that German history may take a slightly more physical slant. Martin's collection of local photographs by legendary artists, *Eivissa-Ibiza: A Hundred Years of Light and Shade*, is out of print, but second-hand versions dot the local bookshops. With such erudition awaiting, I went to Figueretes feeling as though I were heading for the staff room at my secondary school.

Martin picked a seafood place set on concrete tiers dropping down from the main drag towards the beach, and I stepped nervously down to their table where both were enjoying the sunset. My schoolkid fears were rapidly dispelled. Far from a seminar, the dinner became a witty race through island gossip with a healthy dose of local character assassination. Martin was slightly ahead on dishing the dirt, while Emily was prepared to give people the benefit of some doubt, but by the time the main course arrived I felt suitably briefed on the relative levels of incompetence demonstrated by a good half of the island's public figures.

I made a fairly embarrassing hash of thanking the waiter for bringing me my skate. Indeed, it was so bad that I had to repeat *gracias* three times before he understood. His face was so grim at first that I felt sure I must have stumbled on a new form of pronunciation that meant 'your mother is a whore'. As he departed, I turned to find Martin and Emily looking at me with sympathetic but unmistakably teacherish faces. With gently supportive smiles, they offered to correct my hopeless Spanish pronunciation – an offer I felt it would be churlish to refuse. They began by working on my soft Cs – the pronunciation of *gracias* that makes it sound like 'grathias'. My problem, as I told them, has always been shifting out of the soft C at the end; I somehow overshoot so that it comes out as 'grathiath'. They both laughed, so I repeated it a few times, clowning for approval.

Suddenly Martin froze like a cat facing off a mongrel terrier. Had he actually hissed I wouldn't have been entirely surprised. Emily and I stared at him. He practically snarled, then let loose with a string of Spanish words that barked and stuttered like a machine gun. Had I been of a nervous disposition, I'd have worried that he was possessed by demons and was about to start rotating his head while chanting in ancient Aramaic. It turned out the problem was slightly more acute. 'Barcelona trash,' he spat, and I realized he was directing his gaze at the table next to us. I half turned my head and saw a gang of four men with short hair and unusual clothes half laughing at, half stunned by Martin's outburst. I looked back at him. 'They were mocking your accent,' he said grimly, refusing to take his eyes from the foursome. 'Barcelona trash think they're better than anyone else.' He then added something in Spanish that I couldn't directly translate but clearly understood to mean something extremely disrespectful.

For a few moments, I wondered if we would end up in a full, Wild West-style bar brawl, tables crashing on heads and chairs swinging into stomachs. There were four of them against three of us and neither Emily nor I had our dander up. The odds weren't good for our team. In the end, though, the four men wilted in the face of Martin's verbal onslaught, folded up their tents and sheepishly stole away. 'One thing you need to learn,' said Emily, wryly, 'language is something of an issue here . . .'

It might have been worse, she went on to explain, if they'd been trying to teach me Catalan. Language was at the heart of the political agenda and grown men had been known to come to blows over the use of certain words in public places. From the moment Ibiza fell under the rule of the Spanish Crown in 1717, Catalan had been suppressed. This continued until the 1950s, with Franco ruling that speaking or writing prose in Catalan was tantamount to treason. Nonetheless, Catalan intellectuals found, in the 1970s, plenty of peasants in Ibiza's hinterland still speaking pure Catalan and completely unable to understand Spanish. Under the PACTE government, a new generation of fervent Catalan speakers had ended up running the education system and the civil service. If you didn't know a word of Catalan, the chances of your getting a job were slim. The Spanish speakers didn't take kindly to this, the most peaceful reaction being schoolchildren protesting in the Vara de Rey.

Indeed, the old Henry Higgins saying 'When one Englishman opens his mouth, another Englishman despises him' is doubly true on Ibiza. The island communities are divided along linguistic lines. The British, Americans and Australians stick together, as do the Germans; the Spanish avoid the native Catalan speakers, and the French have as little to do with anyone else as possible. There is a hierarchy, and it's complicated. The pure-born Ibicencos are the top dogs, while the Spanish speakers come out close to the bottom. Ibicenco Catalans, for instance, talk Catalan to one another but would much prefer to speak English than Spanish to everyone else.

This state of affairs is further confused by the fact that Ibicenco Catalan is distinct from mainland Catalan. It's so distinct that the island *consell* is punting for it to be recognized as an official dialect by Madrid. Ibicenco Catalan has previously been lumped in with that spoken on Mallorca and Menorca as a single Balearic dialect, but it's a very coarse lumping. Over the last few centuries, there has been little contact between Palma and Ibiza – most of the island's trade was with the mainland – and the two versions of Catalan evolved in very different ways.

For a start, it's rather controversial to call the dialect Ibicenco Catalan. Ibicenco is a Spanish word. Those who speak it call it Eivissenc. The language arrived on an Arabic-speaking Ibiza with the Catalan conquerors at a time when Catalan itself was intensely regionalized. The nobles who took Ibiza for the crown of Aragon came from Ampurdan, Barcelona and Tarragona and the island's language ultimately combined words and forms from each dialect.

After the conquest, Ibiza remained largely in the hands of the ecclesiastical arm of the invading army, which mostly came from Tarragona. Meanwhile, on the mainland, Aragon Catalan came to dominate in a sweeping programme of language standardization, which drove a wedge between the evolution of the two dialects. Today, Eivissenc still employs some Medieval Catalan forms long out of use on the mainland. A strong Muslim presence and regular contact with salt-hungry Genoan sailors added a heavy sprinkling of Arabic and Italian. The definite article, for instance, is *sa*, which you won't find anywhere outside the island. There are also something like a thousand words of Arabic origin in Ibicenco, including place names such as Benirras and Benimussa, derived from the Arabic *banu* meaning 'son of '.

The strong local Arabic influence isn't confined to language. Many aspects of Ibicenco life still carry touches of the Moors. In one traditional local song, the *porfedi*, the singer covers her face with her hands in the style of a Muslim veil and trills with North African-style quivering wails. A recent genetic survey found that Ibiza's gene pool is far closer to North Africa than it is to the Spanish mainland.

The Moors – a mix of Arabs and Berber warriors from present-day Morocco – occupied Ibiza for some four hundred years, and created a vibrant, fertile garden. 'Yebisah is thirty parasangas long and almost as many wide,' wrote the Arab geographer al-Makkari mid-way through Moorish rule, 'and it supplies a great part of Africa with wood and salt. The island is highly populated, and its inhabitants are industrious; it produces all sorts of grain and fruits, but cattle do not multiply there. Grapes, almonds and figs are the things which the natives cultivate and export to the nearby island of Mallorca . . . Since there is much wood, the islanders' main industry consists in making carbon which they take in boats to Barcelona and other Mediterranean ports.' Arab authors refer to Ibiza as the daughter of Mallorca, the Arabic word for daughter being *bint*. It's clear from their description that she is a serious economic entity. Writers such as al-Himyari and al-Kazwini count ten harbours on the island;

barely three exist today. They commend the excellence of the shipbuilding, which they attribute in part to the quality of the local pines, and Ibiza's fruits, vineyards, grapes and raisins, as well as the 'inexhaustible' salt of its pans, come in for high praise.

And yet, in the years before Moorish rule, life on the island had almost ground to a halt. When the Muslim forces arrived, Ibiza Town lay in ruins and the population comprised a handful of farmers eking out their fragile existence, beset by raids from the troubled Mediterranean. The years after the Romans had been tough. When, in the closing years of the fourth century AD, the collapsing Roman Empire was split in two by Emperor Theodosius, Ibiza was part of the less fortunate western half.

Beset by Germanic tribes, Rome began to buy off its attackers. Mainland Spain went to the Visigoths in a deal with the western Roman emperor Honorius, who saw them as a civilized lot in comparison to the reckless and destructive Vandals. Honorius even recruited Visigoth mercenaries to fight the Vandals, who were clearly the worse of two very nasty evils. Having been forced out of mainland Spain, however, the Vandals ended up occupying Ibiza, along with the coast of North Africa. They secured control of the island shortly after taking Carthage and probably did so in a bid to recreate the old Phoenician strategic triangle, using the place as a port of call on long voyages and as a base for controlling the western Mediterranean. It seems likely that they did very little else once there but use the port facilities.

Archaeologists have found almost nothing from the years of Vandal occupation. These light-touch rulers were Christian, but practised a version of Christianity called Arianism, which believed that Jesus was the son of God but was separate, inferior and subordinate to God the Father. When they arrived, the Ibicenco population was almost entirely Catholic. Even so, there is no evidence that the Vandals tried to set up churches or convert the population.

Admittedly they did interfere, and interfere rather drastically, with Ibiza's Catholic Church at one point. In 483, Ibiza's bishop Ophilio was invited, along with his peers on Mallorca and Menorca, to Carthage to debate Catholicism versus Arianism with the Vandal king Huneric. 'Debate' is a loose term. Huneric's position seems to have been 'Catholicism is rubbish, and if you don't convert to Arianism I will kill you'. They didn't, and he did.

Even then, the Vandals don't seem to have built churches or forts or indeed anything on the island. They just berthed and resupplied until 532, when the Byzantine Empire declared war on the Vandals as part of a hopeless dream nurtured by their idealistic emperor Justinian. He longed to reunite the old Roman Empire, to recreate its majestic sprawl and secure the lush farmland of Spain and North Africa for his hungry economy. Devoting much of his empire's resources and most of his time to the project, he was partially successful. Ibiza became his in 535, shortly after he had taken Carthage, which suggests the same old strategic motive.

But the Byzantines didn't stay for long. In turning his eyes from the East, Justinian had shaken his mind free of the problem of his troublesome neighbours, the Persians. Taking advantage of the thinly stretched Byzantine forces, the Persians attacked, pushing into Syria, Egypt and Asia Minor.

They even laid siege to Constantinople, although the strength of the Byzantine navy proved too much for their inexperienced fleet. Finally, Byzantium was saved by the wily and ruthless emperor Heraclius who effectively restored the old frontiers of the two superpowers to their starting positions after almost a hundred years of constant struggle. The long, bitter cycle of war had drained these two behemoths of their money and strength and they stared, exhausted, at each other like weary boxers who no longer care which of them wins the title. Unable to afford its upkeep, Byzantine rule in Ibiza crumbled away.

For over two hundred years, the islands vanished from history. There is no mention of the Pitiuses in any chronicles or records. The archaeological evidence is scant, but the tiny population seems to have operated a kind of subsistence-level anarchism, with no power structures or rulers. What few people remained bumbled along with little outside contact, although the recent discovery of a cache of Moorish coins on Formentera suggests someone was doing business. Perhaps the salt pans kept an all-important trickle of foreign currency running into the island's coffers.

Over in the Middle East, meanwhile, the prophet Muhammad had united the warring tribes of Arab nomads and welded them into a supremely effective fighting unit. After his death in 632, his three successors – the Rashidoun, or Holy Ones – led these skilful horsemen out of Arabia and across Persia and North Africa with astonishing speed. Within ten years they had defeated the Persians and driven them out of modern Iraq, forced the Byzantines out of Syria and Egypt, and swept through North Africa; within another fifty years they had crossed into Spain then up into northern

France where they were finally halted at the battle of Poitiers.

Offering 'Islam or the sword' to all but Christians and Jews – who were 'children of the book' – the Muslim armies swelled in size as more converts joined up the further the original Arabs got from home. By the time they arrived in Spain they were a mixed bag of clans, each fiercely loyal to its tribal leader but content to co-operate in an uneasy alliance. These factions could often fall to in-fighting, and the first two hundred years of Islamic rule in Spain saw two separate kingdoms rise and fall. By the tenth century, however, the Caliphate of Córdoba had been established.

This entirely enlightened and technologically superior kingdom flourished and prospered, extending tolerance to Christians and Jews under its rule, while its cities could boast of sewers, pavements and street lighting and its houses had running water on demand. Great advances were made in astronomy, algebra and medicine, and Moorish scholars translated the works of the Greek philosophers, giving us the texts we use today. Public literacy was public policy. In comparison, London's mainly wooden buildings were being periodically burned to the ground during frequent skirmishes for control between rival tribes of illiterate Saxons, Danes and Norwegian Vikings.

Under the caliphate, Ibiza was rediscovered and re-populated, with farmers from North Africa rushing to till its rich soil. The Moors set up systems of irrigation that survived into the twentieth century and dug the water channels that still serve the salt pans. They founded Santa Eulalia, intensively farming the surrounding valley. They also created an administrative network that divided the islands into the same geographical units the current political system employs. Ibiza Town, known as Yebisah Medina, became a vital naval base, allowing the Moorish kings to control the western Mediterranean and command the maritime routes to and from France and Italy. Pirate raids against Christian shipping regularly set out from Ibiza, and the Balearics operated an independent fleet of some size until the Christian reconquest.

When the Córdoba Caliphate came to an end in 1002, a series of small Muslim kingdoms sprang up in the lands it had controlled. The rulers of these tiny empires, known to scholars as the 'party kings', encouraged the arts as well as the sciences. One beneficiary of this policy was an Ibicenco poet called Abu Ali Idris ibn al-Yaman, known in the Moorish world as al-Yabisi, 'the Ibicenco', or more commonly as al-Sabbini, after Ibiza's famous juniper trees. Although his date of birth is obscure, he died around 1077, putting the majority of his life under the rule of the benign king Ali of Denia and the Balearics.

Al-Sabbini became Ali's court poet, where his job, as with court poets through the ages, would have been to issue verses explaining in elegant detail just how fabulous his ruler was. This was a well-rewarded appointment. Al-Sabbini could freelance outside the court and usually charged one hundred gold dinars for a *qasida* or eulogy. As he told the ruler of Seville, 'The daughters of my inspiration are so highly appreciated, as you know, that he who would wed one of these poems must pay a handsome dowry.'

Only one fragment of al-Sabbini's poetry survives. It was collected by a North African editor, Ibn Sa'id al-Magribi, in a thirteenth-century anthology called *The Book of the*

Banners of the Champions. The book was translated in 1953 and published by the Cambridge University Press, where the translator, A. J. Arberry, gives this version of the only two verses that remain of a far longer work, 'Wings of Wine':

> Heavy were the glasses, though
> They were empty when they came;
> As I lit in them the flame
> Of pure wine, and let it glow.
>
> Suddenly they grew so light
> That they seemed about to soar,
> As the body, gross before,
> Flutters with the new-born spirit.

This ode to alcohol clearly indicates a liberal attitude to high living that would find little favour with today's fundamentalist imams. But then little about the party kings or the Córdoba Caliphate would impress al-Qaeda, even though a return of these lands is one of the claims for which Osama bin Laden sends out young people to die. For one thing, Jew and Muslim lived in absolute harmony. Indeed, some accounts of the original conquest of Spain by the Moorish armies suggest that this was the result of an appeal to their Muslim friends from the Jews of Spain who were suffering cruel persecution at the hands of the Christians.

The benevolent party kingdoms, however, faced extreme pressure from the Spanish Christians gathered in the north of the mainland. Inspired by the brutal slaughter of the Crusades and egged on by the Pope, at the turn of the century they launched the Reconquista, a religious campaign to retake the Moorish lands and expel their Muslim rulers. Under pressure from the north, the Moorish kingdoms buckled. The mainland kings turned to their defences, and for a while the Balearics became an independent kingdom, ruled by the former governor of Mallorca, al-Murtada. His brief dynasty collapsed in 1114 when a Christian raiding party from the city state of Pisa and the increasingly powerful kingdom of Catalonia looted the islands, laying siege to and taking both Ibiza Town and Palma before returning home laden with booty. A convoy of reinforcements from the hardline Islamic Berber tribes in Morocco known as the Almoravids arrived to find the Christians gone and the island's leaders dead. Not to waste an opportunity, they moved in and took over.

The Almoravids were dedicated to a fundamentalist interpretation of Islam and saw the Spanish Moors as corrupt and decadent. Using the Balearics as a base, they swept up into the remaining kingdoms, booted out the effete party kings and set about inflicting their version of the Koran on everyone they didn't kill – except in the Balearics, where the local populace were so outraged at the restriction of their liberties that they rose in violent protest. This led to a twenty-eight-year-long struggle against the Almoravid governor, or *wali*, that ended when the mainland sent out a new man to arrest his predecessor and repeal all the gloomy Almoravid laws.

This new *wali*, Ibn Ganiya, took over the Balearics just as the mainland suffered invasion by an even more fundamentalist group of Muslim Berbers, the Almohads. These warrior monks moved up from Africa and took the Almoravid territories across Spain, ultimately defeating the entire empire with the exception of Ibiza and Mallorca.

Ibn Ganiya promptly declared himself king and started rallying the refugee Almoravids to his banner.

His dynasty's rule was brief – 1143–1203 – but it saw the Balearics operating as an independent military power for the final time. Ganiya's son Ishaq stole the throne from his brother and instantly floundered in a sea filled with diplomatic mines. There were Almohads to the left and Christians to the right, so he responded with an impressively insane strategy. Called to pay homage to the Almohad caliph, he instead launched a Holy War against the Christians and was slaughtered at the height of his tiny crusade. His son Ali tried to maintain the island's independence, launching an equally unhinged attack on the Almohads that lost him Ibiza and then his life. Finally, in 1203, the rest of the Balearics fell to Almohad forces, although this was just ten years before the decisive mainland battle of Navas de Tolosa that clinched the Reconquista for the Christians. The Moors were forced into a long, drawn-out retreat. Ibiza was taken by the Catalans in 1235 and on the mainland only the Moorish kingdom of Granada held out, fending off Christian attacks for over 250 years.

In 1491, Isabel, the Queen of Castile, and her husband Fernando, the heir to the throne of Aragon and Catalonia, built the fortress town of Santa Fe near the coastal village of Malaga to launch the final attacks of the Reconquista. Almost incidentally, they also gave a commission to a strange and obsessive sailor by the name of Cristobal Colón – whom we know as Christopher Columbus – to pursue his single-minded dream of a voyage to the East. As he hurried to his ship, on 6 January 1492 Isabel and Fernando entered Granada and the Reconquista was complete.

Almost instantly, the monarchs turned on those the Moors had protected – the Jews. Within three months of the fall of Granada, an expulsion order was issued for any Jew refusing Christian baptism. Adherence to any other faith but Catholicism became tantamount to treason. Across Spain, Jews fled or concealed themselves, dreading the accusation that could bring the Inquisition to their doors. On Mallorca, fleeing Jews were beaten, robbed and in some cases lynched. Across the water in Ibiza, however, something curious took place.

From the moment the expulsion order was issued, the inhabitants of Ibiza and Formentera closed ranks around their Jewish population. Everyone on the island took part in a sustained policy of shelter, keeping their neighbours' Semitic identity a complete secret. Under Spanish law, any accusation to the Inquisition was completely anonymous, so a dissenting Ibicenco would never have been discovered and could have told on the Jews with impunity. But the accusations never came.

In part, perhaps, this was because of the size of the Jewish population. Even today, about a third of the pre-tourist-era families can trace their ancestry back to Jewish links. Uprooting 30 per cent of the island's inhabitants would have been economic and social suicide. At the root of this defiance, though, lurked the instinctive tolerance of the Ibicenco people. Isabel's expulsion of the Jews, and the existence of the Spanish Inquisition, is held up as a brutal piece of anti-Semitic violence. Which of course it was. But it was hardly exceptional. England had expelled its entire Jewish population in 1290 and refused to let them return for 350 years. In 1370, they were expelled from Belgium. In 1394, they were expelled from France. In 1497, they were expelled from Portugal. In 1540, they were expelled from the city state of Naples, and in 1550 from Genoa and Venice. With the entire continent murdering, expelling and stealing from the Hebrews, the stand taken by the Ibicenco people seems even more incredible. They would have the courage to maintain this position for the next five hundred years. From 1492, the Jews of Ibiza practised their faith in secret – or at least in secret as far as the mainland was concerned. Given that the chief synagogue in Ibiza Town was hidden beneath the chapel of the Convent of San Cristóbal, it's clear that even the Catholic Church on the island happily tolerated this theoretically heretical position.

The Jewish population engaged in dyeing, weaving, the salt trade and even piracy. As a result of the warm co-existence between Jewish and non-Jewish Ibicencos, Jews taken prisoner by Ibicenco corsairs did not have to pay the ransoms normally demanded. Indeed, Ibicenco corsairs often helped Jews to escape the clutches of the Inquisition in Palma. Rescued families were hidden on Formentera, especially in the area around the now ruined estate of Can Marroig, which sheltered Jews from the seventeenth century on and had its own underground synagogue. The policy of protection was highly successful. In 1868, Prinz Luis Salvador of Habsburg arrived in the islands, effectively as the first tourist. He wrote home to his mother about finding the Jewish population thriving, maintaining traditions and customs and playing an important role in the local economy.

In the 1930s, with Hitler's anti-Semitic fury descending on Germany, many Jews fled to Ibiza's sheltering arms. The son and grandchildren of the Chief Rabbi of Bulgaria, Rabbi

Moritz Grunwald, Jean Seltz and the German artists Erwin Broner, Will Faber and Raoul Hausmann were among those who found temporary safety in and around San Antonio. Even after the Spanish Civil War, when many of Ibiza's liberals and left-wingers had been forced off the island, the Pitiuses held a dented shield over their neighbours. In 1942 the Gestapo arrived in Ibiza Town and insisted that the local inhabitants give them the names of all Jews on the island, just as they had done on Mallorca. The Ibicencos refused, point blank, to hand over any information and the Nazis went away empty-handed.

When you ask Ibicencos how this small, rural island could have shown such tolerant and liberal attitudes for hundreds of years in the face of the prejudices of the time, they mostly shrug, baffled by the question. If you push them, they usually say that the islands have had so many people pass through that they are used to strangers. And yet, the same could be said of Mallorca, Sicily and Malta, even of North Africa and mainland Spain. The same civilizations have come and gone, but not all local populations are renowned for their forbearance. It is Ibiza and Formentera that have stood apart, protecting, tolerating and enjoying the company of those the rest of the world scorns and abuses, whatever their colour, faith or sexuality.

This fact was brought home to me in spectacular fashion as I drove into Ibiza Town the day after my dinner with Martin and Emily. On the outskirts, I saw a huge poster dangling above the main road that screamed 'Gay-Fun-Ibz! – Do You Like Fun?' At first I drove on, assuming it was an ad for a new gay club night on the island. Then I did a double take. There was a similar poster hanging on the walls of the *consell* civic hall, a huge centre equally capable of hosting international conferences or primary-school fêtes, and it carried the *consell* logo. It looked as though Ibiza's town council was hosting an event called Gay-Fun-Ibz . . . but, no, that would be absurd. Councils just don't do that sort of thing.

But it was true. After I'd screeched my tyres in a full 360-degree turn and bounced erratically into the civic-centre car park I found that Gay-Fun-Ibz was indeed a council event. I suppose I shouldn't have been so surprised. Ibiza is on record as having extended its hand to gay visitors since the 1960s, and it almost certainly did so before. Locals are proud to claim that men have always been able to walk hand in hand along Ibiza Town's narrow streets with no fear of violence or censure, but news of this tolerance spread through Europe only after London's acting aristocracy had begun visiting the island in the 1950s. Initially, gay visitors stayed in Santa Eulalia, and then, as the package tourists began to dominate, moved down to the more cosmopolitan Ibiza Town. The first gay club on the island, Anfora, opened in a cave in Dalt Vila in the early 1960s, despite a rather sniffy reaction from Franco's Guardia Civil who weren't sure about the legality of men dancing with men. Since then, Ibiza's gay scene has grown. It now supports around twenty bars, a network of restaurants, a couple of beaches and club nights at all the main discos. Most of the clubs and bars that sport the rainbow flag are in Ibiza Town, but you'd be hard pushed to find a place anywhere on the island that wasn't, in UK terms, gay-friendly. Pretty much everyone welcomes gay travellers.

The problem for Ibiza, however, is that this liberal attitude is increasingly common around the world. For almost forty years, Ibiza has maintained its position in the top three gay tourist destinations. This year, the tourism team was worried – the island had almost fallen to number four. Under no illusions as to the value of the pink pound, they booked and promoted Gay-Fun-Ibz as a way of encouraging awareness among gay tour companies and gay-owned businesses.

Inside the Gay-Fun-Ibz complex, it felt like a curious mix of gay nightclub and village fête. The main room looked like a large, modern high-school gym, albeit a school gym filled with stalls run by gay bars and restaurants. On the stage, a DJ pumped out earthshaking house, but the dance floor had a slightly nervous, empty look. Which isn't entirely surprising at about three in the afternoon.

I stopped next to a stall bearing a banner that stated, proudly, BAR MURALLA. The guy serving looked friendly, even though I only ordered a Coke. 'Looks good,' I said, gesturing towards the echoing hall.

He sniffed slightly. 'They mean well, but it hasn't entirely worked.' His accent sounded French, so I asked if he was working the summer here. He laughed. 'I own the bar,' he said, offering his hand. 'Daniel Villedieu. Pleased to meet you.'

Daniel told me that he'd first come to Ibiza on holiday in 1974 when he was working as the manager of a French restaurant in London. At that time, gay life in the UK's capital for those not fortunate enough to be fabulously wealthy or part of the entertainment industry revolved around a few dingy, secretive bars in Soho. These usually operated like private members' drinking dens to avoid violence from gangs of drunken queer bashers and constant police harassment. This, after all, was after the Stonewall riots but before 'Sing If You're Glad To Be Gay', and though individuals might have been out and proud, gay men could still get stabbed in central London just for looking a bit camp.

When Daniel arrived in Ibiza and walked down the town's legendary gay street Carrer de la Verge, which roughly translates as 'the street of the virgins', he could hardly believe his eyes. Gay couples walked hand in hand in the warmth of the evening sun, lively bars opened on to the street with their clients spilling out onto the cobbled stones laughing and dancing, people dressed up in the most fantastic outfits and not one of the local Ibicencos batted an eyelid.

'I was still very cautious,' he told me, 'but one night that holiday I decided to go for it. I dressed all in pink – all my clothes – and walked through Ibiza Town to the Carrer de la Verge. I was almost too scared. My mouth was dry and I kept my eyes fixed on the ground. If I had gone out in London like that I wouldn't have made it to the end of the road. But every person I passed didn't seem to care less. There was no trouble. When I got to the Carrer de la Verge I looked up and just in front of me were ten to twelve queens all wearing the most outrageous clothes and jewellery so that I felt completely underdressed.'

He holidayed on Ibiza every year after that and finally moved out in 1984, not regretting it for a second. 'The only problem is that gay culture is becoming so monotonous and boring these days.' He sighed. 'Everyone dresses the same, has the same haircuts. And it is getting very expensive here. I'm thinking of packing up and moving to Morocco any day now.' I looked around the hall again and asked him if he thought the authorities in Morocco would spend their own money on encouraging gay visitors. He paused, looked at me, then laughed and turned to serve the next customer.

CHAPTER 6

The Pirate

It's known locally as the Egg. People use it as a compass point when giving directions – 'turn left at the Egg' – which can be a little confusing if you don't know what they're talking about because it doesn't look much like an egg at all. Perched in the centre of the roundabout connecting the Ibiza Town road with the seafront at the heart of San Antonio, the Egg is a huge, white, oval stone with its centre carved out and a black, iron ship in its heart. The Egg is a monument to Christopher Columbus, built in 1992 to mark the five hundredth anniversary of his birth. There are two baffling elements here: why pick an egg to celebrate an exploratory voyage to the West Indies, and why erect a monument to a famous Genoese sailor in a popular tourist resort on Ibiza?

The egg bit is easy. It represents a story about Columbus, who was clearly a stubborn and argumentative sort. While waiting for Queen Isabel to sign off funding for his voyage, he fell into a heated debate about the existence of his proposed route. At the height of the row, Columbus exclaimed that not only was there such a route and he could prove it, he could also make an egg stand upright. His audience were understandably sceptical. Columbus promptly brought the egg down hard on the table, breaking the shell so that the underside was flat. *Voilà!* It stood upright. And the table-cloth was ruined.

The Egg's presence in San Antonio is slightly more complicated. Essentially it marks another step in the island's claim that Christopher Columbus was originally an Ibicenco. The claim is based on a hugely extended argument that has raged between Genoa – the generally accepted birthplace of the seafarer – and Catalan and Jewish scholars for over a hundred years. All three sides claim him and do so with the kind of increasing heat and rancour that can only be found in football grounds and academic institutes.

The rebels hold that Columbus was not born in Genoa but arrived there as a young boy. In a bid to prove this, books have been devoted to analysing the smallest details of his life, such as the use of an accent on the final 'o' in one possible surname for Columbus, Colón. People have looked at the date he sailed and the fact that he stayed on board ship for a day before departing, which he might have done to avoid sailing on a Jewish holiday. Documents have emerged, proved things conclusively, and then been revealed as forgeries.

It is true that many of the names Columbus gave to places in the Indies, such as Montserrat, are Catalan in origin. It is also true that he wasn't described as Genoese in any document issued by the chanceries of Castile or Aragon; nor do King Fernando or Queen Isabel ever call him Genoese. The letter of naturalization by which his brother Diego was made a Castilian says nothing about Genoa, whereas all the other surviving Castilian letters of naturalization state the origins of the applicant. Nor did the Genoese ambassadors who were present in 1493 in Barcelona when he was received by the Iberian monarchs refer to him as a fellow citizen when they wrote to Genoa. Due to the salt trade, Ibiza's links with Genoa were incredibly strong. Had Columbus come from the White Island, his family could have had dealings with the Genoese, who came from a busy, prosperous city while Ibiza was a languishing backwater. Moving to the big city would have been a smart way to build the family fortune.

Conversely, there is no single document to back up San Antonio's argument and most historians credit Genoa as the birthplace of the mariner. None of this speculation is helped by Columbus's fanatical devotion to secrecy and his failure either to write anything down or, if he did, to pass his papers on to anyone when he died.

Whatever the truth, it seems strange that the Ibicencos are so keen to claim him as one of their own. More than anything else, it was his discovery of America that really did for the island. The creation of an American empire turned Spain's face – indeed, Europe's face – away from the Mediterranean and out across the Atlantic. From the moment Columbus landed, Ibiza's mainland rulers had little or no interest in maintaining the island as the strategic base that had mattered so much to the Carthaginians, Vandals, Byzantines and Moors. The ships that sailed to the New World had abandoned oars as a means of propulsion. They were sailing ships with smaller crews and larger holds designed to cross the Atlantic in a single voyage. They had no need for regular stops to take on stores. Suddenly, almost overnight, the island became irrelevant.

And now it celebrates that disaster with a giant stone egg.

I drove past the Egg on my way out to a flamenco night at the invitation of Emily Kaufman. Some friends of hers had opened a new restaurant just off the main drag in San Antonio and were putting on regular flamenco nights to pull in the tourists. The idea was meeting with mixed success. They served high-quality Spanish food, so some of the sangria-and-chips brigade who came out for a jolly old knees-up had been put off and it wasn't on the wish list of too many package holiday reps. Nonetheless, word had spread somehow and the restaurant was comfortably busy.

I'd seen flamenco twice before, once in Seville and once in Madrid. Both times I had been stunned into awe-stricken silence. It had been especially impressive in Madrid. I'd stumbled into that flamenco bar with a gang of lads while out on a stag weekend. We'd commandeered a table, ordered up San Miguel, cheeked the staff, fallen off our chairs, stood and made a toast to the bridegroom and then the rest of the room, and generally behaved in that toe-curling way large groups of blokes do when out and about and very drunk.

When the poor flamenco dancer stalked on stage, a tiny sober part of my mind pitied her. We were in no mood to watch some big-nosed Spanish bird stamp about the stage with quivering lips and pouty poses. We were drinking! Drinking! We even had a drinking song! And then something utterly unexpected happened. If I believed in witchcraft, which I don't, I would have been convinced that this woman had cast a spell on us.

As she stormed and writhed about the stage, her face contorted in the throes of agony, and as the singer's mournful wail echoed above the pounding feet and rattling hands, we became transfixed. If fascination originally meant the state of frozen awe faeries could cast on humans simply by the way they looked, well, we were fascinated. Flamenco came up with the gypsies from southern India, where the dances and songs were traditionally performed at funerals. This I could well believe. The woman danced stories of death and loss, of young lives snuffed out, of the pain of mothers and lovers and the despair of existence in a universe without hope.

We stared in silence for the entirety of her show, exploding into applause between each song, until after her final dance we rose to our feet and cheered wildly. Embarrassingly, we then sent her a bottle of champagne, proving you can't fundamentally change the nature of a stag party no matter how much of an artist you are.

When I walked out of that bar, I swore to myself I would never watch flamenco again. That, I concluded, had been the perfect performance. Nothing could ever have the same effect again. To be fair to the San Antonio dancers, though, they did come pretty damn close. The same pain. The same despair. The same love and loss. Of course, the aching beauty of the sunset did distract slightly from the overall tone of nihilism, but I was suitably desolate when the final dance had been danced.

At the end, a small team of dancers shuffled on stage in slightly nervous fashion, dressed in a bizarre costume resembling those weird Greek soldiers in their ceremonial skirts, quaint little hats and bobble-fronted shoes. They carried with them castanets that seemed to have been bought from a joke shop, they were so large. Musicians started up on hand-held drums and quavering pipes and the ensemble wobbled into a strange dance that resembled the formal quartet-style routines of Morris dancers or Elizabethan courtiers. Every now and then, one of the men would leave the main group and begin a series of high leaps and splits, like a ballet dancer exceeding his capacity for jumping, while the other dancers clacked away on the dinner-plate-sized castanets. I was baffled, and turned to Emily for explanation.

'It's traditional Ibicenco dancing,' she whispered. 'Flamenco only came to the island with the tourists. The Ibicenco dancing is probably a blend of Carthaginian fertility rituals and Arabic dancing. There may be some Jewish music in there as well.' The pipes certainly sounded vaguely Hebraic. 'It's taken very seriously here,' she continued. 'In the remotest villages, the young men will still go courting, stand outside their intended's house and perform some of these dance steps.'

It's hard to find an equivalent to the role of traditional dancing in Ibiza. It would be as if in England Morris dancing were not the preserve of strange, bearded men in folk clubs who trill fa-la-la because they genuinely find it appealing. Instead, we would all know the connections between the dances and old country fertility rites and would thus practise as hard as we could because we knew the opposite sex found good Morris dancers to be ideal partners. Almost all native Ibicenco children learn the dances at school, and parents spend fortunes on the costumes for a variety of festivals throughout the year.

That the dancing survives and is taken this seriously is really a tribute to Columbus. Once he'd removed Ibiza's role as a strategic base, Spain all but forgot the island existed. There was almost no need for any self-respecting Spaniard to head out to a benighted rock in the Mediterranean backwaters. As long as the salt kept coming, everything was fine. With little or no input from the mainland, and with Mediterranean trade operating at subsistence levels, Ibicenco culture was effectively frozen around 1500 and it remained almost entirely unchanged for four hundred years. These were very dark years for the island, especially as the void left by the European powers withdrawing from the Med was filled by dark and deadly forces.

The tough years began with the collapse of the Byzantine Empire. The Fourth Crusade saw Catholic forces laying siege to and ultimately sacking the Orthodox Christian Constantinople in 1453. This defeat allowed the powerful Muslim Ottoman forces to expand into the Byzantines' vast territory. Sea battles with the largely naval Christian city states of Genoa and Venice went the Turks' way, and they ended up controlling the majority of the eastern Med.

The Ottoman Empire, anxious to keep pressure on the Christians, began to sponsor pirates, or privateers, in much the same way that the British, French and Spanish were already wont to do. They began to recruit sailors with the aim of creating a pirate fleet, paid for with the booty they were able to take from defenceless Christian shipping. This call to arms was carried west by an especially fearsome Muslim pirate captain called Khizr, the son of Ya'Kub, a powerful Ottoman warlord. Known in Europe as Barbarossa, or Red Beard, Khizr was greeted with unusual fervour in Morocco and Tunisia.

After the victory of the Reconquista in 1492, the Spanish Moors had been forced across the Straits of Gibraltar by the victorious Christian armies. They had fled the land that had been their home for hundreds of years and nursed a strong resentment towards the conquistadors and their successors. Huddled on the coast of a hostile land, they still dreamed of returning, or at least of revenging themselves. Barbarossa took these resentful refugees and created a formidable nest of pirates.

Known to Europeans as the Barbary corsairs, these hardy and savage sea rovers, led by the skilled and strategically minded Khizr, preyed on the immensely wealthy Spanish galleons returning from the rich new lands of the Americas to unload in Seville. As the galleon routes were changed and security beefed up, they also took to raiding the islands and city states of the Mediterranean, including vulnerable Ibiza. The helpless little island turned to the king for support, but found itself largely ignored by a busy and harassed Spanish state. Unopposed, the pirates grew ever bolder, as the Spanish abbot Diego de Haedo recorded:

They very deliberately, even at noon-day, or indeed just when they please, leap ashore, and walk on without the least dread, and advance into the country, ten, twelve or fifteen leagues more; and the poor Christians, thinking themselves secure, are surprised unawares; many towns, villages and farms sacked; and infinite numbers of souls, men, women, children, and infants at the breast dragged away into a wretched captivity. With these miserable ruined people loaded with their own valuable substance, they retreat leisurely, with eyes full of laughter and content, to their vessels. In this manner, as is too well known, they have utterly ruined and destroyed Sardinia, Corsica, Sicily, Calabria, the neighbourhoods of Naples, Rome and Genoa, all the Balearic Islands and the whole coast of Spain.

At the same time, frequent outbreaks of plague scared off traders and limited the ability of the islanders to work the salt pans. The threat of raids and the plague epidemics meant that Formentera was uninhabited from the beginning of the sixteenth century, and at one point Ibiza's population dropped to just five hundred souls.

In 1529, the Spanish realized something had to be done. They sent out eight of their largest war galleys, including the flagship of the Mediterranean fleet, to force the corsairs from the waters around Ibiza. With a comparatively small force of light ships, Barbarossa outfought and defeated them all, capturing seven Spanish ships and towing them back to Algiers. Unable to believe their good luck, the pirates ran wild. They destroyed the walls of Ibiza Town in a sustained bombardment, thus denying Ibicencos any refuge during future attacks.

As a result, the population had to adapt. The first change was architectural. Ibiza is dotted with chains of small, squat, stone watchtowers, built as a first line of defence against the raiders. The towers would light fires to warn of pirate attacks, allowing the residents time to flee into nearby churches, which had to be strengthened and fortified – half place of worship, half military installation. The effects of living under constant threat can also be found in little touches of rural Ibicenco life, many of which are slowly disappearing. The traditional Ibicenco garb for women working in the fields seems, at first glance, to be immensely impractical. For working under the blazing Balearic sun, it's hard to imagine anything more unpleasant than dresses bulked out with endless folds of cloth. This style, however, was created to protect young, attractive peasant women. It was designed to fool seabound corsairs sweeping the island with their looking-glasses into thinking the girl was a fortysomething matron and thus not worth raping.

With daylight raids common and many Ibicencos out of sight of the watchtowers, the islanders developed their own warning system. Until all forms of regional identity were banned by Franco in the 1940s, Ibicenco hunters would call out to one another with a distinctive cry that sounded like a high, clear 'ook'. This call grew out of a curious local whistling language that could get a message from one side of the island to the other in an hour. When corsairs were sighted, everyone could be warned as quickly as possible.

These disguises and tricks were necessary for one obvious reason. While people living in the mainland coastal areas around the western Med had the option of escape – which they usually took, leaving coastal lands barren and deserted – on Ibiza there was nowhere inland to run. In the end, despite all the little devices for avoiding conflict, the islanders realized there was basically no choice but to fight back.

It's not entirely clear exactly when this decision was taken, but the island probably relied on the mainland for defence until Barbarossa died in 1535. Leadership of the corsairs passed to a ruthless cut-throat called Dragut who upped the number, weight and ferocity of attacks. Raiders destroyed Santa Eulalia completely in 1545, so the Ibicencos created a fleet of their own corsairs and started taking the enemy on at sea, succeeding where the Spanish navy had failed.

Ultimately licensed by the Crown, which took one fifth of any booty as a tithe, these plucky privateers grew in skill and effectiveness. Indeed, the island seemed to support an entirely buccaneering population. In the 1640s, for instance, a ship bound for Granada was caught up in a storm and limped into Ibiza Town harbour for shelter. On board were hundreds of kilos of wheat. When the governor realized what was on the ship, he ordered the entire hold to be unloaded and its contents distributed among the people. The empty ship returned to Barcelona and reported the wheat-snatching, so an outraged king put the entire island on trial for theft. Presumably the mainland then realized how tough things were out on the Pitiuses, because when Ibiza was finally made to pay for the wheat it was at a heavily reduced rate.

By the 1600s, the corsairs' power was so effective a protection that Formentera was recolonized and the Ibicencos began a series of devastating attacks on the North African coast. From the late seventeenth century until 1830, a corsair was the career of choice for any ambitious young Ibicenco man. Wealth, adventure and piracy on the high seas – what's not to like?

Ibiza's greatest corsair was Antoni Riquer. Born the son of corsair Francesc Riquer in Ibiza Town's La Marina in 1773, Riquer joined his father's ship at an early age. By the time he was thirty-three, he'd made a name for himself and his ship, the *San Antonio y Santa Isabel*, or the *Vives* for short, around the Balearics. Legend has it that he captured or destroyed over a hundred Barbary ships, but it was his destruction of a British brigantine, the *Felicity*, that made him a national hero on the mainland.

By 1806, the British navy was effectively the ranking naval power in the Mediterranean. Spurred on by the need to protect the overland route to India, and having removed all opposition in the battle of Trafalgar the year before, British ships roamed the full length of the sea, boarding and detaining anyone they liked. This included Riquer himself as a young man in 1799 while he was delivering a cargo of barley to Barcelona. He never forgot the insult.

As well as the fleet, the British licensed their own privateers who were permitted to raid enemy shipping in exchange for splitting booty with the Crown. The most notorious of these hired pirates was Michele Novelli, nick-named the Pope. Born in Italy in 1779 in the port of Ancona, Novelli became a British citizen and captained various Royal Navy vessels operating out of Gibraltar, including the *Sovereign* and the *Eagle*. At the beginning of 1806, he was given command of the *Felicity*.

At dawn on 1 June, Riquer was awake and keeping watch from the walls of Dalt Vila, despite the fact that his ship was lying upside down in the marina for extensive repairs on her hull and his crew was scattered across the island at their respective homes. He spotted the *Felicity* close to shore, sailing – according to Ibicenco historian Isidor Macabich – slowly and insolently past the town's guns flying a red flag

— a sort of nautical slap in the face that demanded the equivalent of a duel.

The fact that he had no ship or crew didn't seem to worry Riquer. He ordered a rush job on the caulking of his ship and started running through the streets of Ibiza Town, knocking up any skilled sailors he could find. When the number proved insufficient, he raided the jail, taking out at least six prisoners to round off a hundred-strong crew. By nine a.m. he was ready to put to sea in a slightly leaking ship with a rough and ready crew of randomly chosen tars and convicts. His seventy-two-ton, three-masted xebec was far smaller than the 250-ton *Felicity*, which sported thirteen large cannon against the *Vives*' nine mid-sized pieces. The news that Riquer was putting to sea to tackle the *Felicity* had spread throughout the town, and hundreds of people lined the walls and the shore to watch the battle. One nervous onlooker remarked that the *Vives* looked like one of the *Felicity*'s lifeboats, but playing to the home crowd seemed to do the outgunned *Vives* some good.

Riquer used his ship's nimble size to weave about and dodge the *Felicity*'s heavy guns, and he closed on the brig as the day wore on. It was a long, slow cat-and-mouse game and it proved impossible to avoid the *Felicity*'s flying shot completely. By four p.m., Riquer had taken heavy damage in the hull, lost his sails and had five of his crew killed, including his father, who was aboard as first mate. Despite this he managed to pull alongside the *Felicity*, too close for the British cannon to wreak any further damage. He quickly tied up to the larger vessel with grappling irons and harpoons, then Riquer's crew showered the side of the brig with the nineteenth-century equivalent of Molotov cocktails

– bottles filled with oil, lit and hurled at the enemy's wooden sides.

The effect was spectacular. The *Felicity* burst into flame, forcing its crew either deeper into the ship or over the side and into the Med. Seizing the moment, Riquer leapt aboard, leading his men into a ferocious hand-to-hand battle with Novelli's stunned and bewildered crew. So wrong-footed had the British sailors been left by Riquer's audacity that the struggle was over in just twenty minutes. Novelli surrendered and he and his crew were shackled and taken aboard the *Vives*, while the *Felicity* slowly sank.

Both captains were questioned by the Spanish authorities, and the record of the sessions survives. It shows that the vast majority of Novelli's crew were from Malta, Sardinia, Portugal, Gibraltar and Menorca. Only one, the severely injured second skipper, was originally from England. As a result, they weren't awarded the status of prisoners of war and were initially ferried over to Palma as common criminals. Riquer himself took on the job, which involved several voyages, but halfway through the process the Spanish government suddenly realized that by endowing the crew of the *Felicity* with POW standing they could exchange them with the British for Spanish equivalents. To Riquer's pique, Novelli was back harassing shipping by May 1807. Apparently, he was especially cruel to any Ibicenco sailors he captured from then on.

Given the significant lack of sea victories in the war with Britain, the Spanish Crown reacted with delight and considerable generosity to the crew of the *Vives*. Two wounded convicts were pardoned and four had their sentences reduced. Wounded crew members and the widows of those lost received a pension. Riquer himself was promoted to second lieutenant and earned a tidy salary of ten gold escudos a month. He also began to play a game that proved far more dangerous than open attack on a heavily armed British ship – he got involved in Spanish politics.

Spain had enmeshed itself in the Napoleonic Wars after signing a treaty of mutual assistance with France against the British in 1795. The two countries had a history of such co-operation, mainly as a result of imperial rivalry in the Americas. A combined French and Spanish fleet had blockaded the English Channel during the American War of Independence and prevented the British sending aid to the besieged Lord Cornwallis, who had been forced to surrender in 1781. Spanish royalists were keen to maintain the relationship in the interests of securing lost territory in Italy.

Napoleon's war, however, was catastrophic for Spain. The British victory at Trafalgar effectively wiped out the Spanish fleet and destroyed the country's ability to function as a great sea power. The land war in Portugal resulted in French troops pouring into the Iberian peninsula, leaving an army of a hundred thousand French troops in the country by March 1808. Napoleon was in control of Madrid. King Carlos had fled. The population rose in protest but the revolt was put down within forty-eight hours by French troops with bloody ferocity. Napoleon installed his brother Joseph on the Spanish throne.

The countryside refused to kow-tow to France, however, and by 1810 Spain's official government had retreated to Cadiz where it was surrounded by French troops. The British, sensing an opportunity, made common cause with Spanish rebels and landed an army in Portugal. The

Peninsular War is famous for the horrors both sides inflicted on each other, and this is not the place to explore its detail, but the Spanish did forge a constitution during the war that ensured some level of parliament and removed some of the king's absolutist powers.

By 1813 the French and the British had left and the Spanish were free to fall on one another. Carlos, who was blamed for the arrival of the French, abdicated and was replaced by his son, Fernando VII. The new king instantly ripped up the constitution and continued with the old system, whereby the Church and the aristocracy controlled the land – 98 per cent of which was owned by 2 per cent of the population – and the king did whatever he liked. Twelve thousand French sympathizers were executed and the Jesuits were put in charge of education.

Unfortunately for Fernando, Spain's American colonies chose this moment to rebel. Exhausted Spanish soldiers had no desire to travel thousands of miles in support of the collapsing empire, and in 1820 an army of reinforcements sitting in Cadiz awaiting transport to South America revolted in the name of liberalism under the leadership of Colonel Rafael de Riego.

Liberal and monarchist forces threw themselves into civil war with gusto. Fernando, welcomed by the population because he had opposed the French, now turned to the French-dominated Holy Alliance to help destroy this dangerous experiment with democracy and restore his total control. They sent a hundred thousand troops to his aid.

Riquer was by now a rear admiral in the remains of the Spanish navy and lived in La Marina, the stretch of Ibiza Town outside the walls of Dalt Vila. Riquer's neighbours were the rising middle class – doctors and lawyers – as well as fellow corsairs. La Marina was firmly behind the rebel liberal government. Dalt Vila, however, was the home of the old families – landowners and old money. They backed the monarchy. The hatred ran deep. Those in Dalt Vila were called *mossons*, a slang version of 'monsignor' that mocked their snooty ways. The residents of the Marina were nicknamed *banyculs*, or 'wet-backs', because they lived so near the water or, worse, worked on the sea. As a *banycul*, Riquer's sympathies were firmly with the democrats and the idea of parliamentary rule. Fernando's violent reaction to Riego's uprising appalled him, and when the French army laid siege to the nearby mainland city of Cartagena, Riquer set about raising ships and crew on Ibiza to support the trapped liberal forces. He secured funding from the town hall, recruited sufficient men and launched a brave convoy of three ships to tackle the might of the 'Hundred Thousand Sons of St Louis'.

Poor Riquer picked the losing side. His adventure, and the adventure of the Spanish constitution, failed under the boots of the French army. Although he promised amnesty, Fernando unleashed a reign of terror against liberals that shocked even the French. Riego was taken to the centre of Madrid in a coal cart where he was hanged, drawn and quartered for public display. The mere possession of his picture carried the death penalty, and hundreds went to the gallows. Riquer himself was hunted down and hauled before the Bourbon authorities, who found him guilty. He was very lucky. In light of his heroic actions as a corsair and his subsequent service to the Crown, he was spared the grisly fate of his comrades. Instead, he was allowed to return to Ibiza, having been stripped of his rank and his pension. As far as Madrid society was concerned, a life spent on Ibiza was as good as exile. Riquer spent his last days eking out an existence in the Marina, broke, tired and bitter.

In 1830, the French army took Algeria and finally subdued the pirates. The waters around Ibiza became peaceful. Normal trade resumed and all was calm. The Ibicencos, however, had discovered a taste for the illicit, knew all the sea routes and had learned some handy tricks for dealing with well-armed vessels. Putting all these skills to good use, the pirates simply switched jobs and became smugglers, mainly running tobacco around the coasts of North Africa and southern Spain to avoid the state's monopoly on the tobacco trade, as well as shipping pigs between Ibiza and Formentera to make a little pocket money on the side. This worked because of a small local difference in the way markets traded on the two islands. Formentera's pigs were big-boned and heavy but were sold on the island by individual pig; on Ibiza, the pigs were small and skinny but were sold by weight. Smuggling fat pigs from Formentera to Ibiza turned a nice little profit. One of the rocks that dot the straits between the two islands is called the Illa des Porcs because the smugglers used to keep their contraband hogs there. The next-door rock is Illa des Penjats, or the Island of the Hanged. This was where the smugglers who got caught ended up.

The era of the smugglers saw the first change in the fortunes of the island since the Moors' departure. In part, this was down to the rising fortunes of a complex and controversial local family, the Matutes. To hear the critics of the Matutes, you would think they were the Corleones; to hear their admirers, you'd think they were the Kennedys. Not originally Ibicenco, their origins are shrouded in mystery. The Matutes themselves believe they are descended from a family of Italian navigators; others say they were Jewish corsairs operating from Morocco who moved to Ibiza to set up in the smuggling game. There is no doubt, however, about the respectability of Don Pedro Matutes, who spent the latter part of the nineteenth century hustling and working to raise the family's status from that of struggling outsiders to pillars of the upper echelons of society. By the beginning of the twentieth century, Don Pedro had become the island's only substantial moneylender, effectively Ibiza's banker, albeit without an actual bank as he was operating privately. His big economic opportunity came in 1914 when the European powers declared war on one another.

With the quality of its pine wood and the requirement of its corsair community for regular new vessels, Ibiza had built up a considerable shipbuilding industry. After the collapse of the pirate trade, Matutes' money had helped the two brothers who ran most of the yards to carry the industry forward, building strong wooden cargo vessels for clients across the western Mediterranean. The yards were commissioned to build for Naviera Mallorquina in Palma as well as shipping companies on the Spanish mainland, and they could handle orders for ships as large as eight hundred tons. Don Pedro himself bought two ships, the *Pedro* and the *Abel*. His first cargo was a shipload of broad beans, which he carried to Marseilles. The business developed from there. When World War One broke out, Don Pedro was in an ideal position to help ship military and civil supplies around the Med. The war made him an incredibly wealthy man, and by

1933 he had sufficient capital to found the Banca Matutes with his three sons as partners. This was Ibiza's only bank until after the Spanish Civil War, and even though mainland banks set up on the island in the 1950s and 1960s, Banca Matutes still carried the vast majority of Ibicenco business until the late 1990s, when it was acquired by the Caja del Mediterráneo (CAM).

Being the island's banker gave Don Pedro and his three sons enormous power. They mixed it in local politics, with one son, Abel Matutes, holding office as mayor under Franco and going on to become a leading light in the Partido Popular.

The Matutes invested heavily in post-war tourism, including the scheme to develop Salinas. Those who were outraged by the plans baffled and annoyed them. Abel described the proposal for Salinas to be protected by environmental laws as 'an initiative that is clearly Communist and totalitarian in style'. Despite the occasional hiccup, the family massively increased its wealth and position with these tourist developments, even if they sometimes sailed extremely close to the wind – as the 1971 Humiliation of the Hotel Augusta demonstrated.

By that year, Mayor Matutes owned his bank, one tenth of the island's real estate, shipping interests, ferry lines and twenty hotels. As this was clearly not enough, he set about building a towering, state-of-the-art leisure complex next to the airport, the Hotel Augusta, which would be the pride of his empire. This immense structure was so tall and splendid that it terrified the wits out of British pilots every time they came in to land. In the end, the pilots' union declared Ibiza airport unsafe and refused to land there. A furious Don Abel called in the Spanish Air Ministry who backed him until the minister himself, former bomber pilot General Julio Salvador, flew into Ibiza to see what was what. The landing petrified the old warhorse and General Salvador told Don Abel that he would have flattened the hotel with a bomb had he had one. Don Abel replied, with some hauteur, that not one brick would be touched. The general flew back to Madrid and closed Ibiza airport to all night traffic until a team of aviation inspectors could deliver a report. This brought about such a slump in visitors to the island that the hoteliers almost rose in mutiny. Graffiti across town accused Don Abel of being the 'Cain of Ibiza'.

Finally, the team reported back: the hotel was unsafe and it would have to be dynamited. In February, the Augusta was reduced to rubble by 650lb of TNT. Don Abel resigned as mayor in disgust, but returned to front-line politics when Spain's 1996 Partido Popular government made him foreign minister. At that time, the worst-kept secret on the island was that Don Abel was the largest shareholder in the Space and Privilege nightclubs. The British equivalent in 1996 would have been Douglas Hurd owning gay Mecca Heaven and the superclub Ministry of Sound.

It's not hard to imagine such a family coming from smuggler stock. Indeed, it would be entirely appropriate if Ibiza's first family had at one point carried contraband. For many on the mainland, that was the defining activity of the island. When the Impressionist Joaquin Sorolla was commissioned by the Hispanic Society of America to paint one picture for each of Spain's fifty provinces, each painting to capture something essential about the area, he chose Ibicenco smugglers to represent the Balearics. In Sorolla's

Las Contrabandistas, the smugglers wrestle with tobacco in a rocky cove on the headland beyond the castle, ready to sneak it past the customs men as they continue Ibiza's defiance of mainland rules and regulations.

Perhaps their spirit lives on. After the flamenco, I stopped off in a bar on the San Antonio seafront for a nightcap and fell into conversation with the girl behind the bar. She was Ibicenco and seemed mildly interested in the nerdier parts of my research to date. When I told her about the salt pans – 'after all, that's why it's called the White Island' – she giggled delightfully. 'Really?' She put her head on one side and smiled. 'I thought it was because of all the coke.'

I asked how much of the drug there actually was on the island.

'Come on,' she said, 'there are drugs all over the island. People come here for the clubs, and the clubs need drugs. It's no different from anywhere else like that. But, you know, it is different from other places as well. No-one gets shot here, for one thing, and there is no mafia.'

I looked doubtfully at her, and she read my mind.

'OK, look, I'll tell you a story. There is a restaurant outside Ibiza where, if you knew what you were about, you used to be able to get your little gram of cocaine with your bill – you know, if you knew what to say and who to say it to. Maybe you still can, I don't know. Anyway, there was this girl from the mainland, a journalist, who wanted a big story, and she went to this restaurant every night and saw a man there, a big-name businessman, and she saw him get his little gram and she saw that he didn't pay his bill. So she ran the story. Front page. Big news. But after that she found it very hard to get things done. And in the end, after six months, she left the island. That's how it works here – people get their privileges revoked. If she had done that story in Las Vegas or Moscow or London there would have been threats or worse and they'd have fished her body out of the river. Here, she just ended up leaving the island.

'OK, sure, there are people on the island who deal drugs and they are probably people from here – don't ask me, I don't know. But if someone came here to try to muscle in, if some mafia came to try to run things, they just wouldn't be able to. They couldn't get anything done, anything at all. It would be impossible for them to live here. That's why there are no guns or shootings on the island despite all the clubs and the drugs. We don't need those things to get rid of people we don't like.

'You have to understand that Ibiza is a place where anyone can come and be whoever they want to be. You can do whatever you want, no-one cares. You can dress how you want and no-one stares. But there is a certain kind of person who is not welcome here – pushy, arrogant, selfish people who want lots of things for themselves. They could be gangsters or they could just be the wrong kind of person. I had an American woman in my building who used to complain all the time, at the post office, in the shop; everywhere she went nothing was ever right for her. So things stopped happening. She didn't get served. Once, she didn't get her letters for three weeks. I had to tell her – you don't get it. If you complain, if you are rude, if you shout, people don't work harder for you, they work slower.'

We looked at each other and I nodded. She seemed a little annoyed, as if she'd been unduly intimate and now realized she'd prefer me to leave. Rather awkwardly, I finished my beer as quickly as possible and walked out on to the water-front where the fishing boats rocked gently in the light breeze. With one of those, I thought, you could get to Morocco in half an hour. And think what you could buy when you got there.

CHAPTER 7

The Artist

The Day of the Drums was the last great flowering of Ibiza's hippy movement. During the first Gulf War in 1991, Ibicencos, hippies and New Agers gathered together around the hippy enclave on Benirras beach in protest at the conflict. Although Benirras faces west, out into the Atlantic rather than towards Iraq where the actual war was taking place, the beach had become a focus for the counter culture because of its drummers. At dusk, especially on Sundays, the drummers would gather to salute the setting sun with pounding rhythms and wild ululations, drumming on into the night in a scene that seemed almost prehistoric in its blend of worship, rhythm and bare skin.

When it came to the anti-war protest, then, there was only one real option: a twenty-four-hour drumming marathon for peace. It was by all accounts an impressive event. Massed ranks of skin tom-toms rolled out a deep, booming thunder that sent a chill down the spine of even the most cynical observer. The drummers continued through the night, fuelled by alcohol, chemicals, caffeine and raw energy, and those that survived still speak about it as if something genuinely changed.

Flushed with success, the idea of this percussive protest survived the end of the war. Dubbed the Day of the Drums, it was repeated every August in a Karmic attempt to spread good vibes to a hostile world. They drummed on through the wars in the Balkans, the genocide in Africa, the violence in Kashmir and the slaughter in the Middle East. In the early summer of 2003, with Iraq torn by conflict again, it seemed an ideal time to hear the drums speak.

I drove down to the beach at around three p.m., locked my car in the tiny car park and followed a wide track down to the beach. Three bars sprouted from the sand, two selling the usual holiday fare but one carrying the Bob Marley insignia that denoted a hippy hangout. A handful of scruffy twentysomethings sat outside, looking tanned and stoned and passing an unduly fat joint from hand to hand. They couldn't have been more hippy if they'd turned up in a VW camper covered in peace signs. One of them was even strumming an acoustic guitar. The wall-of-sound drum experience, however, was nowhere to be heard.

I wandered up to the bar and ordered a San Miguel. 'When does the drumming start?' I asked the girl behind the counter.

She looked doubtful. 'Well, sunset, but they haven't had drumming on this day for two years.' She had a strong northern European accent.

'Why not?' I felt a little let down. 'Surely with another war in Iraq people will want to come down?'

'It's not the war,' she said, looking over my shoulder and almost adopting a conspiratorial whisper. 'It's the nightclubs. They don't like the free parties. Sometimes they use the riot police. It's very bad.'

'Do you think they'll stop this one tonight?' I was looking around the beach for the rows of helmets, night-sticks and heavy plastic shields.

She shrugged. 'I don't know. They stopped it last year, and the year before. I don't know. Maybe.'

I settled down on a wooden bench and waited. The day drifted along lazily, like any summer's day on a sandy beach in a crystalline cove. Families played, hippies strummed and the warm sunlight seemed to throb behind my eyes as the San Miguel was followed by another and another. At eight o'clock the sun was slipping down the sky, promising to set with as much radiant beauty as she could muster, when the first of the drummers stole across the sand.

He had dreadlocks and a large African tom-tom, and he made his way slowly down to the shoreline where he looked out over the scarlet sea like a shaman. Or at least like someone who wanted to be a shaman. I looked back the way he'd come and saw two or three carloads of people hefting drums onto their shoulders. Over by the bar another guitar player had joined the first and their rhythms became more urgent. There must have been ten or eleven drummers getting ready now, and the sun was nearly at the horizon.

Suddenly, from the car park behind me, a car revved hard and switched its headlights on to full beam, which wasn't enormously impressive as the sky was still pretty light. I turned and saw a solitary police car at the mouth of the car park. Two cops clambered out looking, if such a thing were possible, like the opposite of a riot squad. If a really bad B-movie director had been looking for a way to create 'comedy Hispanic cop one' and 'comedy Hispanic cop two', he might have considered dressing his extras like this. Both were slightly overweight and sported crumpled, baggy, green uniforms complete with slip-on shoes and white towelling socks. Their caps were set at an excessively jaunty angle and they had matching moustaches that quivered on their upper lips like ironic parodies of Freddie Mercury at a dead-popstars fancy-dress party.

Fully aware that they were now the centre of attention, Officer Tweedledum and Officer Tweedledee stalked slowly down to the beach, took out A4 squares of white paper and nailed them to trees and posts before retiring to lean on their car and gaze up at the narrow beach road. One or two of the hippies walked up and read the notices, then returned and started muttering among themselves. I wandered over as casually as possible and stared at the nearest one. It was in Spanish, but the intention was clear: no-one was allowed to play music on this beach. It was a non-music beach.

Here, then, was an interesting situation. The drummers on the beach now numbered about twenty, and winding down the narrow road were a number of cars. They were rebels, these hippy kids. They didn't cut their hair. They believed in peace. Perhaps, I thought, they were the spiritual kin of the Seattle protesters and we would see some non-violent direct action. Looking at the representatives of the law, I couldn't really see the hippies losing. Especially not if they were legion, as descriptions of the Day of the Drums seemed to suggest.

But nothing happened. The cops searched the back and boot of every car that drove into the car park, warning the occupants with theatrical hand gestures. The hippies slumped on the beach and stared off into the sun, passing joints around as ostentatiously as possible. Gradually, one by one, the drummers went back to their vehicles and drove off. I sat there alone for a while, then got up and headed towards one of the cafés for some food and water to mitigate the effects of my afternoon drinking. The last thing I needed was to be breathalysed by the forces of repression. Even if they did look like Mexican prison warders in a Brad Pitt movie.

I felt overwhelmingly sad. The Day of the Drums – no matter that its power was directed into the Atlantic, no matter that it had throbbed its message to a world that didn't care – seemed so beautifully Ibicenco. It was an artistic statement of protest and protection, a stylized warning from the shores of an island that had spent the first part of the twentieth century protecting people from war and terror. Its demise had taken something of Ibiza away.

The main beneficiaries of Ibiza's mantle of sanctuary have been artists. After Joaquin Sorolla painted the smugglers, another Impressionist, Rigoberto Soler, dropped in on the island. He was instantly struck by the paintings of a local Ibicenco, Narcis Buget, but refused to believe the soil on the island was really the powerful, vibrant red Buget had depicted; he assumed the painter had ramped up the ochre in a slightly OTT Impressionist style. Buget told Soler he had just painted what he saw, so Soler went out into the countryside, looked around and saw that Buget was right. The colours were almost too vivid. He also realized that the light on Ibiza was perfect for painting, offering the best alternative to the Impressionists' Mecca, Provence. He rushed back to Valencia to tell his artistic friends what he had found.

Throughout the 1920s and the 1930s, Spanish artists such as Soler, Cecilio Pla, Amadeo Roca, Miguel Nieto, Laureano Barrau and the Catalan Ramón Fina flocked to Ibiza. They also spread the word just at a time when the continent's artistic community was facing naked hostility from Hitler's Germany and Stalin's Russia, both of which had very clear ideas about what sort of art guaranteed you a living and what sort of art guaranteed you a place in the camps. Many German artists, especially Jews, and a handful of Russians made their way out to Ibiza as the 1930s progressed, usually on the run from oppression in their homeland. Ibiza was so far off the edge of the continent that they felt safe, sure the SS and the NKVD had better things to do than tramp all the way out there. Besides, who on mainland Europe had even heard of Ibiza outside the weird little circles of artists?

The Viennese Dadaist Raoul Hausmann was a case in point. In 1933, one month after the Reichstag fire, he was declared a 'degenerate artist' by the Nazis and fled Berlin. With a lingering death in a concentration camp waiting at home, he slowly made his way to Ibiza where he found a small community of German artists including the writer Walter Benjamin, the painters Erwin Broner and Will Faber, as well as the Moravian Bruno Beran and the Polish painter Josef Sperber, who showed up with his writer compatriot Vitol Leonard. These exiles met and drank in an old windmill just outside the walls of Ibiza Town that had been converted into a nightclub by a Russian émigré and his two sisters. Sometimes they went to the nearby Bar Puerto, owned by a Jewish refugee, or ate in the Portmany Hotel in San Antonio.

Initially, Hausmann lived near Benimussa in a house called

Can Mestre, close to Faber's place, where Walter Benjamin was staying. He was a familiar sight to the islanders, striding along the winding, unmade roads deep in thought. He met Adolf Schoulten, a German archaeologist who had lived in Spain since 1926, and the two of them would tramp through the countryside, digging up patches of earth in search of Phoenician and Carthaginian artefacts.

In 1934, Hausmann left the island and stayed in Paris, contributing to Man Ray's *NUS* album and showing him pictures of Ibicenco buildings and people, which so inspired the American photographer that he made his own trips out to the island. By July, Hausmann was back in the Pitiuses, this time staying in the village of San José. As well as his dark, slim wife Hedwig, Hausmann brought with him Vera Broido-Cohn, a statuesque Russian blonde who had modelled nude for him for a series of photos taken around the Baltic. The artist and the model had become lovers – hey, this was Dada. A travelling love triangle was just one more flouting of bourgeois morality.

Hausmann paraded around San José in brightly coloured cravats and shoes, always sporting a monocle. He liked to take pictures wherever he went, but on an island still shaking off four hundred years of solitude this didn't always go down very well. 'The peasants are very superstitious and do not like you photographing their house because they believe it brings bad luck,' he wrote in 1936. 'Sometimes you manage to photograph a young woman while she sings, accompanied by a drum, but only with permission of her husband. Even small cameras would be no use in Ibiza because people would notice them and might be offended. Such a thing must be avoided, as the country people are very kind and hospitable towards strangers, loading them down with presents.' This generosity amazed the visitors. The Ibicenco people, even in the heart of the countryside where many families were operating at subsistence level themselves, were immensely welcoming and generous to these artists. They would hand out gifts, offer food and drink, and welcome people into their homes without the least suspicion or hostility.

Hausmann made himself understood with his rudimentary Spanish – a language at which neither he nor his hosts were particularly adept – and in French, which was sufficiently similar to Catalan to help him get by. These faltering conversations enabled him to become especially friendly with two locals: Llorenc Carbonell, who owned Can Llorenc, San José's main bar; and Antoni Ribas, the leader of Ibiza's tiny Communist Party.

Carbonell had served in Cuba during the Spanish-American War under the Ibicenco general Vara de Rey. There he had picked up a taste for fat Cuban cigars; he could usually be found with one wedged between his fingers. He also played the guitar, and would sit with Hausmann singing Spanish folk and South American Creole songs late into the night. Hausmann ate at his bar almost every day, and Llorenc's daughter Catalina recalled his visits: 'When lunch was ready, we would whistle up to his house and all three of them would come down to eat with us. Also Vera, who was a seamstress, would often come to use the sewing machine to either repair clothes or to make new ones.' Hausmann, in return, would entertain the village with Dadaist poems and dances. A few years later, Vera Broido described a typical Hausmann entertainment on a warm evening in Llorenc's bar which, given traditional Ibicenco dancing, can't have appeared as outlandish to the locals as it obviously did to her:

> People cleared space for him. He stood in the middle of the room, took off his shirt – he had an athletic torso – and stood there, dressed only in long baggy trousers. He removed his monocle, which was very out of character, looked around him and called for a kitchen chair, which was brought to him immediately. Only then did he begin to dance. It was like no dance I had ever seen, not even in India or Bali or amongst the Blacks – and certainly not in Europe. He opened and closed his eyes, appearing to contemplate something. His gestures were neither ugly nor beautiful and everything in him moved – his face, his eyes, his fingers . . . In his eyes, all the forms of artistic expression were linked to each other. In this case, it was dance and architecture or, even more, a sort of total construction of the world.

Hausmann travelled all over the island with Antoni Ribas, one of the few Ibicencos to own a car. The machine drew the two men together, Ribas driving Hausmann and his women on long trips down the dusty dirt tracks that criss-crossed the hills. Hausmann would occasionally dart out of the car and rush about the yard of some small *finca*, or country dwelling, measuring and photographing and trying to talk to the people who lived there while Ribas and the women remained in his automobile drinking the cheap, low-quality Ibicenco wine that came in flasks rather than bottles.

Perhaps Hausmann should have seen it coming; a *ménage à trois* can't be attractive for anyone who makes up part of the majority sex. Even in bohemian artistic circles. Antoni was bright, charming, articulate and handsome, and he found seducing the beautiful Vera a relatively easy task. She left the Hausmanns and moved in with him, provoking Raoul into a fit of jealous rage. One night he stormed through the village in fury, searching for Ribas with a large kitchen knife and screaming, 'I'm going to kill him! Kill him!'

By the time Hausmann arrived in Ibiza, his most famous works were behind him. He was forty-seven years old, Dadaism was dead, and he was on the run. He was tired. He was depressed. He was on the verge of giving up. And yet, somehow, the island managed to provoke a new interest in this erratic polymath: he became an expert in the unique design of Ibicenco *fincas*. Although he had no formal training in architecture, he began to submit papers on their design and construction to architectural journals.

The curious thing about the buildings was that they had no designer in the way modern Europeans understand the concept. Most of the houses had been there for so long that no-one could recall their foundations being laid. As families grew, or as a new house was needed, the village would simply get together and build one. The add-ons, and any new houses that had to be built, weren't overseen by any one master builder; instead, they were the products of collaboration, like honeycomb in a beehive. No one person knew all the measurements, no single expert dictated how everyone worked. Each person knew a measurement or a building technique that was useless on its own but, when the whole community brought its knowledge together, became an integral part of the overall design.

The result was a complex building, sometimes with huge, decorative arches stretching across the large communal dining and living rooms, tens of feet high and twice the width. Stairs threaded between a multitude of floors, sometimes straight and true, sometimes short and broken. Doors could appear at almost any level in the walls and lead to rooms of any size. Ceilings could be high or low, plastered or bare wood, while vast ovens and extended stone benches were built into the walls. Indeed, as furniture was an expensive luxury, jutting ledges and tiny niches would serve many purposes – storage, seating or just decoration. Hausmann described the creation of these ambitious co-operative ventures as 'architecture without an architect'. Anthropologists now believe that these square *fincas* with their thick, heatproof walls and strong, pine-beam ceilings were fundamentally Carthaginian in design and execution, suggesting that Ibicencos had been building houses like this for thousands of years, passing on the techniques from generation to generation. In a way it's a shame no-one picked this up at the time. I'm sure it would have delighted Hitler to find that such complex and well-built houses were originally the creation of a Semitic culture.

Towards the end of his stay on the island, Hausmann invested many of his hopes in these rustic dwellings. The Berlin Dadaists hated the Big City. They saw its noise, speed and skyscraper landscape as apocalyptic. In this they were not alone. Their dream of a rural, naturist and agrarian society was shared by thinkers as diverse as the English socialist William Morris and Adolf Hitler himself. For Hausmann, Ibiza had a rare quality as its fabric had not been broken up or destroyed by historical evolution. He believed the ultimate human form was the community, and that early humans had managed to weave their harmonious relations with the world into all aspects of their lives. He thought he had found a manifestation of this on Ibiza, and he hoped it would be the vanguard of a new revolution, the triumph of the community over the horror of the city and the loneliness of the individual. He saw Ibiza as a vast, ideal garden city that could be scaled up into a plan for the world.

His theories attracted strong interest in Spain, especially among a school of modernist architects in Catalonia that included José Luis Sert and Rodriguez Arias. Hausmann's compatriot Broner was also impressed. Sert travelled to Ibiza, and both he and Broner built experimental houses on the island, fusing modernist styles with traditional local techniques. By 1936, both Sert's and Broner's buildings were finished and Hausmann's discoveries were on the verge of sparking an architectural revolution. But within months, Broner, Benjamin, Hausmann and countless others were forced back onto the road, refugees once more. War was coming, and Ibiza's isolation would prove a feeble defence.

CHAPTER 8

The War

Cala de Sant Vincent is a small village in the north-east of the island. It's named after one of Ibiza's little secrets – a wonderful, wide sandy beach sloping softly down to shallow, crystal-clear waters and a wide bay dotted with tiny rocky islands. The feeling is one of tropical isolation. You wouldn't be surprised if a troupe of Balinese dancers emerged with a pop and a clash of cymbals beside you and began their elaborate, writhing performance. All in all, it's an unlikely spot for a war crime.

It took place on 7 August 1936, and it resulted in Ibiza's first death in the Spanish Civil War. The summer was hot that year, and in the Balearics temperatures peak in August. The 7th was a searing Friday, the kind of day when very little moves except the waves and even they seem to fall on the sand with a lazy stagger. The beach at Cala de Sant Vincent would have been deserted in those empty, silent days before tourism. The tiny hamlet sported no enthusiastic sunbathers and the locals saw the sea as the factory floor, a place to fish rather than splash. Those villagers with an eye on the briny were looking out for the boats of family members, returning – hopefully – with the day's catch of tuna, skate, flounder and bass.

In the late afternoon, however, those careful watchers saw a small, overpacked boat chug into view around the headland and slowly make for shore. It pulled to a stop a few feet from the beach and disgorged a small detachment of soldiers who hauled the hull up onto the sand. Although the band looked ragged and ill disciplined, they would have been startling enough for fishing folk who thought a donkey ride to Ibiza Town was a racy and rather too exotic adventure.

Led by a single officer, the troops fanned out into a ragged line, rifles at the ready, and began a slow walk inland. It quickly became clear where they were heading as the line began to curve into a semi-circle around a curious grey concrete house at its centre. This house was unusual, especially by Ibicenco standards. For a start, it was built of concrete where all about was whitewashed stone. Set against the sloping cliffs, it rose in three raked storeys with a pillared porch standing proudly on a raised first-floor balcony. A golden strip of heraldic shields and fleurs-de-lis sparkled beneath the gables.

As the line of soldiers approached, a man stepped out of the building's shadowy doorway and stood on the balcony looking down on the barrels of their raised rifles. He seemed to be expecting them. The officer mounted a few steps to the balcony, they exchanged some quiet words and, without a struggle, the man walked down to join the troops on the track below. The waiting soldiers swiftly surrounded him and marched him down to the water's edge. The only sound was the hiss of the waves and the sharp snap of the officer's drill commands.

Once they reached the shore, a soldier pushed the householder roughly to his knees. With a word from the officer, the troops lined up into a ragged firing squad, aimed their rifles and waited. The officer barked out a short command and the soldiers squeezed tightly on their triggers. An extended fusillade of shots echoed in a percussive rattle around the stone cliffs, and the man fell forward onto the sand.

For a second, no-one moved. Then the officer turned sharply and issued curt instructions to the villagers watching curiously from the edge of the sand. He told them that the body was not to be disturbed and that he would return to ensure his commands had been obeyed. The soldiers climbed back into their launch and ploughed slowly out into the bay, turning south to hug the coast as they slipped from view behind the cliffs.

The villagers crept back to their houses. But the hail of bullets had only wounded the victim. He lay alone on the sand for two whole days, his long, low moans filling the night, before he finally died. The following day he was buried, almost entirely unmourned. In the solitary years he had spent in the concrete house he had been unwilling, or unable, to make many friends. Most people hadn't even known his name. They just called him the Frenchman. Perhaps they felt guilty about leaving him to die, but what could they do? The officer had left strict instructions and, after all, there was a war on.

The story of the Frenchman finds its way into a handful of local books and lives on in fewer memories. I'd stumbled across it in a slim volume by Rafael Sainz, scion of a wealthy mainland banking family who wrote enthusiastically about his dog Mel, one of the local podenco hounds. He described the house as half fortress, half church, planned in imitation of the cathedral at Reims where the kings of France had been crowned. He said it was the hallucination of the madman of Sa Cala, the Frenchman.

It sounded worth seeing so, on my way to Santa Eulalia, I took an enormous detour up to the north-east coast along a narrow, twisting road that climbed and swooped through undeveloped pine forest and low, stepped crop fields cut into the sides of the hills. Every now and then I caught a glimpse of sea; less frequently, the odd villa or *finca* rose out of the soil a few metres back from the road.

For the final few hundred yards into Cala de Sant Vincent the road hit the flat and suddenly widened into an improbable dual carriageway, then spread out even further into a concrete apron that was part car park, part roundabout and part coach turning circle. I ended up stranded in the centre, panicking slightly as a packed Thompson's tour bus bore down on me hooting wildly, before I worked out where to put my car.

The village looked like little more than a service centre for the three or four high-quality hotels that line the seafront, all pale tiles and soft muzak with polite staff and creatively catered restaurants. The staff were especially polite with me, the scruffy non-guest who asked them in broken Spanglish for 'the concrete house, the French house, where the man was shot. In the civil war.' Eventually a young manager understood, took me out of the hotel's back door and pointed along a road I'd originally thought was simply for service vehicles.

This narrow tarmac strip ran in front of the rocky hill that marked the rear wall of Cala de Sant Vincent. Most of the old Ibicenco houses are built up this hill, presenting a dazzling array of white-walled *fincas*, but about four hundred yards along there's an architectural anomaly that looks desperately out of place among the old houses and fake marble hotels.

The French house didn't look quite as imposing as Sainz had suggested. The concrete walls were badly painted and in places the house still looked half finished. The wide double doors underneath the pillared portico were sealed shut with cement and breezeblocks. Around the edge of the roof, tiles tried hard to give a faintly art deco, faintly Egyptian feel, but struggled against the sandy bricks surrounding the cellar and the cold, dead, boarded-up windows. There was a sense of desolation, of empty years having passed, years of long, slow, lonely decay.

I tried to imagine the man who had built it. Back then, before the hotels, the view down to the beach would have been superb, but there must have been countless empty *fincas* on those cliffs. And if not, the villagers would have gladly pulled together and assembled one for a pittance had the new arrival been friendly. Instead, he had withdrawn from them and from the world, trying to create a grandiose temple of safety. All he succeeded in building was a council house crossed with a bingo hall.

His name was Raoul Villain, and he had arrived on Ibiza in the 1920s a hunted and lonely figure. He might have seemed jumpy and neurotic, but he had good reason. Just because you're paranoid, it doesn't mean they aren't out to get you. In 1914, Villain had been an amateur political assassin and had murdered the leader of the French Socialist Party, Jean Jaurès. For much of the European left, this act had helped tip Europe into the First World

War. Villain had the blood of millions on his hands.

Jaurès was a popular and charismatic figure in pre-war France. A democratic socialist who had been elected to the Chamber of Deputies as an independent, he did everything he could to prevent the rising tide of militarism that he foresaw would lead Europe into war. Perhaps naively, he was convinced that international co-operation between the ordinary people of the Great Powers could prevent the impending conflict. Jaurès travelled to Berlin in July 1914 to try to talk German socialists into organizing a co-ordinated anti-war strike with the French working class in a bid to paralyse the two countries' war machines. The discussions proved fruitless, but Jaurès was hopeful that the dialogue could continue and that somehow war could be prevented. Shortly after his return, he was sitting with his friends at a table near an open window in a Paris café when the twenty-nine-year-old Villain, son of a clerk of the Civil Court of Rheims and a fervent monarchist, poked a revolver through the window and shot Jaurès through the head. He died almost instantly. Three days later, Germany declared war.

Villain, described as 'a young aesthete of 29 who was tinged with insanity', was easily traced. In March 1919 he was brought to trial and, despite overwhelming evidence, acquitted. This outraged large militant sections of the European working class, sparking riots and demonstrations across Paris. In fear of his life, Villain fled France. Over several years and via South America, he gradually made his way to Ibiza. There, like so many others who had found the island's position at the edge of Europe a useful place to disappear, he lived anonymously.

His house was designed as a kind of panic room, with strong, thick walls and narrow windows which he hoped would enable him to put up some sort of defence should the need ever arise. Down on money, and with few local friends, the work proceeded slowly, but he was well on the way to finishing when the Spanish Civil War broke out. For a few months Ibiza became the focus of the war in the east and Villain's hideaway ultimately offered him scant protection when Republican troops landed on the island. As he had feared, memories were long.

Standing in front of Villain's house, a few years older than he was when he pulled the trigger and a few years younger than he was when he died, I tried to work out what I believed in strongly enough to kill a man then hide out in a concrete cell through years of terror. Was there anything I had sufficient faith in, anything for which I would walk out to my death without a struggle, without screaming and running and pleading for my life? I don't know if it's the age I am or the age I live in, but I struggled for an answer. I suppose I'm soft and decadent, a corrupt symbol of compromise and consumerism, but it seems to me that there's no idea I could cherish in my mind to such an extent that it overrode my basic desire to live. Raoul Villain was the suicide bomber of his day and somehow he knew that his dream of war and a monarchy for France was something he was prepared to die for, for which he was prepared never to see the sun again, never to sit and laugh with friends, never to embrace his lover.

I've believed in many things in my life – God, music, politics, books, people, ideas – but, at the last, they have always, always let me down. What if I had given my life for them? They wouldn't have cared for my death, not unless it gained them something. So poor, mad, driven Villain pulled a trigger and died for it. If he hadn't, the First World War would still have happened. The century would have unfolded as it did. And maybe his children could have played on the sand at Cala de Sant Vincent.

Villain's death might have been the first of the civil war on the Pitiuses, but it was far from the last. The islands' war started early and ended quickly. It was a nasty, bitter exchange with both sides steeped in slaughter. The population of Ibiza and Formentera was so small – some people believe there were as few as fourteen surnames on Ibiza in the 1930s – that the killing was a family affair. As a result, few local historians will tackle the subject. Although most of the bloodshed took place in Ibiza Town, the story of Santa Eulalia's war is far better known because it was written by an outsider. At the time war broke out, the American journalist and thriller writer Elliot Paul was living there. He wrote *Life and Death of a Spanish Town* about the effects of the war on its population, and it is still the best account of the first days of a much-described conflict.

When Paul arrived in 1934, Santa Eulalia was a collection of around fifty houses grouped along a single road several hundred metres from the sea. Then, as now, the main road from Ibiza Town passed over the island's only river on a broad stone bridge before snaking around the base of a low hill, the Puig de Missa, dominated by the town's church. The church itself was built in the sixteenth century as part of Ibiza's coastal defences against pirates, so it has a distinctly military air.

The Santa Eulalia Paul found was an idyll of rural Spain.

The carpenter was also the vet. Rain stopped work. The cafés were packed late into the night with fishermen, farmers and storekeepers drinking wine, beer or absinthe and singing songs about friendship and cigarettes. The women still wore traditional Ibicenco costume and valued the white skin its protective covering gave them. The bus would come in from Ibiza Town once a day, bringing ice and picking up fish to take back to market. Some of Santa Eulalia's inhabitants would take the nine-mile journey back with the bus once or twice a year; some of them had never dared venture that far. Life was simple and slow moving. The only indication that something was bubbling beneath the surface was the cool reserve between the drinkers in two of the town's three bars, the Royalty Hotel and Cosmi's.

Cosmi's hotel took full advantage of the local licensing laws that are still in effect: bars can stay open for as long as they want provided they close for one hour during every twenty-four. Cosmi Salvador himself worked the afternoon and evening shift, shutting up shop at two in the morning after he had kicked out all the evening regulars – the stonemasons, carpenters and indolent loungers from the international crowd of writers and artists who, like Paul, had moved to the town. His brother Pep then opened up an hour later to serve the fishermen. Just along the road, the Royalty served a better class of patron, the likes of Don Ignacio Riquer, who had English ancestors and a car and who owned most of the land south of the river; Don Carlos Roman; and Father Torres, the priest who went from house to house impressing on the newly enfranchised that to vote liberal was a mortal sin. Some of Cosmi's drinkers suspected him of harbouring arms in a tunnel beneath the church. The bar that locals chose to drink in generally marked out the drinkers' sympathies and social class, although there were a few exceptions. Don Ignacio would sometimes drink in Cosmi's, while internationals could flit easily between the two. Even so, most residents were either Cosmi's people or Royalty people, just as they were either left wing or right wing.

The same tensions simmered across mainland Spain. The country had lurched almost bankrupt into the twentieth century and failed to make much headway for the first three decades. In the 1930s the mainland was basically a feudal society. The vast majority of the land remained in the hands of the aristocracy, who would often leave huge tracts fallow, retaining land simply as an investment. Meanwhile, Spanish peasants were starving, unable to scrape a living on the tiny strips of soil they could till. In Andalucía, conditions were so bad that peasants were forced to eat grass and sometimes squatted in farm buildings since animals were housed better than people.

The country was divided along class, ideological and regional lines. On the left stood anarchist and socialist parties such as the CNT (Confederación Nacional del Trabajo) and the PSOE (Partido Socialista Obrero Español) as well as the Moscow-backed Communist Party and various Catalan nationalist movements; on the right were the fascist Falange party, the red-beret-wearing monarchist Renovación Española, and ultra-conservative Catholics united as the CEDA (Confederación Española de Derechas Autónomas).

The two burning issues for both sides were the thorny question of land reform and the position of the Catholic Church. These were matters of life and death on the mainland, fury over starvation and virulent anti-clericalism leading to constant violent uprisings that were put down with brutal force. On Ibiza and Formentera, however, neither issue was especially high on the political agenda.

As far as land reform was concerned, the two islands had effectively operated under their own rules since the early days of the Catalans. On Ibiza, land was in plentiful supply and tenant farmers were fairly secure in their homes. They could choose which crops they wished to grow, lived rent-free, kept half the produce for themselves, delivered half to their landlord and were expected to provide their own tools and animals. In theory, landlord and farmer signed annual contracts, but in practice, the contracts just rolled over year after year. On Formentera, most families actually owned their own land – a position of comparative luxury. Anarchism, so popular among the landless peasantry of the mainland, had few followers in the Pitiuses.

The position of the Catholic Church was also complicated. Across the mainland, anti-clericalism was rampant. Despite the wealth and political power of the Church, fewer than 20 per cent of the Spanish population attended mass, with the figures down to 5 per cent in the south – lower than in any other Christian country. In Ibiza, few men attended church – Elliot Paul reckoned that barely twenty men from Santa Eulalia would start out up the hill every Sunday and most would only get as far as the café just below the brow where they would sit out the service watching the traffic on the road below – but for women and for those rural peasant farmers who could go for days at a time without seeing anyone outside their immediate family, the church was as much a social centre as a religious institution.

Indeed, Ibiza's right-wing historian-priest Isidor Macabich organized Church-based trade unions to rival the socialist affiliations of the workers in the towns. (Macabich is best remembered for this comment, when asked if he was descended from one of Ibiza's noble families: 'In Ibiza there are no nobles. We are sons of seamen, of peasants or of a bitch.') The Church's power was further strengthened by its monopolistic control over schooling. Even so, the satirical procession known popularly as El Gato, held every year on Ash Wednesday, mocked the clergy with a savage, caustic bite that always outraged the island's conservative newspapers.

Politically, the islands were far from radical. The anarchist parties might have been weak but so was the fascist Falange, which boasted only twenty-five members across both islands before the war. The wealthy in Dalt Vila, the middle classes in La Marina, the landlords and the deeply conservative peasantry were broadly centre-right, while the left was drawn from the intelligentsia, the seamen, the fishermen, dock workers, stonecutters and, above all, salt workers. However, even those who pronounced themselves socialists were gentle in their subversion.

A good example of Ibiza's softly glowing firebrands was one of Elliot Paul's friends, Captain Juan, a fisherman and an Ibicenco Red. He had scarcely heard of Moscow or Karl Marx, had no ambitions for political office and had never made a speech in his life. He wanted his children to be educated by the state not the Church, fallow land to be given to the peasants, an end to official corruption and absolute freedom of speech. Storming the Winter Palace, or even Ibiza's town hall, was not on his agenda. Even the head of Ibiza's tiny Communist Party, Antoni Ribas, spent most of his time before the war cruising the countryside with Raoul Hausmann and seducing Vera Broido.

By 1936, however, subtle dissent was not an option. After a series of tumultuous elections in the first half of the decade, Spain entered that year's poll with the country's thirty-odd political parties formed up into two violently opposed power blocks: the left-wing Popular Front and the right-wing National Front. The Popular Front, which combined anarchist, Stalinist, Trotskyite, democratic socialist and regional parties from the Basque and Catalan regions, swept to power with strong support from the cities and the more rebellious rural parts of the mainland. The Popular Front won in Formentera, although Ibiza, as it had done in every previous election, remained resolutely in the hands of the right.

After the Popular Front victory, Spain slid rapidly into civil war. The Spanish military refused to accept the new Republican government and General Franco's African army left Morocco for the mainland on 17 July to oust the left-wing upstarts. Two days later General Goded, one of Franco's allies and the man in charge of taking Catalonia, seized Palma in nearby Mallorca, kicking off the action in the Balearics.

On Ibiza, Captain Rafael García Ledesma, the commander of the small platoon of infantry stationed on the island, promptly declared for Franco and put Ibiza and Formentera on a state of war readiness. The following day, 20 July, command of the island was passed into the hands of Juli Mestre, a visiting commandant of infantry. He set about recruiting extra support from right-wing sympathizers on the island to add to his rather slim squad of 143 soldiers and managed to muster an additional two hundred men. His volunteers came mainly from the wealthy landowning families, with a smattering of retired soldiers and Guardia Civil officers. It must have been a little like the Home Guard in 1940s Britain – crotchety old soldiers, bank managers and a few eager, youthful Falangists gathered together with a motley collection of hunting rifles, shotguns and whatever weapons the infantry could spare.

These volunteers joined the professional soldiers to mount regular patrols through the islands, although Ibiza's left-wing elements were hardly an organized threat. On Formentera, however, the radical tendency was better organized and was getting restive. The Popular Front mayor, Joán Riera I Yern, had been ousted by the former right-wing mayor Joán Serra I Torres, but his position was tenuous, with a mutinous population and no military presence. Helpfully, Mestre sent twenty-three of his professional soldiers to restore order and bolster Torres.

For the next two weeks, the islands waited. Elliot Paul described the atmosphere in Santa Eulalia – crowds gathering along the main street every day to discuss events, the monarchist Royalty deserted but the Republican Cosmi's packed with left-wing sympathizers keeping up their spirits in the dark times. The Santa Eulalia bus service to Ibiza Town found itself running empty; people preferred to await the worst near their homes and families. In the end, the company halved its service, further reducing deliveries of food. People changed their flashy, insubstantial bank notes for solid metal coins and buried them in the garden.

Rumours took wing and flew around the wide, sunlit streets: the exiled leader of the Guardia Civil had been killed in an aeroplane crash; the uprising had been put down in the major cities; Franco was coming – no he wasn't, he was dead, he was alive . . . The island's newspapers, owned by the Matutes, were pro-Franco and the radio was in the hands of the government. No matter where they turned, it was impossible for the islanders to get any impartial facts.

As tension mounted, a British destroyer was sent from Gibraltar to pick up half a dozen of His Majesty's subjects from the harbour in Ibiza Town. Mestre refused the ship's captain access to any but the six Brits already waiting on the dockside. Outraged, one British painter in Santa Eulalia, Derek Rogers, declared for the Republic and turned his shortwave radio over to Cosmi's drinkers. The BBC offered some hope of accuracy, but the clandestine listeners were shattered as London reported a surge of pro-Franco demonstrations.

During these brief days of phoney war, Elliot Paul, whose sympathies were with the Republic, noticed a strong sense of loyalty to the Republican cause in Santa Eulalia but a stronger sense of loyalty to the town itself. Although there was a healthy crop of left-leaning thinkers few, if any, were steeped in theory. They just thought the time had come to move away from ancient traditions and old ways of living. Very few of them saw violence as the answer. In Santa Eulalia, both sides swore that here they would not start killing one another. Indeed, when Mestre ordered soldiers to arrest Cosmi and other known left-wingers, a kind-hearted Guardia Civil sergeant warned them. By the time the troops arrived, they found their prey had hightailed it out of town and were already holed up in the surrounding hills.

At the very end of July, the Republican air force sent a single plane over Ibiza to drop some leaflets urging the island to surrender to avoid bloodshed. Mestre remained unmoved, but the warning to Ibiza residents to evacuate their city in the name of safety weakened the resolve of his part-time soldiers and nervous farmboys. The majority of his volunteers drifted slowly away while a hysterical Mestre tried to fine anyone leaving Ibiza Town. He embarked on a series of small-scale gestures designed to underline his control, censoring the press, arresting around sixty left-wingers and issuing edicts charging certain, mainly Republican, bars to close at midnight. The latter was uniformly ignored.

Meanwhile, the Republican forces were preparing an invasion of Ibiza to help secure the real prize in the Balearics – Mallorca. It was the largest military operation in the east. On 5 August, two destroyers, four submarines and a troop carrier left Barcelona under the joint command of an air force officer, Captain Alberto Bayo – later to become Fidel Castro's guerrilla trainer – and the anarchist Manuel Uribarry. Uribarry's contingent was pretty similar to Mestre's volunteers – mainly civilians who seemed to be going along for the adventure; Bayo's troops were more formidable, with regular soldiers and left-wing paramilitaries as well as six Ibicenco Republicans trapped on the mainland at the outbreak of the war.

On 6 August, the convoy steamed past Santa Eulalia without stopping and Paul watched them disappear, filled with despair, thinking they had decided to abandon their plans to land. In fact they headed for Formentera and overran the small island's tiny detachment of troops almost immediately, mainly because Mestre's boys instantly surrendered to the two negotiators Bayo had sent to open discussions. Bayo went ashore, commandeered the island's telegraph and sent a demand for a similar surrender to Mestre, as he recalled in his autobiography *My Disembarkation in Mallorca*: 'If you give yourselves up, your lives will be spared. If you want blood, you will have it in abundance.' Five minutes later, Mestre replied, 'The blood you wish to shed will be shed.'

The two destroyers carried the Republican troops to the north of the island and they landed near Pou des Lleo and Santa Eulalia. The force took a few hours to organize itself, and to despatch Raoul Villain's firing squad, then formed up and began a swift march on Mestre's positions in Ibiza Town.

Around this time, an ugly incident occurred for which there are two recorded versions of events. In the nearby village of San Carlos, the priest and his father were murdered by the Republicans. As Elliot Paul tells it, local parishioners attacked their Nationalist priest so he barricaded himself in the church and opened fire on those below. Crucially, Paul's version takes place before the Republican troops landed. An alternative version, preferred in Ibiza, has it that Bayo's passing troops demanded water from the church, which the priest denied them unless they disarmed. The soldiers refused, so the priest's father appeared armed with a rifle. Whichever version is true, the story ends the same way: the priest and his father were hanged from the carob tree that stands outside the pretty village church. Presumably Ibicencos prefer the second version because it has soldiers from the mainland carrying out the execution rather than local rebels. Either way, Elliot Paul's version ends prophetically: an old man recounts the tale and Paul's friend Pep Torres remarks with a sigh, 'Now it never will be over.'

Bayo's march south continued. About halfway down the road they passed the old Roman iron mines, S'Argenta, where they were ambushed by a small detachment of Nationalist troops sent up from Dalt Vila. The skirmish was brief and decisive. The Nationalists fired on the Republicans, killing a number of them, then fled under the hail of return fire. It was the only formal battle on Ibiza of the civil war.

When news of the Nationalist defeat reached Ibiza Town, Mestre's flimsy control collapsed. Bravely, he fled, accompanied by most of Ibiza's richest citizens and Bishop Cardona. Captain Ledesma and the prison warden killed themselves and the sixty-odd leftists held in the castle prison forced their way out of jail.

Across the island, Republican sympathizers joined Uribarry's anarchist troops in routing out and executing almost half of the island's priests. They also turned on a number of wealthy landlords. Don Ignacio, the largest landowner in Santa Eulalia, was taken prisoner but released after petitions from the town's leading leftists, including Cosmi. He had lent money without charging interest, and, so it is said, his wife was such a nag that the men took pity on him for all his years of suffering.

Still, personal vendettas came bubbling to the surface, and several outstanding debts were paid off with a couple of rounds from a rifle. Most of the island's churches were burned, although in two cases – Sant Antonio and Jesús – local people stepped in to save their chapels. But Ibicenco

Republicans were not indiscriminate in their slaughter. The island's most famous literary son, Isidor Macabich, was a notorious Franco sympathizer and energetic right-wing activist. Despite his implacable opposition to everything the Republic stood for, they declared him too gifted to be executed.

For Bayo, the extent of the destruction was too much. He tried to rein in Uribarry's excesses and the two men quarrelled. Finally, Uribarry rather sulkily left the island and took his soldiers with him. Bayo then rallied his troops and embarked on a foolhardy attempt to take Mallorca. With his forces stretched and the resistance on Mallorca far better organized than the indifferent defence on Ibiza, his operation failed dismally. Severely weakened, Bayo realized that he didn't possess the necessary force to hold Ibiza against any kind of sustained attack, and his troops returned to Barcelona.

For several days, between 4 and 10 September, neither side had any serious forces in the Pitiuses. On the 10th, however, a large force of anarchist militia under Juan Yague took control of the islands and overwhelmed them with Instant Radicalism, which included changing the name of the *Diario de Ibiza* to *Workers' Solidarity*. This is the political equivalent of renaming the Kent Messenger Group *Socialist Worker*. Yague's boys also rounded up close to a hundred prisoners from wealthy families and fascist sympathizers, jailing them in the cells beneath Dalt Vila's castle.

Over in Mallorca, the Nationalist troops were supplied and reinforced by Mussolini, who also provided ships and planes. With this Italian support, they prepared to retake the Pitiuses. To soften things up, Italian planes bombed Ibiza

Town, killing forty civilians and damaging a number of buildings including the café Mar Y Sol. The Italians also sent a destroyer to scope out the island. On 13 September, one of Ibiza's young fascist prisoners, holed up in the town jail, saw the Italian flag on the gunboat and remarked to his guard, 'It's our turn now.' In a fit of fury the guard grabbed his gun and shot his prisoner dead on the spot. In the confusion following the sound of gunfire, an alarm was given and Yague's five-hundred-strong contingent panicked. They rounded up the hundred prisoners, including local worthies, priests, military men and right-wing political leaders, and machine-gunned them in a single large cell. All but seven of the prisoners died. You could hear the gunfire all over town. It is a day the island has found impossible to forget.

In the aftermath of the shooting everyone in Ibiza Town packed up and fled, including the anarchist soldiers; only around a dozen people stayed behind. Elliot Paul walked through the town the following day. 'What I found in that formerly most beautiful and prosperous and hospitable city is too bleak for words to convey,' he wrote. 'The inner harbour, smashed fishing boats and fish, belly up and stinking. At the corner, the wreck of the tobacco shop and the gasoline pump. Bloodstains on all the walls. On the broad paseo, one building still inhabited. There stood old Carmen, wife of Sergeant Ortiz, her arm around the shoulder of a woman in black, and very gently lifting the blanket from a donkey cartload of corpses to find one other the woman might claim.'

Ibiza is now so clearly a happy, modern European town that the scenes Paul sketched are almost impossible to imagine. It's like someone describing a bout of ethnic cleansing in Bournemouth. But we've seen the TV pictures of similar events – deserted towns in war-torn countries with bullet-pocked walls, inept pot shots fired by frightened teenagers as the cameras roll. For a few brief days, Ibiza Town was Sarajevo, Freetown or Gaza.

On 18 September the Italian destroyer *Malocello* made a reconnaissance tour of the islands, found them undefended and reported back to Palma. Sensing danger, Elliot Paul rounded up his family and, as internationals, secured a berth on a German destroyer that arrived a day after the *Malocello*. As the destroyer steamed away, Paul saw a schooner from Santa Eulalia called the *Isabel Matutes* passing fifty yards away. On board he saw Cosmi, his brother Pep and Captain Juan making a similar bid for freedom.

It was a timely escape. On the 20th a mixed bag of anti-Republican companies sailed into Ibiza harbour on the Mallorca–Ibiza ferryboat, the *Ciudad de Palma*. The soldiers were mainly Falangists but included a notorious Italian platoon sent to Mallorca by Mussolini who called themselves the Dragons of Death. After landing unopposed, the Nationalists rapidly gained control of both islands. As soon as they had, the Dragons herded four hundred Republicans into the cells in Dalt Vila and slaughtered them all.

Ibiza's left-wingers got the message. Those who could, fled. At first they headed to Menorca, which remained Republican until 1939. When Menorca capitulated they moved on again to France, to Russia or the Americas. Like countless refugees before and since, they set off in little flotillas of rowing boats, sticking close together for security and support.

Among them was Antoni Ribas. He fled first to the mainland, where he was caught and interned in a concentration camp in France. Fortunately, his Russian lover Vera stepped in and managed to pull a few strings. Ribas was released and escaped to Venezuela where, good communist that he was, he became incredibly wealthy, returning to Spain a rich man after Franco's death in 1975. His flight to South America was far from unusual. Large numbers of those from both Ibiza and Formentera fled to Argentina for sanctuary, and it was these refugees whose votes were later claimed during Formentera's Partido Popular election scandal.

Some Republicans failed to get away. Many were arrested and then executed in Palma de Mallorca at the close of the war. And for every one of those who had escaped there was a family left behind. Without the ringleaders to punish, the fascists fell on their relatives, as Artur Parrón confirmed in his book *La Guerra Civil a Eivissa I Formentera*, '. . . because of this [scarcity of available targets] repression centred on activists and sympathisers from the popular base, those with no public importance who should not have feared any particularly harsh reprisals for their involvement. For this reason, Franco's repression was rendered much more indiscriminate and bloody, in that its primary objective was that of creating an atmosphere of terror and collective silence; often times the scapegoat was a relative of the person who had actually played an active political role . . .' In Formentera the purges were, in Parrón's words, 'brutal, of disproportionate violence'. The island's pre-war election results and its left-wing tendencies were well remembered. Eighteen Formenterencs were shot, while at least five died in Nazi concentration camps. Investment in the island stopped altogether, leaving the inhabitants operating at subsistence levels. From 1939 to 1942, Formentera became a concentration camp for political dissidents from mainland Spain awaiting execution. The nickname 'the island of women' probably stems from this time. With so many men dead or fled, the moniker was inevitable.

The right wing's revenge, as in the rest of Spain, was long and drawn out. In his history of the war, Anthony Beevor observed, 'The slaughter did not follow the same pattern on each side. In Nationalist territory the relentless purging of "reds and atheists" was to continue for years, while in Republican territory the worst of the violence was mainly a sudden and quickly spent reaction of suppressed fear, exacerbated by desires of revenge for the past.' After the war, the politics of the islands rapidly fell into line with the rest of the mainland, crushed as it was under the heel of Franco's boot. In Ibiza and Formentera, the Falangist numbers had been tiny before the war; after it, Franco merged the party into his Movimiento Nacional. Joining the Party became the only way to advance socially. With Falangists running Ibiza, executions became a nightly occurrence. As well as eliminating the anti-fascist element, there were plenty of personal grudges settled in the dark of night as those who'd backed the winning side took swift advantage of their new power.

When Dutch artists began to arrive on the island in the 1950s, one of them witnessed a murder in San Miguel. The town's butcher walked into his old friend the baker's shop with a hunting rifle slung over his shoulder. The baker asked why he had his rifle, as the season didn't start until the following day. 'I'm opening the season today,' the butcher said, before unslinging the rifle and shooting his friend twice in the stomach. As the baker lay dying, the butcher calmly walked over to the Guardia Civil station and turned himself in. The investigation was short and the motive readily established. During the war the baker, a fascist, had had the butcher, an anarchist, arrested and imprisoned. It was a long time before Ibicencos opened their doors if someone knocked after nightfall.

As I drove into Santa Eulalia from Cala de Sant Vincent, I was half expecting to see the simple main road and low, white buildings that make up Elliot Paul's map of the place from 1936. I couldn't have been more wrong. I don't think there's a phrase that means 'the polar opposite of charming fishing hamlet', but Santa Eulalia satisfied the description should such a phrase ever come along. There were more jolly-looking British pubs per square mile than I'd seen in most British towns. All sported improbably patriotic pub names – the Queen Victoria, the John Bull, the Union Jack. It's funny how Brits who've left their native country plaster their lives with the flag and surround themselves with images of dead royalty. There was even a cricket league in the town. I half expected to find a group of expats taking Earl Grey tea on the lawn at four with dainty plates of cucumber sandwiches.

I suppose I shouldn't have been surprised. In the 1950s and 1960s Santa Eulalia was known as the 'Raj on the Med'. Shortly after the Second World War, the town became a haven for Brits from the colonial service who were leaving independent India but couldn't bear the climate in Blighty. Or the rationing. Or the blacks. They liked living under a good, honest dictatorship and they were joined, at least until the collapse of the pound in the 1970s, by retired officers who could live large on their comparatively low military pensions. Judging by the crowds packing the pavements as I drove down the main street, called Sant Jaume, the ageing British still held sway, although the Germans were making a decent fist of supplanting them. Cafés offered both full English breakfasts and the German *Wurst und Eier* equivalent. After parking up in a used-to-be-charming square, I found this to be doubly true on the seafront. (Insert your own 'fight them on the beaches' references here.)

On the corner of the square, I was briefly delighted to find that Cosmi's was still standing and that across the road its old rival, the Royalty, had also survived the years. But then I pulled out Elliot Paul's book and examined his map. In 1936 the café now called Cosmi's had been the vaguely apolitical Antonia's Fisherman's Bar; Cosmi's was further down Sant Jaume towards San Carlos. I hoped that Cosmi had returned post-Franco and bought out Antonia to get back into the café game; either that or someone had decided to cash in on the post-war popularity of *Life and Death of a Spanish Town* and renamed Antonia's to get the tourists in. This seemed slightly repellent, so I shook it from my mind and started towards the Marina. I had an American to find.

Since I'd arrived on the island, every third conversation had seemed to include a reference to a man called, promisingly, Mad Mike. Sue, Marina, Emily and Martin had all mentioned him. The Vietnam vet. A shadowy figure. They said he had been in tanks in Vietnam and one had blown up under him; they said he had a metal plate in his skull, a pacemaker in his heart and even a reconstructed lower intestine and rectum. No-one seemed entirely sure where he lived, but he used to drink in M&M's bar in Santa Eulalia, an American-owned place down by the Marina. Just head in there and ask around, I was told.

I had a vague hope that talking to Mike might help me understand Villain, Cosmi, the Dragons and all those who'd fought and died on Ibiza. He'd fought in Nam, man. The big one. The civil war that had shaped the end of the twentieth century the way Spain had shaped its middle. Mike had had all his bones broken then wired together and had hidden away on the island ever since. I wondered what sanctuary Ibiza had offered him after fleeing the conflict and his country and dragging his battered body halfway across the world to find some peace.

M&M's was very quiet when I got there. I could hear the clanging of expensive rigging coming from the massed yachts floating at anchor in the Marina. An American couple in their sixties sat outside chatting. I wandered up to the barmaid and asked if Mad Mike had been in. She pursed her lips and shook her head. 'Not seen him for a while,' she said. 'You could try the Bolt Hole or the Queen Vic. Or maybe the Royalty. He's sometimes in there.' I asked her for directions to the Bolt Hole and she gave them with a strange smirk that slightly unsettled me.

Since Elliot Paul's time, Santa Eulalia seemed to have expanded to fill the gap between the main street, Sant Jaume, and the sea with a New York-style grid of criss-crossing roads. Slicing through these, I became aware that the frisky morning sunshine had given way rather rapidly to a fierce midday wall of fire. With the sun almost directly overhead the low, modern buildings provided little in the way of shade, so I picked up my pace and hoped the Bolt Hole was air-conditioned.

When I rounded the corner and caught sight of the place, however, I could feel my hopes pouring away down my outer thigh. Or maybe that was just sweat. I seemed to have walked into the anarchist quarter of Berlin before the Wall came down. The Bolt Hole was a small, dark bar that seemed to burst out onto the street like a scruffy urchin busking with an overdrive pedal and a huge Marshall amp. Someone inside was playing 'Babylon's Burning' by the Ruts with the volume turned up to 11. A narrow door opened in to spray-paint-graffiti'd walls, a metal pole-dancing pole and three of the drunkest people I'd ever seen at midday. Two of them had faces covered in scars and tattoos, and one, while otherwise intact, had some pretty ropey teeth. As I poked my head round the door, they turned to look at me and the place went silent – or at least as silent as a bar can go with the Ruts on at full volume. Nervously I walked towards them with a big I'm-your-friend smile plastered over my face.

'Hi!' I sounded like a male Barbie tour guide. 'I'm looking for Mad Mike.'

The unscarred member of the trio peeled himself from his stool and stepped towards me, his eyes narrowed with suspicion. 'Why?' he rasped, dangerously.

'Um . . .' I paused as eight hopeless lies ran through my head. Then I decided to tell the truth. 'I'm writing a book.'

Instantly his face cleared, though I noticed with some alarm that his voice continued to rasp. Indeed, every couple of minutes he took an especially deep breath that gave off a nasty guttural rattle as well. 'I've written a book too,' he announced, beaming. 'Come in, mate, my name's Colin. Colin Casbolt. This is my place.'

The men made a space for me at the bar and Colin went behind the counter.

'What do you want, mate? First one's on the house.' I hesitated rather primly and repeated that I was looking for Mad Mike, but he waved my concerns away. 'He'll be along soon. He's always here, or maybe next door at the Vic, but he isn't up this early. Have a drink!'

I asked for a Coke, but Colin insisted on slipping a double vodka into it before introducing me to the other two drinkers in the bar. The man to my left was an ex-Spanish special forces sergeant while the guy with a huge knife slash across his eye came from northern England and had just been released from prison by a court in San Antonio because he'd been caught with thirty Ecstasy tablets on him. He'd spent a night inside and they'd let him out because he told the judge they were for personal use. I was about to start drinking vodka with a man who used to kill for a living and a heavily scarred drug dealer just out of chokey. The day was not developing the way I had planned.

I have to say, I'm not much of a morning drinker. Or a lunchtime drinker. Or even an afternoon drinker. Maybe a quiet pint or a glass of wine with some food. If I start on anything else before seven p.m., you really wouldn't like me. And not in an Incredible Hulk dangerous monster sort of way, but in a rather pathetic, overexcitable and then suddenly semi-comatose sort of way. If I am forced to start drinking around midday, I prefer not to do so in the fierce 37° heat of a Mediterranean day. Within about twenty minutes I was absolutely blind drunk. Trouble focusing, weaving through the empty bar, urinating every ten minutes – the works. The fact that the toilet looked like it hadn't been cleaned that year didn't help to balance my karma.

Eventually, Colin took me outside with a couple of large vodkas and we sat in the blazing sun while he told me his life story and I slurped feebly away at my triple-shot morning refresher. Every so often I would look up and there would be the grinning dealer or the lumbering form of the Spanish special forces soldier. I felt that they viewed my pathetic capacity for booze as in some way effeminate. When Colin passed me a joint and I unwisely dragged deeply, this fear became a deep-rooted paranoia. So, to prove how much of a tough guy I was, I started ordering up San Miguels all round, glugging half of mine down and then taking the glass to the toilet with me on my increasingly frequent visits, where I'd try to tip some of it down the stinking bowl while holding down my rising nausea.

After one trip, I returned to find that Colin had pulled out his book, or rather books. It turned out he was something of a poet. The first, self-published tome was called *Thank God I'm Still a Hippy – Verses from Ibiza*. The title poem began:

> Thank God I'm still a hippy,
> I'm free and wild and trippy.
> A sixties freak of lust and luck,
> A hairy monster – gives a fuck.

He told me he'd come to Ibiza twenty years ago after travelling the world for five years with his wife and kids. He'd partied, cooked, sold stuff, bought stuff and generally scammed about until he'd lucked into the bar. 'And now, mate, look at me. I'm living in paradise.' I did look at him. He didn't look so bad for his fifty-seven years, given that these years had involved almost every drug ever produced, a current lifestyle that included hitting the booze pretty much as soon as he opened the bar, and a rate of tobacco consumption that would have made Phillip Morris weep tears of gratitude. But I guess my image of a man living in paradise was slightly different.

In my head, Stephen Armstrong Paradise Dweller would get up early every morning, head down to the beach for a run, go for a swim, partake of a light breakfast of fruit before . . . before . . . well, before what? What on Earth would I do if I woke up every day and found I had everything I wanted just outside the door with sunshine all year round and endless sandy beaches? Of course it sounds fantastic. It's everyone's dream come true. But I don't think those of us from northern European stock are very good at living out our dreams. I think most of us would get very, very bored very, very quickly. I think we'd do what every English-speaking expat I have ever met in a hot climate does. I think we'd do what Colin does. I think we'd get up every morning, dust ourselves down and head for the bar.

I'm not sure why this is the case. Perhaps we can't bear to be happy. Perhaps the pain locked deep in some part of our background – our genes, our environment, who knows? – means that the only way we can achieve true contentment is through oblivion. That given an unlimited supply of everything, it's the alcohol supply we'd test to the limit. I could see them populating every bar I'd passed on the way to the Bolt Hole. Santa Eulalia was full of them – expats propping up the bar, pissing their pension or some lucky windfall up the wall while the waves lapped gently at the shore outside.

A good friend once sent me a quote from a seventeenth-century writer called Blaise Pascal that read, 'Man finds nothing so intolerable as to be in a state of complete rest, without passions, without occupation, without diversion, without effort. Then he feels his nullity, loneliness, inadequacy, dependence, helplessness, emptiness.' Then, Santa Eulalia seemed to be telling me, he turns to the bottle.

Obviously I don't speak for everyone. I've met some lovely British expats on tropical islands who are completely teetotal. Nary a drop has passed their virgin lips. But there's something about most of us, and our kin in Australia and New Zealand, that points in the other direction. I have a Dutch friend who lives in Amsterdam, and one day I was out walking with her when we passed a man lying unconscious, face down, in a pool of his own sick right in the centre of the Dam Square. He was a young man, well dressed and clearly not down on his luck; he'd just had way, way more than his system could handle. I looked at him with some concern, but Lysette just glanced down swiftly and walked on. 'English,' she said, without a sneer, merely as a statement.

I realized I'd drifted off into my own thoughts and looked up to find I was alone on the pavement. Suddenly Colin popped his head out of the Queen Victoria two doors down and beckoned me over. 'Mad Mike's here!' he yelled, causing all the Queen Vic drinkers in the wide, open windows to turn and look at me as I stumbled to my feet and made my unsteady way towards him.

Just inside the door, sitting in a shady patch on the left, was a gaunt, grey-haired figure with a full, flowing Gandalf beard. A pair of crutches leaned against his bar stool and he sipped at a small glass of lager. His forearms were so thin I could have touched my thumb and forefinger together if I'd tried to encircle them. His eyes seemed pale and far away. If he was mad, it wasn't the rage of a demented Viet vet, shell-shocked and crazy. It was far, far deeper inside.

I stepped up to him, trying to appear as sober as I could, and sat down. 'Do you mind if I sit here?' I asked.

He shrugged.

'Are you Mike?'

'Yup.'

'I've been looking for you. I want to talk to you about Ibiza,' I said.

'What's to tell? Came to Spain, met a girl, came down here, there we are.'

'But weren't you in Vietnam?'

I blurted this out with the sensitivity of a charging bull elephant pissed on vodka. He didn't say a word.

'I've got this book about the civil war in Santa Eulalia,' I blundered on, pulling out Elliot Paul's hardback and waving it at him. 'It was written by an American too.' As if that would make any difference.

Mike's gaze fixed on a spot over my shoulder. 'I don't really want to talk about it,' he said, incredibly quietly.

We sat there for a while, then he got up.

'Look,' he said, his voice so soft I had to lean forward to catch what he was saying, 'I'm busy now. Why don't you meet me at the Royalty tomorrow and we can have a chat.'

I nodded as he pushed past me, lurching on his crutches as he made for the door.

I went to the Royalty the next day, like he said. He wasn't

there. I waited for two hours because I might have been confused about the time, but he didn't show. That night I walked past the Queen Victoria and poked my head through the door. There he was, on the same old bar stool with his crutches and his beer, reading a report on the front page of the *Herald Tribune* about four US soldiers killed in Iraq when their Humvee went over a land mine. I waved to get his attention. He looked up, looked at me for a second, then went back to his newspaper. I didn't see him again.

CHAPTER 9

The Faker

Marina phoned to invite me to another party. This one was a launch. 'It's a new restaurant called La Diosa run by some Argentinians in the middle of the island,' she said. 'It should be pretty good. They've been working on the place over the winter and it's supposed to be beautiful. Come by and pick me up from the gallery.'

Fortunately, the gallery wasn't too hard to find. It faced the yacht club on a long, tree-lined boulevard fenced off to the seaward side by chandlers' yards and to the shore side by expensive apartment blocks. By the time I arrived, Marina was in a bit of a flap. The local TV station was sending over a camera crew to do a piece on the gallery and she was nervous. She wanted a distraction to calm her down, so I tried to ask why she'd come to the island. Again. She seemed mildly put out and told me it was the sort of question you didn't ask in Ibiza.

'People come here for a reason,' she said as she sorted aimlessly through the papers on her desk. 'A few years ago there was a bit of a fuss when the Italian police arrived to arrest a fisherman who'd been living in Sant Rafael for the last seventeen years. It turned out he was a Mafia *capo di capi* on the run from Sicily for all sorts of crimes. They took him back to face trial.' She laughed. 'You know, one of the reasons people come here is because Ibicencos don't ask questions and they don't care what you do as long as they like you. They'll never judge you. Almost all the villagers from Sant Rafael who could travel went over to Sicily to see him in prison. Some of them had never left the island before.'

During her club-owning years, Marina went on, she had employed a door team of two huge German bruisers and their Yugoslavian boss who kept tight control of the place for months. One night she was stopped on the way in to open up by a man in ordinary clothes who warned her that a police sniper was on the roof of the hotel opposite, keeping his gun trained on the three muscleboys. Before she could ask why, the man had disappeared. That night, her door team vanished.

Suddenly, from the street, there was a sharp crash and we both turned. A slim, attractive girl in her early twenties who was struggling with a heavy film camera had collided with the gallery door and for an instant seemed spread-eagled against the glass like a bluebottle on a car windscreen. She peeled herself clear and pushed her way in with a bony brown shoulder. Her name, she told us, was Pilar, and she was the TV crew.

As Pilar set up in the corner, Marina fussed about, clearly nervous, so I took the chance to potter around the gallery and eye up the art. It seemed like anyone who had placed brush on canvas was represented there in some form. The paintings came from the Pitti Arte forgers' co-operative near Florence, run by art expert Giuseppe Salzano. This team of earnest brushsmiths strive away in a Tuscan workshop producing perfect copies of great masters which they sell through a local gallery. The pictures are attached to official certificates 'authenticating' the fact that they are forgeries. Marina's Ibiza franchise was the first one set up outside Italy. 'Nice scam,' I commented, smiling at Pilar. She didn't understand.

After the filming was done, we clambered into the Seat and took off into the heart of the island. La Diosa was in the venue formerly known as the Hoedown Barbecue, a themed country and western big night out that holiday company reps had sold to package tourists in San Antonio for a tidy commission. Making the shift to upmarket eatery sounded faintly risky to me. How many chic and exclusive little bistros have six hundred covers as well as an indoor nightclub and extensive, landscaped gardens? The Argentinian owners had bought the place a year ago and had been trying to open it ever since. They had run into continual trouble with the licensing authorities, who were dealing with complaints from locals dreading another Space or Privilege.

In Ibiza, big venues usually mean big noise and La Diosa was enormous. It seemed to stretch off in all directions, reminding me of an infinite series of fashion shoots with drapes and wall hangings screening off the darkwood tables from one another. Soft, chillout funk played over the speakers and tall, slim, tanned staff glided between the tables dressed in fashionable black clothes that made them look like supermodels slumming it for charity. There was a long, well-stocked bar in the very centre while sofas and plants were discretely dotted around the walls and corners. Indeed, there was everything a good restaurant needs on its opening night except for one thing. Customers.

'I thought this was the opening party,' I whispered to Marina.

She nodded, puzzled, and hailed one of the passing models. After a quick conversation in Spanish, the girl swayed off into the gloom and returned with a broad-shouldered man who fell on Marina's neck like a long-lost brother. 'This is Miguel.' She shook him off and turned to me. 'It's his place.' I smiled and shook his hand. 'He's pleased to see me because my friend James may take a stake,' Marina added sotto voce.

Miguel took us over to a low table and told us we could eat and drink on the house.

'What about the party, Miguel?' Marina asked.

He sighed and stood up. 'Let me show you something,' he said.

We followed him across the large room into the far corner where he took us through double doors and into a concrete antechamber that led off into a grim, industrial-looking nightclub playing hard, pounding house music to absolutely no-one. 'Look there.' He pointed at the floor. 'There are two steps.' We nodded. 'There have always been two steps. For thirty-four years the Hoedown Barbecue was here with two steps. Today, the planning from the council comes over and says it is a health risk and we need three steps, each of which has to have lights so that people can see.' Miguel was so exasperated that he fell silent. 'But, you know, tonight we will build the steps, as they say, and tomorrow they will have no excuse.'

As he said this, one of his staff came running over and

whispered in his ear. He swore and turned to re-enter the restaurant. Marina followed, and I tagged along behind. Instantly you could feel the change in atmosphere. The way the waiters were standing, the hushed conversations . . . it reminded me of teenage parties where gangs of violent gate-crashers were waiting outside with taunts and threats, demanding to be let in.

'What's going on?' I asked Marina.

'Someone has set fire to the sign outside,' she said quietly. 'I think it's probably a good time to leave.'

We drove back in thoughtful silence. I dropped Marina off at her flat then strolled round the corner to look through the windows of her gallery again. Although it was two in the morning, Marina had left the lights blazing, presumably to attract the attention of wealthy passers-by. The merchandise certainly looked impressive: Picasso, Monet, Van Gogh and Klimt paintings stared back at me, looking, to my untutored eye, exactly like their originals. I had to tip my hat to Pitti Arte; they knew how to pick 'em. You couldn't have chosen a better place to set up the first franchise of the world's only legal forgeries. Ibiza, after all, was the home and refuge of the greatest art faker the world has ever known, Elmyr de Hory.

He was born in 1906, the son of a powerful landowning family who lived on a vast estate near Lake Balaton in Hungary. The de Horys were rich and influential: Elmyr's mother's family had been bankers to Habsburgs and his father was the Hungarian ambassador to Turkey. The de Horys ate with silver cutlery off Meissen china and his mother shopped for her clothes in Paris. Materially, the young Elmyr wanted for nothing.

Emotionally, however, it was a different story. Elmyr rarely saw his mother or his father as a child and was brought up until the age of fourteen by his wet nurse, living with her and a procession of governesses in a separate wing of the vast de Hory mansion. He was scared of the dark, and when he went to bed his nurse would sit beside him holding his hand until he had fallen asleep.

Once, when he was five, he woke up in a panic to find himself alone in his large, empty bedroom. His parents were hosting a party in the grand salon of the house and the young Elmyr fled through the long, dark corridors until he heard the low murmur of music and conversation. He burst, breathless, into the party and looked frantically around. His mother was standing in the middle of the room, dressed in a dark red silk suit and holding court to a circle of eager male admirers. Elmyr ran towards her in tears and she picked him up awkwardly. When he went to kiss her, she jerked her face away angrily and put him down, saying, 'You'll kiss my powder away.'

The marriage wasn't happy. Elmyr's parents argued constantly and lived almost separate lives until, shortly after his sixteenth birthday, they divorced. His father took a posting in South America and Elmyr stayed with his mother, attending art school in Budapest. When she remarried a younger man and eased Elmyr out of her affections altogether, he convinced her to let him apply to the Akademie Heinmann in Munich.

After Elmyr finished his studies at the Akademie he headed to Montparnasse in Paris. He enrolled at the Académie la Grande Chaumière under Legros Leger and moved into digs in the quarter. At that time, Montparnasse was the home of Ernest Hemingway, Gertrude Stein, Man Ray, James Joyce, Henri Matisse, Albert Marquet and Ezra Pound. Picasso was a frequent visitor. Elmyr sat at the edge of this golden circle, watching as they drank and talked and argued in the Dome or the Rotonde.

He soon began to exhibit in London, and to pick up commissions for portraits from wealthy English and American patrons such as the Duke of Kent and Chicago's Mrs Potter Palmer. And then war came. Elmyr returned to Budapest, where his years in Paris made him suspect to the pro-Nazi Horthy regime. He spent most of the war in camps and prisons until the Russians arrived in 1944. Facing a grim future under the Soviets – Elmyr's parents had died and the Nazis had looted the family's estates; now the Russians confiscated their vineyards – Elmyr took a handful of diamonds, sewed them into the lining of his overcoat, and set out for Paris. He moved into Montparnasse again, but this time as one of the starving artists with whom he had partied as a wealthy playboy ten years earlier. Some of his old friends were there, and they secured him a handful of commissions painting portraits of rich men's children, but his attempts to sell his own work – landscapes and nudes – came to nothing.

By 1946 he was poor, despairing of his talent and huddled in his studio on the rue Jacob. Then an old friend from London, Lady Malcolm Campbell, popped in to see him, glanced at one of his drawings on the wall and mistook it for a Picasso. She remembered Elmyr's slightly overblown claims that he had known Picasso before the war and asked if he would now consider selling the work. With no money to buy food that night, he agreed, and Lady Campbell paid him £40 – enough to live on for two months. Later that year she returned to Paris and came looking for de Hory. She'd been a little short of cash in London, had taken the Picasso to an art dealer, had had it valued and had sold it for £150. She now felt a little bad about the paltry sum she had offered three months earlier and asked Elmyr to lunch at the Ritz. Instead, Elmyr went to his studio and set about faking more Picasso drawings, which he sold for £300.

With the best intentions, Elmyr used the money to fund his own painting, but found that nothing sold. After the £300 had been spent, he confessed the crime to his good friend Jacques Chamberlain, the son of a Bordeaux industrialist whose collection of Impressionist paintings had been stolen by the SS. Chamberlain suggested the two men travel across Europe with a fresh set of Elmyr fakes that were 'all that remained of my father's collection'.

Initially the trip was a roaring success. The two men, and Chamberlain's girlfriend, rode across Europe in expensive sleeper cars, selling paintings in every major capital. Chamberlain faced the gallery owners; all Elmyr had to do was a couple of hours' work in his hotel room every morning. All was joy, until Elmyr realized he was being ripped off by his friend.

After a furious row, the Hungarian flew to Copenhagen alone. Posing once again as a fleeing Hungarian aristocrat, he offered some more Picasso drawings to a local dealer. The man arrived at Elmyr's hotel with a curator from the Stockholm Art Museum and they questioned de Hory closely. Afterwards they went downstairs to consult and de Hory, convinced they had twigged, spent the time throwing up in his bathroom. Finally they returned and offered him twice the amount he'd hoped for. Worried that a quick call to Picasso's Paris dealer would reveal the truth, Elmyr walked into a travel agency, looked at a map and almost at random bought a one-way ticket to Rio de Janeiro. Once there, he took a quick trip to New York – just a flying visit on a three-month visa. But the fleshpots of Gotham proved too tempting. He stayed for eleven years.

In New York it was the same story as in Paris – the odd portrait, the make-or-break exhibition, some positive reviews and a penniless existence in the Village. Inevitably, he turned to his proven revenue stream. Elmyr made his first fake Picasso sale to Klaus Perls, later to become president of the American Art Dealers' Association. Perls was suckered for a grand, and Elmyr was off. He ranged the country in the role of a dispossessed aristo, unloading drawing after drawing. To boost his sales pitch, he became Baron de Hory. Then he became a count. He also traded as Hoffman, Raynal and – my favourite – Baron Herzog. In Los Angeles he grew tired of Picasso and tried Matisse and Renoir. They were snapped up without question by fashionable Beverly Hills galleries which sold them on to film stars at a 500 per cent mark-up. Three of these paintings somehow found their way into an art museum in Philadelphia.

Although the money was coming in, Elmyr wasn't happy. He felt ill at ease with his career as a faker and couldn't seem to keep the money he earned. Broke, tired and deeply depressed, in 1957 he downed fifty sleeping pills and lay unconscious for thirty-six hours.

Fortunately, his luck held. He was found by a friend and taken to hospital where he remained critical for four days.

Once he'd recovered, another friend called George Alberts offered to lend him his house in Florida so that Elmyr could continue his convalescence. Filled with resolution to get out of the forging game, he accepted a lift to the place with a slim, dark, slightly balding man called Fernand Legros.

Legros's career history was chequered to say the very least. Half French, half Greek, he was born in Egypt, spent some time as a dancer – probably in a gay burlesque show – and was discharged from the French army very shortly after beginning his national service for reasons that remain unclear. On his way to America in 1952 he picked up an American wife, which was good for that Green Card, and spent a few years hustling in New York.

He seems to have possessed a talent for seducing and persuading people. Certainly he was able to impress Elmyr with his forceful personality. While they were in Florida, Elmyr picked up all the bills; when they ran out of money, Legros browbeat him into returning to art forgery. Elmyr also met a young man on the beach, Real Lessard, a nineteen-year-old Canadian student down in Florida for the sun. His happy-go-lucky attitude and cheerful freckly face appealed to the worn-out painter, but once he'd introduced the boy to his companion, Legros moved swiftly, managing the inconceivable double coup of stealing Lessard's remaining cash and becoming his lover in the same day.

Legros took over the financial side of Elmyr's forging and went on to comprehensively fleece the poor Hungarian. Everywhere they went, Legros and Lessard stayed in the finest hotel in town while Elmyr put up at a mid-range business inn. Given that the split was supposed to be sixty–forty in Elmyr's favour, it didn't take a financial genius to figure out what was going on.

After six months, the three of them agreed to fly to Europe. Elmyr went first and tried to shake off Legros, running around the continent until depression prompted him to contemplate suicide again. Just as he was planning his own death for the second time, he went to visit a friend in Ibiza. The island saved his life.

What he found there was a scene unlike any other in Europe. Since the end of the Second World War, the island had benefited from its position on the bohemian axis that ran between Paris and Tangier and had started to attract the young and the creative. By the time Elmyr arrived, the island was filled with artists, writers, actors and musicians from across the world. Germans, Brits, Dutch, Norwegians, French – almost every country on mainland Europe was represented alongside a healthy smattering of Americans. They had come to write, paint and find inspiration, looking for their own version of Gauguin's Tahiti – an island paradise to kick-start their soul. Ibiza had other charms, however: very cheap booze, a well-established credit culture and a very tolerant population. The bohos spent their days drinking and their nights carousing and lovemaking, letting the island wash away memories of the cold, bombed-out cities, the rationing and the grim winds of morally charged austerity that were sweeping through the post-war West.

Despite his distaste for the ever-present smells, Elmyr fitted comfortably into this community of dissolute artists, freaks, drinkers and stoners. For the first time in his life, he felt at home. He would drift between tables at the crowded dockside bars, chatting with the other artists and occasionally picking up bits of rough trade. He had visions of restarting his own artistic career now that he was surrounded by fellow painters.

Elmyr's problem was that he was a bit of a snob. He rapidly decided to orbit around the upmarket end of the Ibiza crowd, watching the bohemian life from the moneyed fringes rather than dumping himself in squalor to search for his muse. When Elmyr's funds began to run out, his own paintings failed to sell yet again, in part because he couldn't bear to slum it with those scruffy beatniks and hated the modern styles. Copying Picasso day in day out had tilted the slant of his own brush and his technique was deeply unfashionable. Broke again, he bumped into Legros and Lessard on a trip to Paris. It didn't take long for him to fall in with Legros's suggestion that they should all just take up where they had left off. Elmyr would return to Ibiza and get back to painting fakes while he and Lessard continued to sell, paying Elmyr a monthly salary of $400.

Legros had decided to dispense with selling to art dealers, which he felt placed too many risky experts in the way of the moneymaking process. Instead he cottoned on to the rapid post-war increase in self-made millionaires who were anxious to move up the social ladder. These people found the haughty art world a little too exclusive for their nouveau money, but were nevertheless after the cachet of a roomful of Picassos. Legros thus became an art dealer himself, jetting around the world to meet high rollers such as the Texas oil millionaire and boss of General American Oil Algur Hurtle Meadows. Legros sold Meadows forty-three paintings over a period of five or six years, and Meadows is one of the few we know about.

It's difficult to estimate exactly how many paintings Elmyr created and Legros flogged during their most productive period between 1961 and 1967, but an estimate in 1969 put the value of the art they forged at $60 million. In today's terms, that's roughly $640 million. The cash enabled Legros and Lessard to buy an elegant apartment in the Avenue de Suffren and, showing a rich sense of irony, to decorate it with genuine Valmincks and Renoirs.

While Legros and Lessard flogged the paintings, the faker was living it up on the White Island. His status had improved considerably. After a big spat over money, Legros had offered to buy some land and build Elmyr a luxurious villa. Elmyr was suddenly a man of property. His monthly $400 stipend was a fairly impressive sum on the island too, and his elaborate tastes in food and clothes were easily met. His romantic inclinations, however, were less well satisfied. Elmyr usually went for young, rough-looking lovers. As Ibiza was packed with undesirables this often led to trouble. Elmyr would form instant, passionate crushes on boys he'd meet at a table at the Alhambra and move them into his villa overnight. The boy would usually stay for a week or so, cared for, fed and showered with presents, then move out as rapidly as he had moved in, owing Elmyr money or having pocketed one or two little items. Admittedly Elmyr was a difficult and demanding companion who could treat people like servants, but his dubious source of revenue meant that he was unwilling to go to the police when his ex-lovers smashed his windows in drunken rages or walked out with paintings and cashmere sweaters.

Meanwhile, Algur Meadows was beginning to doubt the integrity of his dealer, and one day he bumped into gallery owners Frank and Klaus Perls. Meadows asked the brothers to run an eye over his collection and was stunned to learn that at least forty-three of them – the paintings Legros had sold him – were fake. After that, the whole house of cards came tumbling down.

French dealers also spotted errors. A collection of paintings Legros had planned to exhibit then sell were impounded when a security guard wiped off some dust and found fresh oil paint coming off with it. In 1966 the French police were called in, and suddenly the net was closing. Barely one step ahead of Meadows' lawyers, Legros headed for Ibiza with two boys of dubious reputation where they broke into and took over Elmyr's house. Technically, the house belonged to Legros, so when Elmyr went to court to evict him, Legros won the right to stay. Elmyr found himself living in a nightmare. Legros would get drunk and charge around the bars Elmyr loved to frequent waving a gas pistol and having his two companions reveal their switchblade knives. He would throw all-night parties, drink Elmyr's champagne, smoke cheap cigars all over the house, threaten him with violence and 'borrow' large amounts of money. Elmyr finally vanished. A postcard turned up once from Switzerland, but to the transient population of Ibiza's bars he was just another missing person.

Then Lessard arrived, needing to arrange some bits of business with his partner. The conversation became fraught and then violent. Lessard went to the police and both men were sentenced to fifteen days in jail. The Canadian fled, but Legros served his time – not that he suffered terrible privations. Ibiza's jail had improved massively since the turn of the century. Back then there was no court on the island so turn criminals – usually drunks – would have to go to Palma to have their cases heard. Until the boat arrived they would be kept in the old dungeons in the castle up on the summit of Dalt Vila. The dungeon was basically one huge stone room where all prisoners were kept together. The barred windows in the ceiling opened on to the street and prisoners' relatives would come and drop food in – a process that had hardly changed since the Middle Ages. When the island infrastructure was upgraded in the early twentieth century, so were the prisons. Inmates now had a cell to themselves, could cook their own food and were allowed to bring any personal possessions they wanted. Legros loaded himself up with goodies from Elmyr's house, including a hi-fi and towels which he left in the cell for future occupiers, and served his time in relative luxury.

After his release, Legros was escorted to the port and asked to leave Ibiza. His debts had become too immense even for the generous Ibicencos to tolerate. Once removed from the protection of the island, Legros was arrested by the Swiss police. His capture meant Elmyr could return to Ibiza, so in November he reoccupied his trashed villa and cruised to the Alhambra to show his face. For the last time he tried to paint some Elmyrs, but all those years of copying had diluted his style, and besides, fashions had changed. Ibiza's artistic community were unimpressed and the paintings didn't sell.

Having dealt with Legros, the law turned its attention to Elmyr. With French and American lawyers baying for his carcass, the Ibicenco legal system advised him that as far as they were concerned he had committed no crime on the island or against the island. They could protect him from extradition. But they had to be seen to be doing something.

In the end, after months of shuttling between Madrid and Ibiza, Elmyr was found guilty of consorting with criminals and having no visible means of support. He was sentenced to two months in Ibiza jail in 1967. He turned up with his own bed, a deckchair, books, clothes, food and sleeping pills. The rest of the inmates were mainly hippies on drugs charges, and Elmyr hired one of them to be his manservant. He spent much of his time sunbathing on his deckchair in the exercise yard and stepped out of the clink with a nice all-over tan.

As he left prison, however, he was served papers expelling him from Spain for a year. He wandered across Europe, grubbing around for cash, and collaborated with Clifford Irving – an American novelist resident on Ibiza – on the book *Fake!* Amusingly, his time with Elmyr rubbed off on Irving. In 1969, just after publishing his story of Elmyr's life, Irving persuaded a New York publisher to give him a $765,000 advance – roughly $5 million in today's money – for an authorized biography of Howard Hughes in which Hughes would talk, on the record, about all the financial, political, conspiratorial and sexual scandals of his Faustian career.

Irving showed the publishers a contract and various notes in Hughes's own handwriting which he said he had secured from Hughes when the two men had met on a pyramid in Mexico. Handwriting experts testified that Howard Hughes had written the relevant documents and everything was going well until Hughes himself phoned the publishers and denounced Irving as a fake. Irving tried to brazen it out but then his mistres, Danish singer Nina van Pallandt, busted his alibi. The hapless writer had to pay back the $765,000 advance and served fourteen months in federal prison for fraud while his immensely long-suffering wife Edith did two months for her role in the scam.

Meanwhile, back in Ibiza, Elmyr almost found happiness. He fell in love with the appropriately named Mark Forgey, and settled back to bask in the local celebrity his exposure had brought him. Sadly, Legros had one final part to play. He had found Elmyr's diary and started calling everyone mentioned in it, reading unpleasant passages to them over the phone in a constant stream of harassing calls. The French authorities were still hovering and Elmyr was terrified that Legros would provide them with the excuse they needed to swoop. In 1976 he took another overdose, and died in hospital in Ibiza Town.

Orson Welles took up Elmyr's tale and based a highly stylized film, *F for Fake*, on his life. Arriving on the island to make the movie, Welles remarked, 'I came to Ibiza in search of a forger and I find myself surrounded by them on all sides.' The crowded Ibiza scene that had sheltered and nourished Elmyr was one of the strangest in Europe.

In his biography of de Hory, Irving described it thus:

There were beatniks, potheads, artists, writers, actors on holiday, escapees from New York advertising agencies, a couple of Canadian ex-con men who had sold shares in a non-existent asbestos factory and beat it from Montreal only one step ahead of the Mounties, longhaired wives with daddyless babies, German land speculators, a few rich men, many more poor ones, and even a reported Nazi war criminal whose bull neck, beady eyes and kindness to children made him a caricature of what he was supposed to be. Life was strictly on a first-name basis. In case of duplication, people received names like Wanted John and Spade John, Pretty Pat and Hairy Pat, Danish George and Fat George, Eduardo's Karen and Carl's Karen. Elmyr, of course, was original – 'man, dig *that* cat!'

One American, known only as Al, boasted that he was on the run after a large bank robbery committed back home. He certainly spent like a thief, building a large dollar-sign swimming pool next to his villa and flashing his cash around town like a sailor on a spree. In the end the haul wasn't big enough to last, and when his money ran out he was hustled off by the Spanish police, presumably to be handed over to the American authorities.

Al wasn't the only man with a dark past. Ironically, given that Ibiza had sheltered Jews and Jewish artists fleeing Nazi Germany, it now sheltered Nazis, hiding out under Franco's protection. The mysterious German known as Otto was almost certainly Otto Skorenzy, and a number of low-ranking Nazi officials skulked around the island until tourists began to arrive in the 1960s. As a result, the two questions you didn't ask on Ibiza were what someone's surname was and what they did for a living.

As well as the dubious community, there was the artistic community. The Germans came first, led by Raoul Hausmann's friend Erwin Broner. Broner had left Ibiza as soon as the civil war broke out to fight with the International Brigade in Barcelona. After the fascist victory he fled to Hollywood where he worked as a cameraman, returning to Ibiza in 1952 and living on architectural and film commissions from the US. As other German artists arrived, Broner founded the Grupo Ibiza '59 with Erwin Berchtold, an artists' collective that operated around the Hotel El Corsario in Dalt Vila. Together, Broner and Berchtold recruited the likes of Hans Laabs, Katya Meirovsky, Bob Munford, Egon Neubauer, Antonio Ruiz, Bertil Sjöberg and Heinz Trokes. Broner later wrote, 'In 1959 we felt the necessity to unite on Ibiza those artists that subscribed to the international avant-garde, those who had, despite resting on the island, a cosmopolitan outlook. Our catalogues, our invitations were summarily praised not just for the efforts of our group towards the artistic reputation of this island, that is on a soil that united many artists with progressive ideas and which generated a collective outlook.'

In 1958, almost the whole of bohemian Amsterdam, the Leidsepleinscene, fled the gloom of post-war Holland to sup at Ibiza's cup of plenty. Among them was the actor Anton Kothuys, who organized 'happenings' to entertain the island. One night he read out *Krapp's Last Tape* by Samuel Beckett in its entirety from the flat roof of a house at the heart of the old town. All the streets, upper floors and rooftops around were packed with people, foreigners and Ibicencos, watching as Kothuys delivered his piece.

Irish playwright and former IRA man Brendan Behan also lived in Ibiza Town during the latter half of the decade. He acquired a notorious reputation for drunkenness which, given the general level of alcohol abuse on the island at the time, was no mean achievement. It's rather akin to Keith Richards suggesting that you ease off the hard living as he's getting a bit worried about you. Behan would stagger through Ibiza almost permanently pissed, singing in Gaelic and trawling the narrow streets of the old town with Irish friends searching for Brits to beat up.

American writers, including promising talents such as Paul Brunswick, began to arrive from the US East Coast. They were fleeing McCarthy and the Korean War and followed Hemingway's dreams to Spain, drifting down to the Balearics because of the promise in New York circles that 'in Ibiza you can live for ever on credit'. Some of these Americans were war veterans, many of them injured or shell-shocked, and they roamed the island with an unsettling gleam in their eyes.

Because Franco's fascist Spain was still under a UN embargo and few ships docked in Spanish ports, Europeans crossed the continent by train while the Americans took tramp steamers to Paris or Tangier and on to Barcelona. There they would catch the *Jaime I*, a long, low steamship with one tall funnel and a crane amidships for loading bulky cargo which sailed overnight to Ibiza once a week. The *Jaime*'s promenade decks and cabins smacked of faded Edwardian glamour. The bar sold absinthe, the powerful, vaguely hallucinogenic aniseed spirit made from worm-wood. Determinedly decadent, these young bohemians fell on Van Gogh's favourite tipple with the result that the faded cabins and promenade were usually swimming in green vomit as the artists caught their first dawn view of Dalt Vila.

For those with money there was the possibility of flying, but few took that option, and not just for reasons of cost. Ibiza airport, a converted civil war air force base, was little more than a wooden hut with a gravel runway. It looked more like a refuelling station in the African veldt than a European international airport. The planes that worked the route were converted bombers and the pilots were often erratic, shell-shocked war veterans. This could bode ill. Passengers waiting to board would watch the more damaged pilots downing liquid courage by the glass as they prepared to fly the rickety crates. Sometimes passengers would cancel their flight on arrival after hearing the pilot singing lustily as the booze got the better of him.

The Ibicencos were delighted to see these foreigners. Ibiza was still struggling to recover from the devastation of the civil war. With a huge section of its population missing, having fled or been murdered, there were empty *fincas*, deserted farms and quiet, mournful villages across the island. Ibiza Town was tiny, just Dalt Vila, La Marina and a handful of other streets. The main square, Vara de Rey, petered out after a hundred yards and became a dusty road with a customs post to deal with islanders bringing their livestock into the market. The town's population was barely ten thousand. There was no gas, little electricity, few proper roads, water from wells rather than taps, and most cooking was done on charcoal.

The islanders' traditional tolerance meant they didn't mind the eccentricities of the artists. They also knew that they badly needed the foreign money: the 1950s saw the island risk famine several times after harsh winters or poor summers. Franco himself had no interest in supporting the island through its hardships. His only real interference was to ban its native tongue and forbid ingrained cultural traditions such as the 'ook' hunting call.

Franco's view of Ibiza was shared by mainland Spain. It's best summed up by the British writer Laurie Lee, author of

Cider With Rosie, who went to live on Ibiza. 'I came to finish a book because I write on wine and it's cheaper,' he wrote in his autobiography. 'You got there by slow boat full of beatniks and Germans. I had no notion what to expect, I knew nothing about Ibiza, and the young gentlemen from Palma in their blue dacron suits had coughed when I asked them about it. "Very rough and brutish," they said. "Very backward. No cars and no society."'

Being ignored had its advantages. The beats and bohos were usually left-wing and struggled with the moral dilemma of patronizing a fascist country so soon after the death camps. But Ibiza was so far removed from Franco that they remained there with ethical impunity. And although these foreigners were struggling artists by northern European standards, on Ibiza they were millionaires.

The most immediate beneficiaries were the bar owners. The Dutch and the Germans favoured Estrella's while the Brits and Yanks opted for Domino's, although everyone would switch when the postal steamer came in. In Ibiza Town's formless week there were only two events on everyone's timetable: watching the *Jaime I* dock and waiting outside the post office in the Vara de Rey for letters and, more importantly, cheques from home. Waiting for the post involved gathering in one of three bars: the Hotel Montesol, which lingers on today in a pale reflection of its former fashionable self; the Alhambra, which was mainly peopled by wealthy Ibicencos taking coffee; and Clean Domingo's, so-called to distinguish it from a nearby bar nicknamed Dirty Domingo's after a young American girl made a fuss over an unwashed coffee cup. So amenable were the staff at Clean Domingo's that on cold winter days waiters would pop over to the post office hourly to find out if the letters from the mail boat had been sorted. Perhaps this was less altruistic than it sounds. Almost every visitor to the island was living on some form of credit and the only hope the Ibicencos had of getting paid was a longed-for cheque from home.

One bar, Juanito's Bar Bahia, was legendary for the size of the bills it allowed its customers to rack up. Juanito would even lend the starving artists money. The downside with Bahia was that it offered so few dishes – basically chicken or sole. One Dutch artist, Hans Sleutelaar, was so poor he ate only at Bahia. Eventually he became anaemic and had to be prescribed iron pills.

Allowing huge tabs wasn't just a way for the bar owners to extract money from their foreigners. There was a sense of honesty and fair play that permeated all aspects of Ibicencos' lives. Street musicians would return money to foreigners who threw more than one peseta into their cup; fishwives would ask customers to tot up their own bills and then accept that payment on trust. If an Ibicenco found something in the street that didn't belong to him, he would take it to the side of the road and leave it in a prominent position in case the rightful owner came looking for it. John Scott, ADC to the governor of Gibraltar, once stayed on the island to recuperate from hepatitis and twice he left his basket on the beach with all his money and valuables. Both times it was discovered by Ibicencos, peasant farmers scratching out a living who wouldn't have seen the amount of money he routinely carried in a year of hard graft. Both times they sought out Scott and handed the basket to him completely intact.

The only real problem for the artists was that Ibiza seemed to close down their talent almost instantly. The combination of golden beaches, eternal sunshine, an incredibly low cost of living – it was possible to winter in Ibiza for about £300 – and a community of similarly inclined souls meant that most people spent most of their time drunk or stoned. 'We had a sign on our door saying "authors at work",' wrote Hans Sleutelaar, 'but we didn't do a thing.'

Perhaps the most tragic of these wasted talents was the New York writer Stephen Seley. Born in Newark, New Jersey, in 1915, his father – who had fled Russia to avoid the pogroms – was a lawyer with connections to the mob. Indeed, he'd handled the divorce for the wife of Vito Genovese, the *capo di capi* on whom Vito Corleone in *The Godfather* was based. As a result the family was hugely wealthy and the young Stephen was chauffeured everywhere.

Rebelling in spades, he joined the American Communist Party in 1930 and avoided national service during the Second World War by hiding out in Mexico City. On his return, the House Committee for Un-American Activities was in full swing under Senator Joe McCarthy. He was promptly blacklisted and found it impossible to get work – not that it can have troubled him too much. Before being blacklisted, Seley had held down only two jobs for a grand total of four and a half weeks.

He moved into a dive in Greenwich Village where he got to know Jackson Pollock and managed to get his first two novels, *The Cradle Will Fall* and *Baxter Bernstein, A Hero of Sorts*, published. *Baxter Bernstein* was an anti-war polemic that *Time* magazine compared to the works of James Joyce, a comparison that inspired Seley to follow Joyce's footsteps out to Paris.

At first he was denied a passport due to his party membership. In the end, however, his extremely well-connected father managed to pull some strings and Seley secured his papers. (There is an apocryphal story, almost certainly initiated by Seley himself, that after being refused the passport he met Joe McCarthy in a waterfront bar and called him 'piddle puke'.) With the phrase 'the American James Joyce' ringing in his ears, Seley arrived in Paris and began to write pornography for Maurice Girodias at the Olympia Press in Paris for $1,000 a book. At the time, the Olympia Press was employing writers of the calibre of Jean Genet, Terry Southern and J. P. Donleavy who were writing filth for cash under a variety of pseudonyms. Seley wrote as R. B. Burns and his book, *The Ordeal of the Rod*, was issued to new writers as a kind of template for creative pornography.

In 1956, Seley travelled to Ibiza and discovered absinthe. He was to remain there for the rest of his life, living on the Calle de la Virgen and drinking his talent away. He once said that the rarest sight on Ibiza was a used typewriter ribbon. 'I sleep on a mattress on the floor of a little whitewashed room with a cold water tap trying to write just a few lines that will sing down the centuries,' he told journalist and novelist Peter Kinsley. 'Just one good poem and I'd be happy. But I'm bogged down here, bogged down and broke and living in a dump.'

His torrent of words had become a trickle, and he published his only Ibiza work, *The End of Mercy*, in 1969. The book bombed. Seley was now living on money from his father and his brother Jason, an academic. This wasn't unusual. Most of the foreign residents on the island were living on some kind of handout, whether in the form of disability allowances, cash from a wealthy family, war pensions or a trickle of earnings from the novels, paintings or films they had managed to push out.

Despite Seley's slim means of support, endless drinking binges and maudlin foul-mouthed rants, he was protected and cared for by the islanders, whether expat or Ibicenco. They knew him as Steve Primero, Steve the First, to distinguish him from the other Stephens on the island. One bar owner, a powerfully built lesbian called Wauna whose eponymous dive was halfway down Seley's street, once broke a bottle of gin over the head of a colonel posted to a cavalry regiment on the island when he launched into a stream of anti-Semitic abuse aimed at Seley. She got away with it in Franco's authoritarian state because no red-blooded Spanish colonel would admit to being bottled by a woman. When one of Seley's girlfriends dumped him and ran off to Paris, he drank himself into an insensate rage, grabbed all the chairs from outside the Hotel Montesol and the Alhambra and threw them into the middle of the Vara de Rey, then took one final chair, walked across the square and threw it through the window of the post office, shouting, 'There, what do you think of that?' The clerk just looked up and smiled. 'Thank you, Señor Esteve,' he said. 'We needed some fresh air in here.'

For the other artists, Seley was an endless source of entertainment, striding the streets of Dalt Vila and La Marina in his old greatcoat, forever planning an English-language newspaper or fulminating against some aspect of Ibizan life. 'And why the hell are we in Spain?' the writer Jan Gerhard

Toonder had Seley cry in his book *Hannibal En De Ratten* while slamming his fist down on one of La Estrella's iron tables. 'You can't eat the food and you can't fuck the women!'

Perhaps the reason Seley was so well looked after was that on an island where most people lived on tabs that were rarely paid off he was essentially honest and always paid his way. He would do almost anything to ensure this reputation was maintained. When Clifford Irving was in trouble over his Howard Hughes scandal, Seley vouched for him publicly to the local police and the international press men in exchange for a handsome payment from Irving. After using Irving's money to pay his debts, he took the remainder and paid for a room at the Hotel Noray in Ibiza Town. He spent the weekend there with a bottle of absinthe, closed the shutters, stocked up on copies of *Le Figaro* and *L'Equipe* and pretended he was in Paris again.

The saddest moment of Seley's self-imposed exile – he used to say he would go back to America only when there was a black female president – was the story of Rebecca. An ex-girlfriend from Greenwich Village wrote to him in the early 1970s and told him he had a seventeen-year-old daughter, Rebecca, conceived during their brief fling. She had promised to tell the girl who her father was when she was seventeen so the time had come to tell him as well. Neither mother nor daughter wanted anything material from Seley, she said, but the girl was very excited now that she knew who her father was. She had read all his reviews and was anxious to meet him. She was proposing to fly over to Ibiza the following spring.

After getting her letter, Seley stopped drinking spirits and declared himself 'on the wagon'. Admittedly, in Seley's world view this allowed him to continue to drink wine, which he didn't regard as booze, but for a world-class dipsomaniac he made quite a sacrifice. His abstinence lasted for months until a St Patrick's Day pub crawl with two US Second World War vets – Native American Marines captain Frank Taylor and a black sailor and former boxing champion of the Sixth Fleet known as Nick – threw him off the wagon with some force. At the peak of his binge, hair dyed green in honour of the day, a waiter thrust a telegram into his hand. It was from his daughter. She would be at the airport in an hour.

Seley staggered off to meet the plane with Frank Taylor in tow and a scrunched-up photograph of Rebecca in his pocket to help identify her. They soon spotted her in the crowd and for about two minutes there was a genuinely touching interchange between father and daughter. When soused, however, Seley was cantankerous and belligerent and he managed to pick a fight with Rebecca almost instantly over the colour of his hair and his generally dishevelled appearance. His drunkenness didn't help.

The three of them caught a cab back to Ibiza Town in frosty silence. When they got there, Rebecca stepped out of the car, turned her back on him and started off towards a group of hippies sitting by the harbour watching the boats coming in while toking on Moroccan hash pipes. As he watched her go, she glanced back and said, with real venom, 'One screw on Bleecker Street doesn't make a daddy.'

Seley stayed off the wagon and on the island until one night in 1983 when, walking down the Calle de la Virgen, he suddenly stopped in his tracks and clawed at the wall next to him. Startled drinkers turned to see his face turn purple as he slid, unconscious, down into a doorway. Paramedics arrived and diagnosed a massive stroke. Seley was rushed to Can Misses clinic where he came round at three in the morning with a doctor looking over him solicitously.

'Get me a brandy,' he said, and died.

His dream had been to write something that would 'sing down the centuries'. Today he rates just two mentions on Google, both of them referring to his books in passing as part of a web page devoted to other authors. It took a long time, but I finally tracked down a shop in the US that stocked a second-hand copy of *The End of Mercy*. The title page was signed by the author: 'For Shane Lynagh with very best wishes. Ibiza 1969.' It's the story of William Mercy, an American living in Paris, and it begins: 'Mercy arose. Mercy attended to Nature's needs. Mercy attended to needs unnatural. Mercy descended. On the boulevard Mercy decided not to take the way that he took. Mercy decided.'

About halfway through, Seley puts himself in the book: 'he saw that foppish young American who was always drunk (he claimed to be a writer; what was his name? Steve Seeley? Seely? Sealey? Sealy?; no, it was Steve Seley; probably he was a Jew) whom he'd avoided ever since he'd been here. Still, he had to admit the guy never did intrude.'

The book ends with this curious exchange, all by itself on page 222:

'To what do you attribute your success, Mr Seley?'
'Failure'*
this asterisk's for fun
so is this one
and this?

simply rhymes with parenthesis, now) closed
and that alors? Left lying on the floor of Mercy's . . . mind?
it (mercy, too) WILL arise in Volume Two, when we'll try again
*alors . . .

But, of course, there was no volume two.

CHAPTER 10

The Hippies

Down on the south-east corner of Ibiza lurks a small patch of coast with a large enough aura of spookiness to make the Bermuda Triangle seem like a nice spot for a fishing expedition. Within a square mile of sea and shore there's a towering offshore rock called Es Vedra – which, if the legends are true, must have 'Land Here' painted on it in UFOese – and Atlantis, an ancient Phoenician quarry that has somehow sprouted countless carvings, mini-altars and childish idols dedicated to a thousand unnamed gods. The most phlegmatic of travellers have felt something quiver in their bowels as they've approached these two sites, conveniently gathered around an extremely attractive beach called Cala D'Hort, and the whole area has become a latter-day temple to unspecified magic ever since the hippies stumbled on the island and found it to their liking.

My guidebook stated that there were only two ways to reach Atlantis: by boat, which is problematic as there is nowhere to moor so one person has to stay with the craft, or by descending a steep and rocky cliff then sliding down a sand dune several hundred yards long. Those with heart conditions or the plain lazy, it warned sternly, would be ill advised to attempt the descent. Now I'm as lazy as the next man, but the opportunity to see some genuine cast-iron Rockwell weirdness was too good to turn down. Hurtling down a seven-hundred-yard long sand dune at the peak of the midday sun, however, sounded like mad dog and Englishman insanity, so I was up at seven and parking my car on a rocky slip road near the Cala D'Hort by eight.

And there I encountered my first problem. Atlantis is deeply unofficial, part of the island's recent counter-cultural history rather than its love affair with the ancient world, so no *consell* signposts mark the route. I had to push along the increasingly unstable slip road following signs to the Torre des Savinar, one of the watchtowers built in the eighteenth century to guard against pirates. This tower, perhaps because it overlooks both Atlantis and Es Vedra, has a chequered occult history in itself. Most recently, about two years earlier, a young French boy climbed to the top, surrounded himself with magical symbols and burned himself to death.

The book said that the path to Atlantis veered off to the left some distance before the benighted tower, and that was about as specific as it got. I made two false turns before finding a clearing in the scrub that seemed to be blocked by a chain-link fence. Following the fence to the cliff edge led to a short, sharp drop onto a shingle slope. It required careful navigation as there seemed little to stop the unwary dropper continuing all the way to the crashing waves on the rocks below. Having slithered precariously down, I made for a cliff face on my right and clung to its reassuring rocks as I slid and stumbled on.

It was a tough path to follow, winding through sharp,

spiky bushes and treacherous tree roots that seemed to leap up and pull your heels away when you were least expecting it. Every now and then one of the branches would tickle my ear, and then, as I turned, its comrade on the other side would come up behind me and hit me over the head when I wasn't looking, which seemed a cowardly thing to do. After about twenty minutes I was extremely hot, hugely irritated and ready to jack the whole thing in when I suddenly broke through a wall of branches and collapsed into a small clearing.

For a moment I lay there, enjoying the short break from my struggles. The clearing was sheltered from the sun by a thin screen of bushes that cast a gentle shadow over the whole area. On the right there was a small cave cut into a sheer rock wall which had a sleeping bag and a pillow spread out on its sandy floor. Beside the cave stood a sort of makeshift table covered in bottles, and above the table was an immensely complex carving. I focused on the network of fine lines and saw that it was an intricate rendering of the Buddha. It must have taken days to do. The Buddha squatted benignly at the centre of a vast spinning wheel with hundreds of fine interwoven spokes. All around the outer rim of the wheel flames licked and danced in a seamless ring, broken only by a swollen, voluptuous crown that encompassed the Buddha's peaceful head.

It suddenly became clear that the objects on the table beneath were offerings, probably for the Buddha; but then I recalled that this clearing was supposedly haunted by a witch. Maybe the trinkets were for her, to keep her happy. I felt I had to give something, but in the name of nimble climbing I had divested myself of almost everything save car keys and a bottle of water. I was just checking my pockets again when I heard a rustle behind me.

I jumped, and turned towards the noise. At the far side of the clearing crouched a young man wearing only a loose pair of canvas shorts. He must have been in his early twenties with deeply tanned skin, a full beard and long, unkempt hair like the ghost of a youthful Ben Gunn. I wasn't sure how long he'd been there. He might even have watched me as I blundered into the clearing.

We looked at each other for a minute, then he turned away and started fiddling with something in the palm of his hand. I couldn't see what it was and I didn't like to stare, so I turned and surveyed the rest of the clearing. When I looked back he was watching me again. It was as if he was the keeper of the clearing.

I had nothing for his table, and it seemed a bit off just to push on past him in my heedless pursuit of pleasure, so I walked over and offered him my water bottle. He smiled his thanks and took a long, deep draught, then turned back to whatever it was in his hand. It seemed as if the encounter was over, so I turned and began my final descent.

At one time, in the late 1960s and early 1970s, the path to Atlantis was a busy one of pilgrimage for the long-haired and tie-dyed travellers who flocked to Ibiza's shores. And there were plenty of them. In the era of peace, love and understanding, Ibiza was one of the top three destinations on the hippy trail, up there with Tangier and Goa. The hippies came to Ibiza in the footsteps of the beatniks, who arrived in the 1950s in search of beach parties and jazz. The author Janet Frame, whose autobiography was filmed by Jane Campion as *An Angel at My Table*, arrived on the island with the beats after fleeing a psychiatric hospital in New Zealand where the doctors had threatened her with a lobotomy. She met an American painter called Bernard, lost her virginity to him and 'felt at peace within my own mind, as if I were on an unearthly shore'. Bernard 'called on other Americans, many of them exiles from the McCarthy regime . . . We attended recitals of music and poetry at the French Institute. We wined and dined, with the men and women living with their chosen partners in the sensuous sensual kind of luxury enjoyed by the lotus eaters.'

In my afternoon walks or cycling I marvelled at the way the clear perimeter of the island unfolded before my eyes. I wrote an ecstatic letter to Frank Sargeson. Ibiza, I said, was all they claimed it would be and all I dreamed. I felt it contained within me and when I had explored the beaches and the salt mountains I cycled past the fields of clay where the clay surface opened its red vein, at the pottery works, and leaving my bicycle, I walked to the wooded interior of the island, to a mass of light-green pine forests where, Catalina and Francesca warned me, the bandits and wild men roamed.

The first of the hippies, originally called *peluts* or 'hairies' by the Ibicencos, were also on the run. This time it was the Vietnam War. By the early 1960s Norwegian and Swedish charities were offering help to draft dodgers and deserters, funding their air fare to Scandinavia and providing them with shelter when they arrived. The kids who came from the south and west of the US, from California or Texas, were grateful but found the harsh winters of northern Europe almost unbearable. In the mid-1960s, two GIs who had deserted from a German base went down to Ibiza on the say-so of a man they'd met in Berlin. They found the Ibicencos friendly and the way of life cheap so they wrote back to their buddies in Sweden saying this was the place – an island in Spain, away from the mainland, outside the political influence of Madrid and drenched in so much sunshine it felt like California.

Gradually, the peaceniks drifted down. The first arrivals were quiet, gentle people. They would gather in the cafés and sing, spending the nights reading, smoking marijuana and talking about the trauma of Vietnam. These kids were often well looked after by their parents, who would send them regular money to pay the bills they were racking up with Ibiza's bar owners and shopkeepers. As a result, they were known on the island as 'hippy checks', people with a hippy mentality and appearance but with a cheque coming from Daddy every month.

The draft dodgers were followed by the European hippies, whom the Ibicencos called hippy-hippies to distinguish them from the wealthy Yanks who paid their way. Where the American hippies stayed in and around Ibiza Town, the Euro-hippies took to the hills in the north of the island, staying around the villages of San Carlos and San Juan. They hired *fincas* in the countryside, old farmhouses that had long been deserted by Ibicencos fleeing poverty and starvation, and set up mini-communes or small family-sized groups. Some lived on the Agua Blanca beach which had fresh water coming out of the rocks. Nearby San Carlos had a little supermarket to buy basics, and the local bar, Anita's, came out for the hippies very early on.

The hippies lived an idyllic life, similar in many ways to that of their Ibicenco neighbours. With few cars and only a handful of buses it could take a day to walk into San Carlos to pick up post from Anita's; shopping trips to Ibiza Town could take two days or more. Scores of people would pile into one of the few cars on the island, drive into town, shop, meet people, go to a party, fall in love and then come back two days later along a dirt road, the car packed with vegetables, picking up hitchhikers along the way and driving very, very slowly. Back at the *fincas*, however, the hippy lifestyle diverged from that of the peasant farmers around them in no uncertain terms. The hippies walked around naked, drinking and smoking and generally behaving in a way that would have shocked polite society across the Western world. The countryside Ibicencos, on the other hand, barely batted an eyelid. 'They are not as we are,' one Ibicenco, José Colomar, told a reporter from *Newsweek* in 1971, 'but we like them here. We've been invaded by all sorts and everyone has left their stamp. There's room for them too.' The Ibicencos even toked on joints and grew their own cannabis to puff and sell. It was the expat residents who responded badly. 'Right away they detract from the beauty of the island,' the British actor Terry Thomas told *Newsweek*. 'They want to make themselves look ghastly.' 'They come on sort of like bohemians,' added the American bar owner Arlene Kaufman, who ran Ibiza Town's most popular bar, La Tierra, 'but they know nothing about what they are supposed to be into. They are 100 per cent American and 100 per cent full of shit.'

At the height of the hippy influx, the island was so important and so filled with those in search of peace, love and drugs that the inevitable hangers-on began to arrive. Dealers locked onto traditional Ibicenco smuggling routes to bring hash over from Morocco. Rock stars keen to grab some counter-culture kudos – Mike Oldfield, Frank Zappa, Joni Mitchell, Robert Plant and Pink Floyd among them – started to buy up places, although their villas had running water and the odd swimming pool. And, of course, spiritual quacks and weird religious movements sent their recruiting teams out to work the towns and *fincas*.

Alongside the likes of the Hare Krishnas in Ibiza Town, the island was selected by the Bagwan Rajneesh cult as its European base, workshop centre and recruitment hotspot. The cult was a vague mish-mash of Western psychotherapy and Eastern mysticism with a strong appeal to the spiritually confused. It had begun in India in 1969 and spread out along the hippy trail with astonishing speed. Working out of San Juan, the cult's followers were familiar figures on the island, sporting red robes and a necklace of 108 beads which had an attached picture of their enigmatic leader Bagwan Rajneesh (you've got to love a guy who names his cult after himself). They spent their time recruiting earnestly among the kids at yoga classes and full-moon parties.

And it wasn't just backpackers who donned the red of Rajneesh. The British actor Terence Stamp spent some time on the cult's ashram on the island in the 1970s. Stamp was sucked into its orbit by his interest in yoga and his work on an organic farm near San Juan. He later made a swift about-turn, saying he'd never really believed all that culty stuff, but the actor in him was fascinated by Rajneesh. While he was still a member, however, it must have been slightly alarming to head out to the White Island and find Terence Stamp trying to recruit you to his cause. It would have been a bit like Jude Law selling *Socialist Worker* in your high street.

To be fair to Stamp, Rajneesh was an interesting character. He was an Indian academic who had taught philosophy at the University of Jabalpur during the 1960s. One day, at the end of the decade, he found himself on the receiving end of a blinding revelation that Jesus Christ had not in fact perished on the cross, as had been believed for the best part of two thousand years, but had survived the crucifixion and subsequently decided to move to India. Realizing that the Lord was calling, he jacked in his job and began preaching his views to the crowds of stoners stumbling about India at the time. Possessing the requisite blend of charisma, drive and a mish-mash of ideas filched from other religions with a nice contemporary twist, the boy done good. His cult prospered, locking smartly into the beginnings of the self-help school of religion so ably cashed in on since by the likes of Scientology.

The principles of the Bagwan Rajneesh cult, such as they were, could be found in the workshops it ran. On Ibiza, these took place in venues across the island, combining the wilder techniques of Californian therapy with a form of Indian meditation. In the two-day encounter session 'Who I Am', for instance, up to a hundred cult members gathered in rooms near Santa Eulalia and faced one another in pairs. One would ask questions and the other would reply. These roles were swapped every fifteen minutes for an astonishing forty-eight hours. Sessions would begin with periods of hyperventilation or forced rage and end with dancing, laughter, weeping, fights, kisses and cuddles. These work-shops were supposed to help the individual to overcome repression, lower their personal inhibitions, develop a 'state of emptiness', and attain enlightenment. The person then would have 'no past, no future, no attachment, no mind, no ego, no self'. As with all cults, the workshops had the completely unintended side effect of bonding the workshoppers so tightly to the group that leaving became emotionally difficult and paying for further workshops seemed like the only way forward.

In 1981, the now wealthy cult's global headquarters moved from Poona in India to Antelope, Oregon, in the US. Here, their leader became aware of the therapeutic experiments West Coast psychoanalysts were conducting with the drug Ecstasy. After the chemist Alexander Shulgin had rediscovered the drug, originally synthesized by a German chemical company in 1914, some American therapists conducted sessions with it, feeding MDMA to their clients at the outset and claiming that this was as good as five months of therapy.

For Rajneesh, this was too good a chance to miss. As the drug was still legal, he started to use it in his workshops across Ibiza, handing out pills at the beginning of 'Who I Am' sessions to 'facilitate' emotional bonding. One can only imagine the scenes as a hundred people plugged to the gills on hallucinogenic amphetamine variants were locked into a single room for an entire weekend endlessly repeating the same questions to one another again and again and again.

After years of this sort of stuff, the cult finally collapsed in 1985 and Rajneesh was deported from America following allegations of mass poisonings, tax evasion and attempted murder. The communes were disbanded and the disciples fled. Rajneesh's reputation had to be under some sort of threat anyway after his apocalyptic predictions of the destruction of Tokyo, New York, San Francisco, Los Angeles and Bombay had failed to materialize in a baffling 'world not ended' shock.

Rajneesh was far from the only bonkers guru to head out to the Pitiuses to feed on the credulous. The world's foremost trepanning advocate, Dr Bart Hughes, lived around San Juan at the same time, doing his best to encourage people to drill holes in their skulls. He believed this would increase the flow of blood to the brain and thus bring about a higher state of consciousness. He was generally unsuccessful, which proves that the 1960s weren't as messed up as everyone claims, but it must have been a bit tricky navigating the streets of San Juan on a Saturday morning with drill-wielding trepanners to the left of you, deranged red-robed cultists to the right of you and the usual hippy detritus beneath your feet.

The sights and sounds of the hippy invasion were captured on celluloid by German director Berbet Schroeder in his 1969 film *More*, which boasts a soundtrack by Pink Floyd, recorded in their Formentera studio. The plot is a doomed love story that ends in drug addiction and death, and its inevitable path is easy to predict from the outset. But Schroeder shot Ibiza with a loving lens, showing a deserted, alien and beautiful island closer to a dream of Africa than Europe. Ibiza Town was small and Moroccan, its white houses and narrow streets barely reaching down to the harbour. The cafés on the Vara de Rey were filled with hippies, drinking coffee and Coke and trading speed pills – legal in Ibicenco chemist shops at the time – for acid. Up north, he filmed parties that took place by the 7km sign outside San José, where people smoked and danced – incredibly badly – to bongos and pan pipes. When Schroeder was interviewed for *Image et Son* in 1969, the journalist asked why the film took place on the island. He replied:

> Ibiza may be one of those centres where the representatives of the avant-garde of a new civilisation are experimenting with a new way of life. It is more primitive, more spiritual, and its main goal is no longer a quest for a pre-existing culture, but a total opening, an intense communion with Nature, human as well as cosmic. It is also, for the film, the idea of being trapped on an island in the sun, which is very powerful mystically and psychologically. The ideal in Ibiza is that everything is beautiful in its simplicity. With a few sheep-skins and some carpets, you can make a palace, and in fact that is what this new group of people who live there are doing.

Most of the time, the hippies and the islanders co-existed peacefully. Sometimes the hippies helped with the harvest or lent a hand down on the farm and were paid with salad, fruit or potatoes. One group of hippies asked an Ibicenco family if they could live in a cave on their land. The farmer's wife was so worried about their health that she brought them a meal every evening, even though the family had little to eat themselves. When the hippies left, they put hundreds of pesetas in a box in the cave, more than enough to allow the family to eat for a year.

It wasn't all harmony and joy, though. Just outside Santa Eulalia a hippy called Blind Bob – because he had one eye – rented an old house from an old man and started to take in paying guests. There was no running water so the bushes became toilets, and the commune dwellers began to steal fruit and vegetables from nearby farms. Stoned hippies would wander into town stark naked and take the clothes they wanted from shops on the main street. Eventually, in July 1971, the owner of the house approached Bob and told him his friends had to leave. Surrounded by his acolytes, Bob told the landlord where to go, so the Ibicenco reported the commune to the municipal police. These unarmed beat cops strolled along and tried to have a quiet word with the *peluts*, but they were mercilessly laughed back down the hill by the fifty stoners lounging around in the *finca*. Local patience finally snapped. A squad of Guardia Civil stormed up the hill and forcefully evicted everyone at gunpoint. The hippies came down to the main square and were milling around in a somewhat confused state when suddenly the Guardia Civil appeared again. The resulting fracas so upset a tourist on the island, John Onley from Exmouth, that he wrote a letter to *The Times* about it.

Sir, The guarded official reports of the Ibiza hippy arrests call for some comment. I was in Santa Eulalia on Friday July 16, on holiday with my wife, and witnessed – in fact, became marginally involved in – the Guardia Civil action.

There were an unusually large number of hippies about the town. On Friday, a crowd came in from their 'commune' for a celebration of some sort. An open-air party aroused the hostility of local onlookers, who tried to break it up with a hosepipe and improvised weapons. This sparked off the fighting which caused the local six-man police force to call in the Guardia Civil. But long before the Guardia arrived, the party had broken up and the hippies were dispersed in groups about the town.

The largest concentration, about seventy or more, was at a small bar just off the main street, normally filled by Spaniards. We passed the bar about 9.30 p.m. A few blocks away in the Plaza d'Esana, we saw a force of about 30 Guardia.

The Guardia put a ring around the street junction and approached the bar from both directions. Shots were fired into the air and on to the ground. I saw no-one hit. Without any warning, the Guardia set on the hippies, flung them into the street and began to beat them with truncheons, batons and handcuffs. There was no provocation and no resistance from the hippies. Many walked forward with their hands above their heads, but were still attacked by the ring of Guardia before being arrested. Some were beaten to the ground, others chased across the street and clubbed as they tried to escape. The violence was savage, premeditated and totally unnecessary. The whole operation was evidently designed to be punitive and deterrent.

Some of the crowd regarded the spectacle as a free bull-ring entertainment and assisted the Guardia in the execution of their duty by barring the way to fleeing hippies and push-ing them back into the arena.

When the hippies had been rounded up, the Guardia dis-persed the crowd, not large, as by now caution had overcome curiosity for most people. One man turned on me and angrily waved me away, probably because I'm tall and bearded and my indignation must have been obvious. I moved back only a few steps, wanting to see what would happen to the arrested. He charged at me and hustled me on my way. As I tried to keep my balance and begin my retreat, he followed up with a swinging blow from a pair of handcuffs. I now have a dark tan and a darker bruise on the shoulder as evidence of the anomalies of life in Spain.

A small incident, by international standards, and a rare irruption of brutality into a placid and friendly atmosphere. But 50 battered young people were taken to Palma gaol, many, no doubt, like the ones we saw corralled outside Santa Eulalia police station, wondering whatever they are supposed to have done. For us it was a disquieting insight into the ways of violence and a reminder that Spain is a police state. Yours sincerely, John Onley.

Of course, the point of Spain's Guardia Civil has always been that its troopers are posted as far away from home as possible, to ensure that no mercy ever stays their paramilitary hands. As a result, the Santa Eulalia Guardia would have been mainland Spanish, not Ibicenco. Many locals were as outraged as John Onley; even the priest of San Carlos made public his support of the hippies over the police.

The peak of the hippy influx came in 1973, but the scene survived long after the trend had died out in the rest of the Western world. Around hippy hangouts such as Anita's, a trickle of tourists kept the old vibe going. As late as 1988 there would be at least fifty or sixty people sitting on the street outside the café bar most nights, smoking joints, playing the guitar and singing. In 1989, the San Carlos police finally moved them all on. In the end, that's what happened all over the island.

Take the free parties. The great legacy of the hippies is

Ibiza's current reputation as an island of music, drugs and hedonism. Both Pacha and Amnesia began as hippy hangouts and the spectacular club parades through Ibiza Town began with the peacock *peluts*, but it was the free party movement that really helped draw the counter-culture to Ibiza and establish it as a place where anything could happen.

The movement started around the time that Pacha and Amnesia opened, in 1974. Before that, parties were in houses or around a bonfire. A French hippy-entrepreneur called Anant got hold of one of the first sound systems loud enough to be heard in the open air, brought over a tent from Morocco and organized parties near San Juan. At first he managed to attract a hundred or so people, then a couple of hundred, then a thousand. By the 1980s there would be five thousand people dancing on top of a mountain or in a secret valley. Invitation was by word of mouth alone. There were Benirras beach parties where everyone was naked and smoking, drums pounding all night. The Can Punta hilltop near San Juan, the caves near Cala Conta and an abandoned bull-ring near San Agust were regular venues.

As the 1990s dawned, however, the Ibicenco authorities got fed up. They were persuaded to act by complaints from locals about the noise as well as grumbling from the island's clubs – including Pacha and Amnesia, the traitors – who saw free party punters as lost door revenue. The cops arrested Anant and expelled him from Spain. Cat-and-mouse games between party promoters and the Guardia Civil usually went the way of the authorities. The Day of the Drums was outlawed. A new wave of trance enthusiasts tried to keep things going, but the accidental death in 2001 of a regular who cliff-jumped onto some rocks at a party near

San Agnes shocked the diehards into acquiescence. The free parties have all but stopped now, and there are only a handful of hippies left.

For a while, some of the hippy celebrities stayed on. Nico, the model, film star and singer with the Velvet Underground, moved back to the island in 1985, cleaned up her smack habit and released a surprising hit album, *Camera Obscura*. On 18 July 1988, however, she went for a bike-ride across the island and vanished. A local man eventually found her unconscious body beside the road and rushed her to the Cannes Nisto Hospital, but it was too late. She died at eight p.m. of a brain haemorrhage. Now the only reminders that this was the European capital of the hippy movement are the Eco-Café in San Juan, parties and hippy markets at Las Dalias outside San Carlos.

In a way, I felt this absence more keenly than that of older civilizations. While the ancient world is commemorated with affection and even the poet al-Sabbini has roads named after him, the hippies haven't had time to filter through into the Ibicenco mainstream. They probably never will. Although the clubs and bars and DJs that draw in so many holidaymakers, celebrities and wealthy liggers owe their existence to the frail idealists who fell in love with the desolate island, the desire to remove their scruffiness has prompted Official Ibiza to step uneasily away from their memory. Daniel Speigel, the German hippy who runs the Eco-Café, can still walk into any night in any club on the island for free, but the free love and free party scene has been roped off and corralled into submission.

As well as leaving Ibiza the clubs, the music and the party culture, the hippies opened the island up. Although the artists, actors and beatniks came to visit, they were all members of some kind of cultural elite. They wanted the island to remain their own private members' club. The point about being a hippy was that you just had to turn up and be; there was no earnest beat poetry to write, no pictures to paint, no career on the stage to fulfil. When they came to the island, they were the first of the everymen to do so. In a sense, they were the first real tourists. Most people came to Ibiza to escape but, after the first wave of draft dodgers and vets, the hippies just came to see what was going on.

As with other civilizations that came and went, the hippies' temples remain. Atlantis, of course, is one of them. As I plummeted down the sandy bank towards it, I could see strange, *Blair Witch*-style piles of stones standing on rocks to my right and left. Some were only a handful of pebbles, but others were three, four, five feet high. They had faces carved onto them and shapes and patterns had been etched into the ground. At the bottom lay the old quarry, half filled with water. In there, the carvings proliferated. Every wall, every surface had concentric circles, or stars, or moons, or curious runes and laughing faces. Wire and string criss-crossed the space, festooned with hanging wraps and knots. On the rock above, stones marked out letters, numbers and mystical signs, laid out as if on a cosmic helipad. Everywhere there were more piles of rock; sometimes they formed little arches, sometimes twigs were twisted into shapes and placed in the middle of the piles. It was deathly quiet, the only sound the waves lapping against the shore, and even though the sun was approaching its midday peak, I felt a chill run through me.

Suddenly I didn't want to be there any more. I started up

the sandy slope, but found my legs slipping and sliding back down. For every step forward I slid another step back. It was as if I were being pulled back down to Atlantis, as if the very earth refused to let me escape. My calf muscles were aching and exhausted after barely a quarter of the climb. My throat was burning, desperate for water, but there was no purchase, no place to stop. Had I flung back my head to take a drink I felt I would have pitched backwards, sliding and falling until I collided with the rocks below.

I gritted my teeth and grabbed at some loose roots poking out from nearby rocks, then hauled myself up until I reached Ben Gunn's shelter. He regarded me coolly as I gasped and spluttered, pouring water down my throat and over my face like a goon in a desert war film. I offered him a swig and he took it gratefully, then we stood while I struggled for breath, he politely smiling as my heaving chest slowly calmed down. A thought hit me. Perhaps this was the original Vanished Boy, the feral clubber who lived like a nomadic herdsman of yore, scavenging from the detritus of modern hedonism. Perhaps now I could ask him why he did it, what he was doing here. Gently at first, so as not to alarm him. I'd just ask him a casual question, then wham! pounce on him like an investigative terrier. I smiled again.

'It's very beautiful down there,' I ventured. He nodded equably and kept his smile fixed in place. I panted for a few seconds more. 'Who carved the Buddha?' I asked. He shrugged, and carried on smiling. I pointed over at the bedding in the cave. 'Does it get cold at nights?' He looked a little puzzled. 'At nights, is it cold?'

He shrugged. 'Why would I know?'

'Don't you sleep here?' I persisted.

'Oh no,' he said. 'I've only been here one hour.' He pulled a packet of cigarettes from his pocket and offered them to me. 'Smoke?'

Feeling unreasonably disappointed, I clambered back to my car and hopped round the corner to Cala D'Hort, the beach that overlooks Es Vedra. This rock's mythology is partly the result of hippy homage – it appears on the cover of Mike Oldfield's *Voyager*, and the rocker used to live over-looking its barren splendour until he sold the place to Noel Gallagher – and partly something deeper. Sailors and scuba divers report compass needles swinging wildly and gauges giving insane readings as they approach. Countless UFOs have been seen over Es Vedra in the usual array of shapes: cigars, discs, balls, you name it. One German estate agent insists that his car's dials go haywire when he gets near the rock. He believes this is because Es Vedra is a source of huge magnetic power, the tip of the dragon's tail from the heart of the Earth.

In 1855, a conservative Carmelite friar by the name of Francisco Palau I Quer was exiled from Catalonia to Ibiza. He took a small boat and rowed to Es Vedra where he spent a week meditating and drinking nothing but the rainwater that dripped from the roof of his cave. Within hours, a series of powerful visions began, as he described in his book *My Relations with the Church*:

> The day passed and the night came. The sea was at peace, the air very soft, the sky somewhat overcast by dense black clouds . . . the moonlight was very dim. And I saw in front of me, coming from afar, a shadow whose distant countenance I could not perceive; and it was coming closer to me. As it

drew nearer I could make out what it was. The figure came alone, and was as white as the moonlight itself; and the figure represented a girl of 16 years, all white, all lovely, all amiable. At the moment she arrived the heavens opened and in the radiant sunlight I saw who it was that I had before me . . . I was aggrieved that I couldn't see her with the clarity I wished: a veil covered her face, but was transparent . . . she was silent and so was I, but a dumb voice was speaking and possessed words.

The legends go back even further than this. Es Vedra is, they say, the island of the Sirens, the tempting singers who crop up in *The Odyssey*, Homer's epic story of Odysseus's voyage home to Ithaca after the Trojan War. His crew berth on an island owned by a sorceress called Circe who promptly changes half of them into pigs. Odysseus gets help from the ever-busy Hermes and manages to turn the tables on her so that she agrees to release his men. Odysseus then settles down to enjoy an extended bout of lovemaking, but this time with a woman to whom the rules of nature simply don't apply. Perhaps surprisingly, given the immense range of possibilities available to the pair of them, Odysseus finally leaves. Circe then warns him about the Sirens – sea nymphs whose song is so beautiful that all who hear it cast themselves from their ship and swim to shore, either to drown or to be devoured by said nymphs, depending on the version you read. The only way for the nymphs' spell to be broken is for a man to sail within earshot and survive.

The scheme Circe suggests to Odysseus to confound the Sirens is so incredibly simple that one has to doubt the mental agility of the countless generations of mariners who had previously dived to their deaths. She tells him to put wax in his crew members' ears and then have them tie him to the mast and refuse to release him until the threat of Es Vedra has receded. This passes off without incident, although Homer makes quite a play of Odysseus's begging and pleading to be let free as his men attend to their oars until the Sirens are out of earshot. With one man having heard their song and lived, the poor nymphs cast themselves onto the rocks and perish.

For those of a less classical bent, Es Vedra is also a movie star, having appeared as the god-in-a-rock known as Bali Hai in the movie *South Pacific*, some of which was filmed on Formentera. For the believers, of course, using Es Vedra in a Rodgers and Hammerstein musical is a bit like using Stonehenge for a scene from *Fame*.

The rock is invisible from most of the island, not because of a powerful UFO cloaking device but because the high surrounding peaks of Llentrisca, Sa Talaiassa and the Roques Altes block the view. As I rounded the corner of the narrow road leading down to Cala D'Hort, however, it burst into view in spectacular style.

Although the sky was clear, a tiny ball of mist remained hanging in the air just in front of the rock's peak. Looking a little like a half-scale model of Gibraltar, it seemed to cast its presence all over Cala D'Hort, and I was barely able to tear my eyes away. The beach was packed with Euro-tanners – bikinis cut high, Speedos cut low, the crystal waters filled with gym-toned bodies – but the imposing presence of Es Vedra held my gaze.

In the middle of the beach, a sign offered a motor dinghy for hire for two hours. Two hours was an ideal time, the sign urged, for self-driven tours of the rock. Admittedly the hire was for an exorbitant sum, but it seemed that fate was slapping me around the face in her bid to get me out to see her limestone wonder. Or at least fate was presenting me with a man called Bruno who'd lend me a boat for £40.

With the bored expertise of the true professional, Bruno talked me through the use of the lifejacket and warned me that landing on Es Vedra was illegal. Then he pushed me off and the boat picked up speed until it was bouncing nicely along, jumping out of the water every couple of metres as I breasted each peak of the surprisingly high swell. The rock seemed a long way off, and I kept my eyes turned off to the right, keeping an eye on a pleasure boat packed with tourists that was ploughing towards me through the briny. As a result, when I finally reached the shadow side of Es Vedra it suddenly seemed to tower over me as if from nowhere, its pale rock face filled with caves and holes so that it resembled a pitted skull looming with menace.

There were no signs of life, although there are supposed to be goats living there. Yellow bushes and shrubs sprouted on the lower levels, and the rock above alternated between the pale, sickly hue of a Hollywood corpse and a harsh black rock that looked as if it had been scorched by flame or laser. On the far side was an unmanned lighthouse. It took me a good twenty minutes to complete a circuit and the clump of cloud was still there when I spun round the final corner. I hadn't seen a UFO, or a vision of the Virgin Mary, but I could see why Es Vedra freaked people out.

I pulled slowly in to the beach and Bruno came to hold the boat steady while I stripped off my lifejacket and exchanged a few seamanly words with him.

'Funny old place,' I said. 'I bet you've seen some weird stuff, working on this beach. Ever seen a UFO?'

He coughed, or maybe he guffawed. I couldn't really tell. 'You want to see UFOs? I'll tell you what you do . . .' He was now leaning over the gunwale; I looked at him with, I hoped, the correct mix of interest and worldly cynicism. 'You go to that restaurant for dinner tonight' – he indicated a two-storey whitewashed building that jutted out from the cliff wall onto the beach – 'you eat, you have four gin and tonics, and then you smoke two joints and look out to sea and you will see UFOs.'

He met my eyes evenly and I tried to combine interest, excitement and sophistication in my expression.

'You know what they are?' he continued.

My face gave up the uneven struggle and just gawped. I shook my head.

'Look.' He pointed out to sea, up at the masts of the yachts where red lights twinkled even in the afternoon sun. 'The lights. Bobbing and moving. I was there last night and there were two guys in front of me. I don't know what they were smoking but they thought they saw glowing red space-ships all over the rock.' He laughed. 'UFOs,' he repeated, scornfully, pulling the boat into the shore.

I hopped out, slipped on the sand, almost fell, righted myself and strode off as manfully as I could.

CHAPTER 11

The Host

On an island where decadence and bohemianism have been cultivated into an art form, Sandy Pratt is a legend. Bar owner, cocktail server to the fabulously famous, father confessor to the great and good as well as the weak-willed and morally dubious, Sandy deserves to be the high priest of the island. His watering hole, Sandy's Bar, has served martinis to Laurence Olivier, Errol Flynn, Denholm Elliott and Elizabeth Taylor. He found accommodation for Diana Rigg and Terry Thomas. He downed chasers with the crowned heads of Europe and lived to tell the tale.

A man like that just had to be found, although it took me a while to track him down. Sandy sold his bar years ago, and it subsequently closed in the 1970s. I couldn't find him in the phone book, so short of stopping everyone on the street and asking after him I wasn't sure what to do. Ibiza's jungle drums, however, can beat loud once they're sure you aren't the law, and just when I'd given up hope someone slipped me his phone number. When I called, he was politeness itself and invited me to join him for dinner that night at Es Pins, an Ibicenco restaurant concealed among the pine trees on a quiet road near San Juan. 'It'll just be me and a couple of old friends,' he said. 'It'll be fun.'

My map was woefully inadequate and I was shockingly late. By the time I'd been shown to Sandy's table, the starters had come and gone. Sandy – a slim, fair man with precise features and a gentle voice – introduced me to his companions. There was an elegant sexagenarian called Babs Urquhart – one of the Urquharts of Craigstone, Sandy explained proudly – and the English painter Peter Unsworth with his wife Jenny. They all said hello with such cut-glass accents and old-school politeness that I felt desperately suburban. I could feel my voice travelling up a couple of social registers as we all shook hands, and I think I actually said 'splendid' at some point.

This accent fluidity is a recurring problem for me. I oscillate from fake posh to fake cockney completely unconsciously, depending on who I'm talking to. Most of my accents are embarrassingly unconvincing, so that I usually sound like Dick Van Dyke when shopping in street markets: 'How much, mayte? Absobloominlutely lahverly.' With posh, I'm slightly closer to the mark, but it seems to take my voice a little longer to get there. If anyone was paying attention, they would actually hear me grinding up through the gears of social class like a novice HGV driver trying to cope with ten shifts instead of five. Most of the time I am completely unaware of the transition, which is clearly a blessing, but sometimes it becomes horribly apparent, adding an unseemly blush to my strangled vocalizing. Tonight was one of those nights. I was sure everyone had heard my south London vowels when I gasped out an excuse for my tardiness and was now puzzling over my impression of Little Lord Fauntleroy. In a bid to avoid the horror, I hid behind the menu in grim silence.

The food was traditional Ibicenco, a cuisine with more than a generous spoonful from every passing visitor. The Phoenicians' salt fish survives, as do the pork, the sausages, the olive oil and the seasoning of the Romans. There's rice, saffron, spices and vegetables from the Arabs, codfish from the Basque salt buyers and Catalan sauces such as the *sofrito* (oil, onions, tomato, garlic, parsley, pepper, paprika and bayleaf) and the *picada* (garlic, parsley, red pepper, saffron, almonds). In the end, I ordered *sofrit pages*, a dish that is to the Ibicenco what roast beef is to the Brit or apple pie to the Yank. It's a heavy, meaty casserole with lamb, pork, bacon, potatoes, cinnamon, saffron, paprika and pretty much everything else you could find on a farm, all mixed up and cooked real slow. And it's incredibly good, even though you can actually feel your arteries furring up from the lard and oil base.

I surfaced from behind the menu to find Babs talking everyone through her early-evening cocktail party. She had been quaffing sundowners with a dowager duchess and Lady someone-whose-name-I-couldn't-catch. It seemed there was a whole colony of titled Brits with holiday homes in the middle of the island, some of them remnants of the 'Raj on the Med' Ibiza of the 1970s, some from the altogether more decadent 1950s – proving that if the British aristocracy know one thing, it's how to have a good time.

The steaming *sofrit pages* arrived, and as I ploughed through its rich mix of fuck-you-Weightwatchers flavours, the talk turned to Peter Unsworth's exhibition in nearby San Juan. Peter divides his time between London, Norfolk and Ibiza, exhibiting just as happily in San Juan's church hall as he does in west London's East West Gallery. His latest show featured portraits of the strange local Ibicenco hound, the podenco. These dogs used to run wild on Ibiza, although nowadays they're mainly kept by farmers or specialist breeders. Originally bred as a hunting dog for the exclusive use of the pharaohs, the podenco's head was the model for the ancient Egyptian sculptures of Anubis, the jackal-headed guardian of the underworld. Those tall, pointy ears and long, sharp snout still have a slightly creepy feel for those who've watched too many bad mummy horror movies. The dogs came to Ibiza with the Phoenicians, adapted to the island gleefully and have survived for a few thousand years while their cousins from North Africa gradually died out. Ibicencos hold them in as much affection as dog enthusiasts, who are starting to breed them all over the world, so Peter's paintings were flying off the walls and he thought he was looking at a sell-out.

Obviously it was all great news, but it made me feel a tiny bit uncomfortable. I mean to say, what on earth was I doing there? Dinner with one of the Urquharts of Craigstone, a fashionable society painter and the man who ran Ibiza's showbiz set? They don't prepare you for that at Ravensbourne comprehensive. I struggled for some witty Wildean epithets then gave up, sat back and opened my mouth only when I had some food to put in it. At the end of the evening, Sandy asked if I'd picked up all I wanted from them. I shook my head miserably and he smiled like a kindly headmaster. 'Pop over tomorrow,' he said, as wisely as only a barman can, 'and we'll start from scratch.'

It was a slow, quiet Sunday afternoon when I went to his Vara de Rey flat. A gentle wind gave brief respite from the heat, but few people were taking any risks and the streets were almost empty. I rang Sandy's bell and waited. It took him a while to answer the door. His right leg was giving him trouble, he told me, so would I mind if he lay on the sofa while we talked? I hadn't noticed his stick at dinner, but when I saw him relying on it as he led me through to his sitting room, he suddenly looked terribly frail.

The sitting room was delightfully cool, with high ceilings and white walls lined with bookshelves and paintings, many of a younger-looking Sandy, his fine features given fresh beauty by youth and the painter's eye. I sipped a glass of water as he reminisced, every now and then taking out a book of old photos to show me how Ibiza had looked before tarmac and tourists.

One of the first celebrities to visit after the end of the war was Errol Flynn, and, in a way, he set the tone from then on. Errol had had a tough few years and when he came to Ibiza he was looking for a place to get away. An arrest in 1942 over statutory rape – sex with a girl under eighteen – had led to an acquittal but also to the mocking phrase 'in like Flynn'. He'd decided to stay in Hollywood during the Second World War and took out American citizenship so that his Australian nationality wouldn't lead to a call-up. This, of course, went down badly in the post-war years and the quality of the scripts he was offered started to slide. He was drinking heavily and was fed up with the constant sniping, so in the early 1950s he took his two-masted schooner *Zaca* and high-tailed it for the sanctuary of the Balearics.

In 1953 and 1954, Errol was a regular in Ibiza Town. He would berth *Zaca* along the waterfront and come ashore with his entourage, which sometimes included Prince Bertil of Switzerland, uncle of today's Spanish king Juan Carlos I. They would drink in Casa Pepe, a little bar in the fisherman's quarter, eat in the Royalty in Santa Eulalia, and party in the Mar Blau nightclub up on the cliffs behind Ibiza Town.

Of course, this was Franco's time, and Flynn was an American citizen. Memories of the US blockade of fascist Spain still rankled. The island's police commissioner had to accompany Errol wherever he went, keeping tabs on his behaviour and reporting back to Madrid. The commissioner's son, Mariano Juan Farragut, is the editor of the *Spanish Naval Review* and he recalls his father's tales of Flynn drinking, womanizing and carousing all night while poor Farragut Senior sat smiling politely in his uniform, sipping his beer slowly.

What Errol found, he liked, and he spread the word. At the time, Hollywood stars such as Elizabeth Taylor and Ursula Andress were drifting between the South of France and Tangier, dripping glamour and attracting the dubious attentions of the early celebrity photographers. They were delighted to find an island unknown to the paparazzi. Both came and stayed; Andress even bought a house in the countryside. Flynn also told the American writer and director Howard Sackler, soon to become the author of Pulitzer Prize-winning boxing classic *The Great White Hope* and the creator of the Indianapolis monologue from *Jaws* quoted by boys of all ages ever since ('if you look into a shark's eyes, they're like doll's eyes, lifeless eyes').

When Errol tipped him off, however, Sackler was a jobbing screenplay hack. He came over to Ibiza, rented a house, and set about changing his fortunes. Something came together for him on the island because he ended up producing the script for the stage version of *The Great White Hope*. In order to make money while working on the script, he began directing Shakespeare plays on vinyl for the New York-based Cadmon Records, owned by two Greenwich Village girls who had followed Dylan Thomas around Soho and made a famous recording of him reciting *Under Milk Wood* when he was completely pissed. After making a bomb out of that, they paid Sackler to direct Shakespeare's complete canon, employing the cream of London's acting talent.

Sackler ran back and forth between London and the Pitiuses, directing and writing. He told various actors about his Ibiza hideaway and they began to drift down themselves. First came Robert Stephens, Maggie Smith and Charlie Kay. They liked it and rented their own villas. The following year saw Diana Rigg and John Mills arrive. Then Robin Maugham took a place outside Santa Eulalia, near Sal Mineo's house, and was soon joined by Leslie Phillips, Nigel Davenport and Terry Thomas. By the time Laurence Olivier took a place in 1965, Ibiza's reputation as the most fashionable place in Europe was secure.

By the mid-1960s most of London's acting aristocracy either owned places or took villas or *fincas* for the summer. Being actors, they liked a drink and they liked to socialize, so they needed a local where they could down London-style cocktails and, on an island with such a primitive infra-structure, use the bloody phone. They chose Sandy's.

'I arrived in 1954, at the beginning of August.' Sandy spoke quite softly and it was sometimes difficult to hear him above the gentle hum of traffic from the square beneath his open windows. 'I'd never heard of the place before, and I was supposed to be passing through. I was supposed to be studying law at Trinity College, Dublin, but I was so mad about Ibiza that I decided to live here.'

He built his bar out of a derelict house at the edge of Santa Eulalia. For those foreigners who were avoiding the reckless artistic mayhem of Ibiza Town, Sandy's Bar rapidly became the centre of the world. With one of the few telephones on the island, Sandy became postmaster, call taker and even ersatz agent to most of the thespian community. Once he got a contract signed for Nigel Davenport. There had been a frantic phone call from Davenport's agent worrying about a deal that had to be done in the morning.

'Go ahead and sign it,' Sandy said.

'You can't say that without speaking to him,' the agent protested.

'Well, I had lunch with him yesterday and he said he liked it,' Sandy replied.

There was a pause. The agent said, 'Are you sure?', Sandy was, so the paper was inked.

'The actors were very serious people – John Hurt and Ian McShane, real artists and craftsmen,' Sandy explained. 'One novelist I knew said that my bar looked like a cross between a gallery in Bond Street and a bus stop in Afghanistan. I was very pleased with that. There were lots of writers and painters too, but they were less successful than the actors. I have a whole shelf of signed books written on this island and all the pictures in my flat were painted here.'

By the late 1960s and early 1970s Romy Schneider, Terence Stamp, Roman Polanski, Goldie Hawn, Nina van Pallandt and Niki Lauda had all bought houses on Ibiza. As had the Bee Gees. They, too, came to escape, to go somewhere they could be themselves without anyone pouring scorn on their ways. Diana Rigg liked to sunbathe nude in her garden; Terry Thomas could deal with his Parkinson's disease in private; Errol Flynn was avoiding the whispers in Hollywood; Freddie Mercury could romp into town without fear of censure. Ibiza's phlegmatic toleranc offered them sanctuary from prying eyes and gossiping tongues.

As proof of this, Sandy showed me a photo taken outside the Hotel Montesol in the Vara de Rey. There's a girl walking towards the camera, about six feet tall, looking like a Scandinavian goddess. She has long, flowing blond hair and she's wearing an ankle-length hippy coat wide open in front. Underneath, she is completely naked. Nothing on at all. An old Ibicenco woman is walking past her, dressed all in black, hair tied up with a ribbon, and she doesn't even turn to look at this naked Valkyrie striding across the main square in town.

One of those who sought this calm protection to the very end was the actor Denholm Elliott. I'd always associated him with his 1980s roles in films such as *Raiders of the Lost Ark* and *Trading Places* in which he played a rumpled, doleful, basset-hound Englishman. He seemed to represent the respectable wartime generation who kept a stiff upper lip, made do and mended, did the decent thing and ironed their Sunday best. I hadn't realized his existence had been so lascivious. Although I knew he had died of AIDS, I hadn't properly assimilated just how huge were the bites he took at life.

Denholm came from a reputable upper-middle-class family and went to a minor public school, where he was in 1933 when his father was killed in Jerusalem. He flunked the first year of his course at the Royal Academy of Dramatic Arts shortly after the outbreak of war but acted in plays while a POW in Germany and turned this into a promising career as a romantic lead in the West End after demob. He was taken up by Peter Ustinov and Laurence Olivier, who helped him secure work and an attractive contract with Michael Korda that propelled him into the front ranks of London talent. A brief marriage with a starlet made him a favourite with the gossip columnists and work on Broadway secured his reputation in New York.

There, he met the aspiring model-cum-actress Susan Robinson, nineteen years old and just making her way into the profession. They dated, he proposed and, as the wedding drew closer, decided to make a confession. 'I've been in love with other women, of course,' he told her one night in a small, secluded New York restaurant, 'but I want you to understand something: I've had male lovers. Does that shock you?' In her biography of Elliott, *Quest for Love*, Susan says she replied, 'The women and men you have loved are part of you. If it wasn't for them, I might not love you as much as I do.'

The couple tied the knot in London in 1962 and spent their honeymoon in Paris and Barcelona before heading out to visit some friends on Mallorca in a swish Mercedes SL 190. The friends had left a note saying they were staying in Ibiza and would the couple like to join them. They'd never heard of the place, but honeymoons are a time for adventure so they decided to give it a punt, as Susan recalled:

There was one boat a week, and today was the day. At first we assumed we would have to leave the Mercedes in Majorca. But no, there was space for a car somewhere between the crates of live chickens and the sheep pens. We bought our tickets and, because this was an overnight trip, reserved a two-berth cabin which turned out to be designed for one berth for a very small person.

To say that our fellow passengers were of peasant stock is no insult. Dressed in the style of a mediaeval painting, they stayed close to their animals and provisions. The journey was evidently a big event in their lives, the equivalent of an excursion to the big city. The next morning we were out on deck in time to see the island come into view. As we approached the harbour, the sun was rising over the battlements high on the cliff above Ibiza Town. It was quite the most gloriously exhilarating sight. When we looked at each other, we both had tears streaming down our cheeks.

They soon found Howard Sackler and his contingent of theatre folk, as well as the Danish pop stars Nina and Fredrick. The beaches were empty, the accommodation cheap and the locals charming. Denholm immediately decided to buy a house. Initially they nosed around the coast, but deals kept falling through as the canny Ibicencos had already sensed a tourist boom. After some frustrating failures, the couple wandered into Sandy's Bar where Sandy advised them to buy a patch of land away from the coast and build their own villa. He too could smell the tourism boom and knew the couple were looking for peace and privacy. They duly found a patch in the hills above Santa Eulalia and set about constructing a family home.

It was at about this time that Denholm's roles began a slow transition from romantic lead to faintly mournful or seedy loser. His hangdog face and exquisite ability to portray failure and disappointment struggling under a formal, respectable exterior secured him part after part after part. He flew around the world making films, from Tripoli to Washington to Camden Town. Susan waited on Ibiza, guiding the creation of their dream home and looking after two children, Mark and Jennifer.

On his travels, Denholm found himself tempted by the availability of sexual adventures on overseas movie sets. He used to say that his favourite place was the departure lounge at Heathrow. In *Shooting the Actor*, Simon Callow describes an unnamed actor who later turned out to be Denholm. The passage gives some idea of his proclivities:

For him, filming abroad is perfect, a God-given opportunity to follow his romantic inclinations. He feels ill at ease and unlovely in England; abroad he blossoms. His pursuit of sex is all-consuming, but one would hesitate to describe him as promiscuous. For him there is no such thing as casual sex. Each encounter is an overwhelming transcendence: what Holy Communion is to a Catholic, an ecstatic reunion with God. And he seems to have provoked great romantic commitment from his anonymous lovers. He may never see them again, but in the moment they give their all. It is love, of a sort.

He always moves me with his stories of trysts and couplings: a time in Morocco when a young man had fallen for him on sight and stood under his window, singing for over an hour till my friend, jet-lagged and exhausted, nevertheless rose from his bed and joined the stranger for hours of love; the time in Haiti when as a challenge to him the brothel keeper had produced a hunch-backed dwarf as a potential partner, and how the dwarf had made love more beautifully than any man he had ever known, and later, when my friend was leaving, had sought him out at the dock to bid him goodbye.

Here, in Zagreb, he has somehow found the centre of sexual activity, a sauna, and has brought a young man back to his hotel. But the young man was cold and unloving and didn't give himself; what's worse, when he left, he had stolen a radio. And my friend's romantic heart was bruised, not for the radio, but because the god hadn't descended, and life is too short to waste a single night, a single hour of love.

By 1971, Denholm's infidelities were beginning to resemble a cross between Roman decadence and a Brian Rix farce – *Whoops! Caligula*. He had two long-term boyfriends – David, a London shop assistant, and Edwin, recently arrived from Barbados – and an on-off dalliance with an unnamed young actress, as well as maintaining relations with his wife and family. Through all this he tried to keep Ibiza sacred, a place where his incessant desire for romantic fulfilment could be kept at bay. His life there was close to respectable. Susan owned the Red House gallery in San Carlos with Diana Rigg. The Elliotts would drink cocktails at Sandy's, socializing with the Oliviers, Robin Maugham and Rigg, hosting and attending dinner parties and downing champagne on the terrace at sunset. 'There was something about Ibiza that encouraged excess while somehow making us feel we were immune to the consequences,' Susan wrote.

Sometimes, Elliott's other life would intrude. Lovers turned up at his door, trying to wrest him away from Susan's arms; his children would criticize some wild aspect of the island's nightlife, sending Denholm off into a defensive rage. During one of these outbursts, prompted by twelve-year-old Mark's disparaging remarks about a flamboyant local character, he raged at his son that he, Denholm, was bisexual, had made love to both men and women and had been in orgies where everything went on. 'Does this make you care about me less?' he berated his stunned boy.

As Denholm's 1980s acting renaissance flourished – Spielberg took a liking to his twist on the English gent – his sexual appetite increased. By now in his sixties, his rate of pursuit grew ever faster and the new risks the 1980s brought seemed only to feed his hunger. In 1984, he was diagnosed HIV positive; although he did his best to work right up until the end, it soon began to affect his performances. He took a part in a David Mamet play, *A Life in the Theatre*, but was hospitalized with bronchitis after just three months. He went on to develop a multitude of AIDS-related illnesses and returned to Ibiza, effectively to die. Susan would help him into a chair on their patio where he would sit and watch the sunset. Only Sandy and Leslie Phillips were allowed up to the house to see him, although Susan would spend time with Queen guitarist Roger Taylor and his wife Debbie to let her grief flood out. The Taylors understood. In a curious piece of synchronicity, Freddie Mercury spent the summer of 1991 staying at Roger's house on the other side of Ibiza as he neared the end of his struggle with AIDS. Freddie would move only between the bedroom and the pool, and spent every evening watching the sunsets. Freddie died in November 1991; Denholm died in October 1992.

He was the last of the old guard. Almost everyone from the fifties and sixties set had by the early 1990s either passed away or sold up, having become too successful or having got divorced and decided not to return with their new partners. Tourists started poking around their houses. Sandy sold his bar when 'it became overrun by drugs. Because I didn't use them and my friends who took them weren't sure about me and as a result it became a problem. No matter how fond you were of someone who used drugs, there was always that wall, glass wall, between you and them. And so the bar lost its feeling of being a sort of club. More and more people came in who I wasn't interested in at all, so I got bored with it. I became a gardener.'

Susan still lives in the Elliott villa, but Diana Rigg's rural dreamhouse was demolished to make way for a grim modern suburb called Siesta. The stars don't head to Santa Eulalia any more. The likes of Jade Jagger and her supermodel friends Linda Evangelista and Elle MacPherson are all up in the hills near San Juan; DJs such as Pete Tong and Eric Morrillo have villas near the clubs. There's nowhere you can go and just bump into Elizabeth Taylor. Except, perhaps, Pike's Hotel.

Pike's picked up where Sandy's left off. It's the hotel the stars choose when they're in town to party as it's secreted away down a little country road just outside San Antonio. The day after my visit to Sandy, I booked in for a couple of nights to see how much of the celebrity magic remained. The car park certainly did the place proud when I pulled in. On one side there was a white limo and on the other a wide pimp-style Cadillac. In reception, photos of the fabulous festooned the walls: Freddie Mercury, Kylie, Sade, Naomi Campbell, Jon Bon Jovi, Grace Jones, Van Damme – all in family-album holiday snap poses, grinning by the pool, or in the bar. In one corner there was a young George Michael, tanned and topless, sharing a joke with a man sporting a huge moustache.

In fact, the more I looked, the more I saw of Moustache. He seemed to be in a good 70 per cent of the pictures with his arm around legends and wannabes alike. As I filled in the registration form, I asked who he was. 'That's Tony Pike,' the receptionist told me. 'You want to meet him? He's in the bar.' And he led me through a maze of Arabic courtyards and gardens dotted with snug little outhouses and sizeable villas. Each lawn, each building was connected to all the others by stairs and paths that interlinked and weaved so confusingly that it was like walking through an Escher painting. We passed a pool and a pool bar, a gym, an outdoor hot tub and another outside bar filled with lanterns.

Finally we arrived in front of Tony Pike and I had the over-powering sense that I was in the camp of an ancient Arab potentate whose mercy controlled my survival. He sat tall and regal at the pool bar, sipping coffee and watching me with careful eyes. He looked so astonishingly like a younger Rupert Murdoch that when he replied to my cheery intro-duction in an Australian accent I had a vague sense of reality slipping out of reach.

Tony Pike is probably the closest thing to royalty Ibiza has. It was his hotel's ability to entertain that kept the rich and famous coming to the island long after Sandy's acting set had fled. Pike himself arrived in Ibiza in 1978 after a nineteen-year adventure that involved shipwrecks, bobsleigh accidents, military service, hard drinking and three marriages. Until he set foot on Ibiza, the longest he'd stayed anywhere was five months. In 1978 he'd just divorced wife number three in the South of France and was feeling a bit lonely and rootless when a mate of his suggested he take a week on Ibiza because the girls were out of this world.

He went over for a week in March, then – completely out of character – booked a *finca* for three months. A week later, he was driving a jeep along a dirt track with his mate when he saw two girls hitchhiking up the road. 'One was fugly – you know, not just ugly, but fucking ugly,' is the way he tells it, 'but the other was beautiful. I told my mate, "I don't fancy yours," and we stopped to pick them up.' Tony's target was Lyn. They went out for dinner that night, he told her he was just out of a divorce, she told him her husband was an alcoholic, and before the evening was out they were in the middle of a holiday fling. When her two-week stay expired she went home, and that, thought Tony, was that. But about three weeks later she turned up at his front door with a suitcase saying she was just going to stay with him for one more week. She never went home.

The heady mix of Lyn and the White Island meant Tony put down roots for the first time in his life. He even bought a house – this nomad who had spent money only on boats. The lovers found a derelict farmhouse and decided to build a hotel. Tony had two sons by his previous marriages and the three men built the place pretty much themselves. Lyn helped – 'I told her that shifting sand would keep her boobs firm' – and the locals pitched in, but Tony designed the place. 'That's why some of the walls aren't straight. I don't know how to do straight walls.' He slapped his thigh as he told me, roaring so hard with laughter that I worried he was going to fall off his bar stool.

When Pike's Hotel was just about ready to open, the goddess must have smiled on him. Pike's first guest was an American by the name of Bo Palk – the managing director of MGM Studios. Palk was supposed to be with a house party near Santa Eulalia, but the house was full when he arrived so he needed somewhere to stay. And pronto. Pike's wasn't quite ready, but Palk showed up anyway. Tony was just finishing the bathroom when Palk checked in, so they asked him where he wanted his toilet.

Palk clearly knew a few people because the next thing Tony knew a guy called Andrew Napier Bell came out to his place scouting for a video shoot. Bell loved Tony's hotel and decided to film the whole thing there. His band was an up-and-coming British duo called Wham! and the video was for their single 'Club Tropicana'. Tony got on famously with George Michael and was persuaded to appear on camera playing the barman. Suddenly Tony was in there with the music industry and everyone started coming out to stay.

Alongside George Michael – 'Everywhere he goes there's eight gorillas bundling him in and out of cars, but when he stays here he comes alone and gets a cab to Amnesia to go dancing' – the Americans came out too. Joan Baez was a regular. 'One night, there's maybe forty people in the restaurant and she just starts singing this love song. Everyone stops talking, and I swear I fall in love with her as she's singing it. A bit later, she was leading a kind of conga line round the pool, everyone just dancing to her voice.' Julio Iglesias also loved to visit – 'always does his exercises round the pool, I don't know why' – and Kylie's a summer fixture.

'Lovely girl. First came here about six years ago. Still rings up at the last minute and asks for a week and if I've only got one night she takes it anyway. She doesn't get on well with women, but she gets on great with my wife.' And, of course, there was Freddie Mercury.

'He was something else, Freddie,' Tony said, his voice dropping slightly. He seemed to lose focus and gripped the bar for a second. 'The most incredible bloke I've ever met. You know, he first performed "Barcelona" here on the island in the Ku club with Montserrat Caballé, but the first ever time he sang it was in this bar. Right here! He had his forty-first birthday party in my hotel. When I asked him what the budget was, he said "Budget? Oh do fuck off, Pike. I want the works and I want it to be remembered for years to come."'

The only guy who ever did a runner from Tony's hotel, according to Tony, was Wham!'s Andrew Ridgley during the 'Club Tropicana' shoot. Over the years that followed, Tony became friends with Grace Jones, and one year he was helping out as her tour manager when they bumped into Ridgley in Spain. Tony had told Grace the story, and she unleashed a stream of invective at Ridgley. 'I was saying, "No, Grace, it's fine."' Tony's eyes sparkled with joy. 'But she always had a healthy range of Anglo-Saxon words, did Grace.'

He broke off as a tall, stunningly attractive woman came round the corner with a cute little boy who pottered over and bounced onto Tony's lap. 'This is my son,' he said proudly. 'Twenty months old.' He took the woman's hand. 'And this is my wife, Dounia.' I stood up and shook her other hand, convinced I'd seen her before. Of course! She was the woman in the photos in reception in the hot tub with Kylie.

I'd assumed she was a model. Dounia shook my hand politely, said something to Tony and took the boy off. He watched them fondly. 'She's from Casablanca,' he said. 'I met her when she was twenty-three. I told her my life story and she said, "I want to be Mrs Pike number five." I said, "You've got to be crazy," but there it is. She's twenty-eight; I'll be seventy next birthday. She pretty much runs the place these days.'

'How do your sons feel about that?' I asked, thinking that she looked set to be running the hotel for quite some time. It was the worst thing I could have said.

'My son . . .' He faltered, suddenly looking old. 'My son was murdered. In Miami, five years ago. It was over this hotel. A guy wanted to buy it and he'd gone out to Miami to meet him. He was murdered an hour after he landed. They caught the bloke who did it and he's been inside for two years. He wanted the hotel, he wanted to be me, he wanted to be Tony Pike, but he couldn't. I'm Tony Pike. I'm me.'

We sat in silence for a minute as I fumbled for something to say, and it was a relief when his wife appeared to say that the TV man had come to see him. 'I'm sorry, mate,' Tony said, pulling himself together. 'The TVs here are cack; we need to get plasma screens and satellite dishes. I've got to see this guy about it.' I thanked him, shook his hand and wandered off to find my room, feeling a little odd.

My room was called Sunset. It was behind the middle of three darkwood doors on the second floor of a small rustic-looking outhouse. There was a modest sitting room with a huge antique mirror, plush sofas and a CD player that didn't work. The bedroom was enormous, and the bathroom was decorated in a vaguely Moroccan style with a curtained bath nestling behind a low arch.

I'm a big fan of bathrooms. If done right, they can be the best room in the house. During my college years there was a student house called Caddy's – after the pet shop it squatted atop – which had a raised plinth in the centre and a wide, deep sunken bath big enough to fit three. I once saw a bathroom that took up the entire top floor of a tenement in Edinburgh. It had a huge old iron tub positioned so that the occupant could gaze across the Gothic vista of the Athens of the North as they scrubbed away at their corns with a pumice stone. But this arched temple of bathing was now leading the pack.

Although, actually, Pike's depressed me a little. For some reason it made me want something I'd never really wanted before: it made me long to be famous. I imagined how fantastic it would be to be famous and successful, with a bag of cash and a sack of cocaine, darting around the lamplit pathways with my other gorgeous, famous friends, just like George and Kylie. I wanted to bathe in my bathroom of delight, slip on a magical, glittering designer shirt, then bump into Robbie as I left my room, the two of us having a light bite before jumping into the limo and being whisked off to Pacha.

And why not? I thought. I might not have Kylie next door, but getting into Pacha was something anyone could do. It was just a matter of ironing a shirt and pretending to be fabulous. I could do that. I'd read *Heat*. Although, frankly, my evening didn't start too fabulously. I stubbed my toe while filling the bath, and as I hopped around swearing I managed to bang my head as well. I'll bet Julio doesn't get ready like that. I also revealed my suburban soul by arriving at Pacha at eleven p.m. There was no queue and the street was deserted. 'We don't open 'til midnight,' the doorman said, with a knowing sneer.

I sat outside in my car for a few minutes, but I could see the doormen watching me and smirking. Feeling more than usually pathetic, I started the engine and drove off to find a beer. When I returned, fashionably late at one a.m., the street was packed. The paying queue seemed to snake off into the distance, and although I could see it was moving at a reasonable speed I figured I'd be lucky to get in before two. So I did something I'd resolved not to do: I went to the doorman and told him I was writing a book and I'd like to get in on the guest list, please.

He looked incredibly doubtful and told me I'd have to speak to Danny Whittle. After a few minutes a stocky, shaven-headed bloke came round the corner and shook my hand. 'Why don't we go to my office?' he said, in a friendly but hard-edged Scouse accent. I followed meekly behind, wondering if I'd pushed it too far on my first attempt at blagging.

Pacha is Ibiza's oldest surviving nightclub and the only one that stays open during the winter. Its owner, Ricardo Urgell, had run clubs called Pacha on the mainland from 1966, but in 1972 he moved to Ibiza and built the club in the style of an Ibicenco *finca* on a patch of low-lying land across the harbour from Ibiza Town. Photos from the time show a barren and desolate stretch of ground dotted with pools of sea water. Few people thought a club so far outside the city could compete with Lola's, the island's only nightclub, secreted in the walls of Dalt Vila. Today, Ibiza Town has stretched its arms out to embrace Pacha, and hotels and apartment blocks now surround the venue. Urgell guessed right.

Danny Whittle sat me down in his office and told me these facts, which I scribbled down assiduously and ostentatiously to prove I was no conman, then waxed lyrical about the celebrities who passed through the doors. In the 1970s, Pacha played host to hippy parties scented with patchouli oil and was the favoured haunt of Pink Floyd and Mike Oldfield when they lived in the south of the island. In those days the club was a single room, the little bar punters now enter through; today it has twenty-eight bars. Oldfield and Floyd have been replaced by U2, Mariah Carey, Puff Daddy and Mick Jagger. Elle MacPherson loves to pop in for a boogie.

I asked if I could see inside, and he walked me through a maze of corridors, bars and dance floors. If he'd opened a door into Narnia I wouldn't have been entirely surprised. 'The plan is to move the whole place upmarket.' We stopped at a bar and he ordered rum and Cokes. 'Now that they've opened the new marina, all the ferries and cruise ships will be docking and the old port will become like Monte Carlo. The price of buildings in the old town is shooting up, and you can't get a mooring for this summer. They'll come here to party. It's always been a party island. The Roman legions used to come through here for some R&R on their way back from northern Europe. They'd stop off in Ibiza, visit the whorehouses, get a bit tipsy, then head off to Italy to see their wives.' We laughed. Danny sighed. 'To be honest, they could get rid of 25 per cent of the tourists and the island would be the better for it.' He pulled a face. 'Don't get me wrong, I'm grateful to San An for looking after them. Everybody needs to be sixteen and to go abroad for the first time, throw up and get sunburned. San An looks after those kids. There are police everywhere, the bar staff know what to look out for. No-one gets left in a gutter and, given all the drugs and booze and cheap scooters and sea, no-one dies. Which is a miracle, and a credit to the town. And there's only 5 per cent of those kids that get up to mischief and then only in about three streets in the West End. But that 5 per cent gets all the press and the remaining 95 per cent of the island is ignored. The island's overcrowded as it is in August. We wouldn't miss them. '

A lot later I walked down to the harbour to find my car. It was after three a.m., but people were still turning up to queue outside. I drove back across to San Antonio feeling culturally jet-lagged, having ended my evening as others were just starting theirs. On the way back into Pike's garden, I noticed a plaque on the trunk of a tree standing by the gate that I hadn't seen earlier. I stopped, leaned over the low wall in front of the tree and read its inscription:

Anthony Dale Pike
1955–1998
In loving memory of eldest son Dale. Here a portion of his ashes are laid to rest while the remainder flow within the currents of his beloved Pacific Ocean.
May his spirit strive no more but rest within this tree in peace and tranquillity.
I loved you, my son.

CHAPTER 12

The Hotel

My first visit to Ibiza was in 1973. I don't have many clear memories of it, but I do know we stayed in a Thompson's hotel near San Antonio where there were kiddie talent competitions I was too shy to enter and a beach with some curious grey slime that smelt a bit funny. Our first day there was the day of the FA Cup final, Sunderland v. Leeds, and about 50 per cent of the hotel's population were from Sunderland. Their holiday rep was in floods of tears as she tried to usher them on to the coach to the airport with barely an hour before their flight while they were all crouched around a transistor radio by the pool telling her in no uncertain terms to let them be.

I remember going to the toilet in the hotel foyer at some point during our stay and, on trying to leave, pulling the handle off the outer door. Being a rather slow but faintly hysterical child, I instantly assumed that I was now trapped for ever in this pale, tiled room until starvation claimed my emaciated frame. I began to cry with despair, sobbing huge, deep, body-wrenching sobs, convinced that I was permanently separated from my family. I even sank down to the cold ceramic floor and had so abandoned myself to despondency that I almost failed to notice a grown-up pushing open the door and stepping into the room.

'Wait, wait!' I cried desperately. 'Don't shut that door!'

He looked warily at me and answered – in English, fortunately – 'Why not?'

'Because I've broken the handle and we might never get out,' I gasped through the tears.

He took the handle from my damp palm, inserted it into its rightful place, closed the door and then opened it again.

'Oh . . .' I said, awkwardly. 'I thought I was trapped.'

He looked at me as if I was mad and walked on into the toilet. With as much pride as I could muster, I stepped outside.

I'd half hoped to find my old hotel this summer. Perhaps I could walk into that very toilet and with one shout of laughter banish the scared little boy who sometimes still emerges when things get too much, still feeling trapped in that toilet, sweating and wanting most of all to cry for his mother. First, however, I had to get to San Antonio. And that was bad enough.

The road from Ibiza Town to San Antonio is the nearest thing the island has to a dual carriageway. It's a wide, single-lane road but every couple of kilometres, usually as the road begins to climb a hill, a second lane emerges, sensibly designed for the use of heavy lorries or older cars. The dream of the planners was clearly a neat line of happy motorists efficiently separating themselves according to the strength of their engines and proceeding up the slight incline in an orderly fashion.

In practice, of course, it doesn't work like that at all. The Ibicencos, as a rule, are patient, law-abiding drivers who tend to stick to the 60km/h legal speed limit. Inevitably, therefore, these brief bursts of twin tarmac act as periodic overtaking lanes for pedal-to-the-metal boy racer holidaymakers who can't stand the steady pace of island driving. As the extra lane approaches, the tension in the huddled clump of cars is palpable. Some inch slightly forward as their drivers apply a little preparatory gas, others slip back after an unduly early gear change down. It's like the starting line for *Wacky Races*, with an equally eclectic set of vehicles from top-down jeeps to beaten-up mini-vans.

Entering this frantic jockeying without understanding the subtext can be like poking your head over the top of a slit-trench during a firefight. Suddenly everything explodes around you. Cars leap out of line on all sides, the ones behind you hooting madly, the ones in front roaring off in a cloud of dust. As you panic and attempt to pull back into the slow lane, the massive petrol tanker that blindsided you as it rumbled into your old position blasts you with its sonorous air-horn, causing you to jump out of your skin and apply the brakes, further infuriating the eight pissed teenagers in Daddy's hire car tailgating you like a magnet. You try to pull ahead of the tanker, but it's got momentum, and you realize you can't drop back without physically fighting the adolescent Ant Hill Mobsters who are now so far up your arse it must be getting dark. There's nothing for it; you have to join the charge.

As you grind the stick into third and stomp on the accelerator, you curse yourself for being so cheap when hiring the car. This thing must have a lawnmower engine, it's moving so slowly. And nothing is supposed to whine this loudly. Is that smoke you can smell? Is the oil about to boil out, spraying your windscreen with black death? But no, suddenly the engine is doing its job. It's OK. You start to ease forward and for a brief second you relax before noting, with mounting horror, that this new overtaking lane is coming to an end. Whereas at the outset the slow lane was the add-on, sprouting out to the right from the main carriageway like a tree trunk split by lightning, now it has become the heart and soul of the road. It's you who's in the upstart off-shoot and you have to battle to rejoin before you overrun and hurtle into the oncoming traffic.

Of course, the tanker won't let you back in. The driver finds he can't see your frantic waving, and just smiles slightly as he savours his victory. The teens behind are only too keen to see you spin and crash, so they maintain their pressure on your tail. Finally you trump them by slowing right down until both tanker and insolent mob have shot ahead, all ten of them – they seem to have multiplied – snottily offering you hand gestures you don't really understand.

Weakly, you rejoin the stream of traffic and wait for your pulse to slow and the clammy sweat to dry from the palms of your hands before, sweet Jesus! Look out! There's another two-lane nightmare only ten feet away. And this time the lane on the left is the new lane. What does that mean? Who indicates where? Why didn't I get the bus? And then you see the Columbus Egg and realize you're saved. For now.

I'd booked a cheap and cheerful package dive called the Hotel Abrat for my San An stay, anticipating a hankie-on-head, 'Una Paloma Blanca' return to my youth. When I got there, however, it reminded me of arriving at a place I'd stayed in when struggling along the Ukrainian Black Sea coast some time after the fall of communism. I'd wound up in Yalta in a former sanatorium patronized by leading members of the Central Committee of the Soviet Union. The rooms were heavy and dark, with Bakelite telephones, dark wood-pulp fittings and booming tiled corridors outside filled with stamping, yelling babushkas. How the comrades had holidayed there and still thought they were winning the Cold War had baffled me. Until I checked into the Hotel Abrat.

When the Soviet leader Yuri Andropov saw the massed ranks of swimming pools as he flew into LA, he is supposed to have said, 'Now I know that communism has failed.' Had he checked into the Abrat, he would have sensed victory. The hotel had clearly been flung up in the 1960s, presumably by the sort of labour the Ukrainians dismissed as too cheap and shoddy. The foyer was gloomy and barren, its harsh strip lighting providing a startling glare that failed to penetrate the shadows but painted everyone with a yellowish tinge. But then, that could be said of many 1970s hotels.

Where the Abrat triumphed was in the details. The lifts were slow, creaked alarmingly and gave no indication as to what floor they were on. My room sported fake pebble tiles and a sickly green over MFI brown decor. If I wanted to stand on the bathmat, I had to make sure my knees were touching. Halfway through running a bath, a lump of metal fell out of the tap and the water supply spontaneously switched to the shower nozzle. No matter how hard I tried, I couldn't get the bath to run again. The ping-pong room was a musty underground garage without any light bulbs. Interestingly, the Abrat had three stars on its sign outside. I assumed they'd painted them on themselves.

Still, it offered half board – breakfast and dinner – for a miserly sum (which seemed increasingly exorbitant as I realized that the electricity in the room didn't work properly) and it was within walking distance of the fabled West End. For the first night there I spent half an hour bashing the bathroom taps with my shoe to work up an appetite and descended promptly to survey the bill of fare.

It's easy to mock the food in a package holiday hotel. It's been done countless times before and will be done countless times in the future. I'd probably have given it a go had I not been so depressed by it. There was chicken and chips, omelette and chips, and paella and chips. You gathered your selection from a buffet counter that somehow made everything look as if it had been there for days. Perhaps it had. Each mouthful sank to the bottom of my stomach like a ball of pond goo, and even the cheaper-than-cheap San Miguel I washed down to remove the taste couldn't cheer me up. The harsh strip lighting seemed to suck conversation from the air. Couples who'd walked into the dining room laughing and flirting became subdued. I toyed with the idea of getting a pear from the fruit bowl, but somehow the desire to move had been drained from me. I sat and stared at the puce tablecloth, trapped by despondent immobility, until by sheer force of will I grasped the table edge and hauled myself to my feet. Making it to my room seemed exhausting, and I lay on the bed watching a Spanish gameshow for a full forty minutes before I recovered the energy to stand.

When it ended, I pushed myself out of the room and roughly bundled myself downstairs to the hotel disco. There I stopped, aghast. In the corner of the room sat an organist working his way mournfully through 'Ob-la-di Ob-la-da' and – I promise you – 'Viva España'. He looked a little like John Lennon would look today. And I don't mean had he lived. The room was empty apart from two middle-aged couples holding hands and looking out of the window, oblivious to Old Hairy's chuntering chords. I ordered a beer but, as I sat on the bar stool, I could feel the old lethargy stealing over me. Perhaps this was the Hotel California – I could check out any time I liked but I could never leave.

With a mounting feeling of panic, I grabbed my bottle and headed for the door. I knew there was only one thing that would lift me out of my mortal quiescence: I needed the full-throated roar of one hundred men singing Robbie Williams songs while their girlfriends puked in the toilets. The West End was calling me. But first, sunset at the Café del Mar.

This Ibiza legend was an outpost of bohemian dreaming in the days of the late 1970s when San Antonio was still holding on to the last vestiges of its respectability before the arrival of Club 18–30. Whenever strays from Ibiza's large international hippy community wandered into San Antonio, the mayor would, in the manner of a sheriff from the deep south, run them out of town. He might, if he was feeling generous and well-minded towards humanity, allow them to stay for a couple of days, but at some point his patience would snap and he would have the local chief of police round them all up, put them on a bus and send them back to the hippy colonies in the north.

At that time, the Café del Mar was a tea-and-toast place on the edge of town. José Padilla was the café's DJ and he created and perfected the art of playing a sunset. His record selection was timed to coincide with the moment the sun touched the water. He would mix up influences and tunes, styles and performers, so that the mood of the crowd built towards that brief but heartstopping moment when his music would soar and climb as the disc bubbled into the sea. Padilla took the Café del Mar from the status of 'just another place to have a beer and a bite' to a name that, when attached to CDs of gentle, ambient house, could become a global brand. And yet, he had been so badly treated – specifically, so badly paid – by the owners of the café that he had quit in the mid-1990s and had given up DJing professionally.

Since Padilla's departure, the accepted stance for residents and old Ibiza hands is to say, in a slightly offhand way, 'Oh, I haven't been to the Café del Mar for years. It's become so commercial now.' This attitude appears to be an essential ingredient in all conversations about Ibiza, and especially San Antonio. In 1933, Walter Benjamin wrote to the Israeli thinker Gershom Scholem complaining that Ibiza had become too noisy and packed with tourists, that the special magic of the island had gone and that it was all over for him. In 1963, the Dutch writer Hans Sleutelaar 'was lying on the beach and thought, ugh, how things have changed here'. Presumably, when Pliny the Elder described Ibiza as a 'good source of figs' in AD 77 some Roman centurion told his friend he was never going out there again now that Pliny had commercialized the place. I, on the other hand, had never been to the Café del Mar.

My flight from the Abrat meant I was early. When I got to the café everything was very quiet. Initially, I felt the naysayers had been right: the café looked a bit like Croydon. Since the days of tea and toast, it had been gobbled up by San Antonio. It now stood in the ground floor of a large concrete apartment block, and the terrace, which until 1993 was the only chillout terrace in town, was now part of a long line of clubs and bars known, inevitably, as Sunset Strip.

All the bars had their own souvenir shops, selling the same sort of rubbish as most souvenir shops – T-shirts, keyrings, plastic tat – but also pushing endless trance compilation CDs usually sporting the name of the venue. Café del Mar boasted the largest store, the size of a small record shop, packed with rack upon rack of heavily branded Café del Mar chillout albums. When I arrived, the store was packed and there were just enough people to fill every available chair out on the concrete terrace, forcing me to choose between sitting inside or sitting on the rocky beach. So I poked my head round the door, and recoiled in horror.

The interior was spectacular in the way that a warthog pressing its nose against your face is spectacular. Designed in a difficult blend of Moroccan, art deco and Eurotrash, it was like being trapped in an inside-out wedding cake. There were a variety of levels, linked by little staircases, and each level had a mismatched collection of sofas, couches and daybeds that looked like Ivana Trump's attempt to fashion an exciting harem look for her bathroom. I now realized why the terrace had such appeal, paid top dollar for a San Miguel, and sat on a rock at the foot of the beach stairs determined to hate every moment of this nightmare.

And yet, somehow, I didn't. The music was the banal bonking chillout house music I'd been dreading, the beer was expensive, and there was only one toilet cubicle for each sex so there was always a queue, but there was still a slight, lingering hint of magic in the air. Perhaps this was down to the crowd. For one thing, it was so international: German,

Italian, French and Spanish kids mixed peacefully with Kiwis, Aussies, Yanks and even Brits. Which was something of a surprise.

The Brits, after all, are the fearsome king predators of San An's fragile ecosystem. The former fishing village has been a British resort since the 1960s. It's the home of *Ibiza Uncovered*. It's Club 18–30 and geezer chic, full English breakfasts and pound-for-a-pint offers, brawls on the highway and high-rise hotels. But as the Brits came down to the strip, the cocky stroll slid away and the hard, pinched eyes softened imperceptibly. They sat side by side with gangs of German teenagers, drinking beer and resolutely failing to exchange insults, just like lions at a waterhole lapping alongside herds of gazelles. When a frail, bespectacled French youth tripped and fell onto two burly lads wearing Arsenal tops, I truly expected either blood or expletives to flow; instead, they helped him to his feet and all three had a communal laugh. The scent of love, peace and spliff filled the air as everyone settled down shoulder to shoulder to watch Mother Nature's oldest show.

The sky was hazy, there was a low level of cloud and the music selection was faintly cheesy, but the spectacle worked its charm. In part, this was down to the audience. Looking at the beach around me, packed with kids from countries that had carpet-bombed one another's cities less than one human lifespan ago, whose grandfathers had fought each other with tanks, guns and bayonets, I felt the things you're not supposed to feel in these troubled times: I felt hopeful. Perhaps, if mass tourism has a purpose, it is this: to let nations sit side by side on beaches without trying to kill one another.

When it comes to mass tourism, Ibiza went first. And when it comes to Ibiza, San Antonio went first. It is the crucible of Ibiza's ongoing experiment with tourism. San Antonio built its first hotel, the Hotel de Portmany, in the early 1930s on the edge of the town's tiny fishing harbour. The name was taken from San Antonio's full honorific title: San Antonio de Portmany, pronounced Portmayn, from the Roman name for the town, 'Portus Magnus', or great port. The German painter Will Faber had a small house nearby and he agreed to decorate the hotel, using a mix of Cubist, Dada and Expressionist styles and employing large murals and frescoes. Old black and white photographs show a three-storey building in a simplified Spanish colonial style with wrought-iron balconies around both upper floors. A short patio leads out on to a dusty, unmade road with a pretty collection of small fishing boats bobbing in the water across the track. Ominously, the quay is stacked with what appears to be a large pile of breezeblocks – development already under way.

The early tourists arrived in the same way as the artists, by boat from Valencia and Barcelona, and they arrived in little more than a trickle despite the high praise heaped on the island by the decamped literati. In October 1934, for instance, a total of eleven Brits visited the island. This fledgling industry collapsed completely with the outbreak of the Spanish Civil War, and the Second World War made matters worse. Although, had the tourists struggled through there would have been nowhere for them to stay. From 1936 until 1945 all Ibiza's hotels were occupied by the Spanish army. Even when the soldiers left, the lack of electricity, water and tight rationing hardly added to their attractions.

In 1947, the boat between Barcelona and Ibiza restarted its weekly service, reconnecting Ibiza to the mainland after eleven years of isolation. In 1950 the UN embargo on Spain was lifted, and by 1951 the *consell* felt bold enough to guess at a tourist presence of 1,120 in San Antonio. The majority of these tourists were French, from church groups which organized subsidized trips around Catholic countries – the only holidays most ordinary French people could afford.

The first Thomas Cook brochure to include Ibiza was *Spain & Portugal 1953*. The stilted sales pitch read: 'In addition to Majorca, the largest of the group, we also offer a holiday on the less frequented island of Ibiza where old customs still continue.' A fifteen-day holiday including two nights in Barcelona on the outward journey, seven nights at Ses Savines hotel in San Antonio and one night in Barcelona on the homeward journey cost £38 14s. 0d. (roughly £680 in today's terms). The fare included return travel tickets – third class to the Spanish frontier, first class on steamers from Barcelona to Palma and back, second class elsewhere – full-board accommodation at the hotels, including gratuities and taxes; luggage costs; and the services of Thomas Cook's representative from London to Barcelona. Air travel (tourist class) between London and Palma was available as an optional extra. In 1957, 14,356 tourists crossed to the island. The following year saw the military aerodrome founded during the civil war make the transition to a small local airport, offering flights to mainland Spain. In the 1950s, this organic trickle of visitors contributed nine million more pesetas to the island than Ibiza's entire agricultural exports, which included rabbits, eggs, barley, fish, almonds and, of course, salt.

Then, in 1959, General Franco had something of an epiphany. At the time he was still trying to work out how to rescue the country's struggling economy. Spain had gone into the war as a backward, semi-feudal society, and what little industry it had had was badly damaged by the conflict. In the late 1940s Franco had needed foreign capital, but there was a UN boycott in place. Building an internationally competitive manufacturing base would have been prohibitively expensive, but he had unspoiled beaches and he had cheap labour so the answer was right in front of him. In 1959, it finally slapped him round the face – tourism. And by an extreme stroke of luck Franco realized this possibility just as the jet-powered passenger plane made mass tourism possible.

Prior to the jet, it could easily take twenty-four hours to get to Ibiza, overland by train or via a rickety flight in a twin-engine plane that required several refuelling stops to reach the French or Spanish coast. That meant at least seven hours to Barcelona followed by an overnight ferry. This is why the island was exclusive to the bohemians, the artists and the intrepid middle classes. The jet engine and Franco's cheap labour changed that for ever. Ibiza started to compete with the traditional tourist resorts of France and Italy, and made its pitch not on quality but on price. And, of course, that determined who it targeted. The ideal customer was someone who didn't have the sun at home and who didn't have that much money. The market was instantly decided: the British, traditionally the cheapest tourists in the world.

Franco gave loans and grants to build hotels; he allowed foreign charter airlines to compete directly with the state airline Iberia; he even created the first cabinet post for a tourism minister. He divided the planning into national and regional levels. The regional plans were fairly laissez-faire, and regions were split up significantly. Many of the smaller regions, such as Ibiza, could not afford proper planners so buildings went up under the influence of mayors and civil servants with differing objectives. Had planning been carried out at the level of the autonomous community, e.g. by Catalonia, then things might have been better. But Franco was very wary of the regional bodies, which he strongly suspected of trying to destroy the Spanish nation.

As Franco's plan took effect, a beach in Ibiza was suddenly two to three hours away from cities in northern Europe. This opened up the island to people for whom travel to the rest of the world was not that interesting in and of itself. Indeed, they had found it slightly intimidating. The train, the boat, the next train, customs at every point – sod it. We're going to Blackpool like we did last year.

Once the jet can take people in a hermetically sealed tube from a suburb in Manchester to a sunny Spanish beach, then people who want a familiar experience rather than an adventure can also take a break in the sun. Given their yearning for the familiar, their desire for rest and recuperation above questing for some ersatz local truth, it follows that they want Manchester on the beach with them. But in bringing Manchester in its entirety to a beach in Ibiza, mass tourism brought all the social problems of Manchester along as well.

The bonus for Ibicencos was that tourists whose lives were spent on council estates were well prepared to put up with the dodgy plumbing, sporadic power failures, unfinished hotels and absence of concern for the environment.

They simply wanted somewhere warm and cheap to escape the Pennines rain. So they went. In 1950, Spain had a total of 1.3 million visitors; in 2001, it had 76 million, 14 million of whom came from the UK. And with their money, Spain modernized. It was exposed to democracy and wealth, and when Franco died in 1975 the country emerged like a butterfly, ready to become a fully functioning modern European country.

This pattern, the Spanish model, is largely mirrored by the development of each new generation of low-cost mass-market destinations, from Greece to Thailand to Bali, Kenya and Croatia. The ingredients are usually the same. A strongly authoritarian government looking for foreign currency sees mass tourism as an instant panacea. The industry develops with great speed and corners are cut on environmental standards, planning standards, building standards and labour costs. The government says, 'OK, we know the environment is important, but right now it's a cause for the rich. We have more serious problems: feeding everybody; creating jobs; building up foreign exchange so we can nurture other industries. Our nation of computer programmers has to come later.' The dollars, euros and pounds start to flood in, but with them come problems.

Take any agrarian or fishing-based economy with a strong local community and then plonk thousands of tourists right in the middle without asking the locals what they think. The fishermen's children suddenly find themselves working in a hotel as little better than servants, getting abused by brash foreigners who wear what they want and do what they want even though every word they speak shocks and offends. Sex. Drink. Immoral coupling. The beach is now polluted so there's no longer any fish. No-one could be a fisherman even if they wanted to.

Long-term resentment is inevitable. In Greece, there has been real conflict between tourists and local people, recently manifesting itself in rape, violence and murder. It's no coincidence that terrorist targets in the post-9/11 world include the touristic. In countries with orthodox religious populations, tourists often represent all that traditional cultures despise.

Of course, the Western tourist industry wasn't expecting this reaction, in part because the first places on the mass-market agenda were the Balearic Islands. These pioneering case studies offered no precedent for the unpleasantness experienced in other destinations since. The wonder of Ibiza is that in the face of the mass influx of drink-sodden north-ern Europeans it didn't offer any conflict at all. Especially as Franco's plan altered the island for ever.

In 1961, Ibiza was playing host to 41,000 visitors; by 1971 that had reached 350,000. San Antonio began to acquire the high-stacking hotels that characterize a modern resort, and the authorities even built a bull-ring, something that has no place in the island's Catalan culture. From 1967, when the airport opened to international flights, to 1973, the island witnessed *la gran explosión hotelera*. In 1961, there were eighty-six hotels on the island; by 1970, there were 256, mainly low quality, thrown up in nine months and financed by the tour operators. Instead of Ibicencos fleeing to South America, the island began to import workers from Andalucía to keep up with demand. Even the series of bankruptcies that swept through the low-cost tour operator industry in 1974, triggered by the petrol crisis of 1973, couldn't stop the holidaymakers from coming. 'So now to Ibiza something resembling a miracle has happened,' Laurie Lee wrote in *I Can't Stay Long*. 'Without labour or seed, floating harvests of wealth now fall on this sterile island. Only a few years ago its people were dying in the street, now everyone is plump and busy. How this could have happened, how long it may last, are things too uneasy to ask.'

By the 1980s, tourism accounted for 90 per cent of the local economy. Spain entering the EU in 1985 created an additional problem for Ibiza's cash economy: the arrival of VAT. Island hoteliers tried to avoid paying it for as long as possible, but succumbed after threats of prison sentences. Passing on price rises to tourists led to a minor slump. This still rankles, and the PACTE's Ecotax introduced in May 2002 stirred up the old resentment at new duties. Most hoteliers paid the Ecotax themselves, or gave customers free drinks to compensate, rather than face another backlash.

There was a further problem in store. In the early 1980s, Club 18–30 made a fateful deal to rent out a job-lot of rooms near the West End. At that point, the West End was a British-theme-pub corner of a standard-issue Spanish resort. The Ibicencos described what happened next as the arrival of 'los hooligans'. The British became famous for drunken rampages through the streets while waving Union Jacks and singing football songs. Tour guides would lead pub crawls in conga lines through the West End. Ibicenco hoteliers took to charging tour operators extra at the start of the season to cover the damage their guests would cause. Ibiza's problem was exacerbated by its low-rent hotels, which offered too many rooms and resorted to dramatic price-cutting to attract visitors. Hotels had to choose between bad guests and none at all. Tragedy was inevitable, and the murder of a young Andalucian by British thugs in San Antonio in 1989 shocked the entire island, although the mayor of San Antonio anxiously smoothed things over and did his level best to maintain good relations with the British tourist industry.

Of course, the murder took place in the West End. Almost every frame in the notorious *Ibiza Uncovered* documentaries was shot around this tiny collection of narrow streets. When Michael Birkett, the British consul on the island, resigned his post in 1998 it was the behaviour of the West End kids that he described as 'degenerate'. I was boarding a six a.m. flight to Ibiza two years ago when a party of British kids heading for San An threw up at check-in. They'd been drinking since eight the night before to get themselves ready for the West End.

'The first images which give rise to reflection in San Antonio are the interiors glimpsed through open doors and parted bead curtains,' the German philosopher Walter Benjamin wrote in the early 1930s.

Even through the shade the whiteness of the walls is dazzling. And in front of the rear wall there are usually two or four chairs, arranged in the room according to a strict, symmetrical order. There is much to be learned from their way of being there, with their simple form but strikingly beautiful canework and extreme dignity. No collector could display precious carpets or paintings on the walls of his vestibule with more assurance than the peasant who displays his chairs in this bare space. But also, these are not just chairs.

Their function changes whenever a sombrero is hung on the backrest. And in this new composition, the woven straw hat appears no less precious than the chair.

As I wandered through the West End post-sunset, it was still the interiors that gave rise to reflection. Dark and pounding with bass rhythms or a facsimile reproduction of an English pub, the venues lined the narrow, pedestrianized streets one after the other: the Cat and Parrot, the Beaver Bar, Joe Spoon's Irish Pub, Capone's VideoKaraoke. Outside each stood a crowd of employees – not bouncers, but proppers. They weren't there to keep people out, they were there to get them in. 'It's two for the price of one!' 'Free double vodka with every beer!' Cheerful young Brits assail you every five yards: cheeky Scouse geezers, scantily clad London hip-hop chicks, cocky Scots in combats and smiling northerners offering free drinks, the best music and all the fun you can have – every one of them flirting for Britain. 'There's a special on turbo shandys,' a brunette with a cut-glass accent said, waylaying me.

'What's a turbo shandy?' I replied, revealing my age.

She blinked and almost lost interest right away. 'Half of Stella and a Smirnoff Ice.'

I declined and headed down the hill towards the seafront, feeling desperately out of place, when suddenly I stopped, blinking in the neon light. There in front of me was the Hotel de Portmany. Still standing and still looking as fragile and beautiful as ever. Her walls were white, her shutters green, and the old 1930s sign was still painted in yellow. She wasn't entirely unravaged by the debauchery around her: the ground floor had been gutted then filled with cafés offering twenty-four-hour GutBuster English breakfasts and a cheap boutique called, mockingly, Hippy Republic. A strange hope filled me: perhaps I could check out of Stalag Abrat and into one of Faber's Dadaist rooms.

Scouting round the outside of the building revealed nothing that looked like a hotel reception. I walked into one of the cafés and found a young, cheerful barman called Alex who spoke perfect English when I tried my feeble Spanish on him. Was the Portmany still a hotel? I asked. No, he said, not for years. So what was upstairs now, I wondered. Nothing. What, offices or flats? No, nothing. It is, how do you say it in English? Derelict? Yes, that's how we say it. Derelict.

He was curious: why did I want to know? I told him I'd heard it was one of the oldest hotels on the island. One of the oldest, yes, he said. But not *the* oldest. That was the Hotel Montesol in Ibiza Town. I told him I knew the place he meant. His face lit up even further. 'You have seen it? It is beautiful. It was done by a very famous architect. I cannot remember his name, but he built my great-grandfather's house as well in San Rafael. The house and the hotel are both protected. They are so beautiful.'

I pulled the book of old photos out of my jacket and we flicked through to see the pictures of 1930s Portmany. 'Look,' Alex said, pointing out through the door, 'the sea used to come up to just outside.' We looked out towards the port now. They'd been reclaiming land outside the Portmany, it seemed. There was a square and a kids' playground and then a dual carriageway before you got to the day-trip boats now. And where the old mule cart had been there was a fat man throwing up.

As I walked out from under the Portmany's fragile balconies, a strange resolve filled my aching heart. Why should
I mourn the death of the past? The island clearly didn't.
Ibiza soldiered on, and so should I. There was drinking, fighting and dancing out there. It was like an old Western frontier
town and I was moping around like the feeble sawbones
stranded when his horse died of thirst. But no more. Given
the strapping muscles on these drunken teens, beating them
was out of the question. I would join them. I strapped on my
metaphorical gun belt and prepared to duel the best drinkers
in town. Hell, I'd survived Colin Casbolt. What could these
schoolkids throw at me?

I settled on the Scottish Pub, mainly because no-one tried
to offer me a free Taboo and lemonade if I chose to spend
my euros with them. Starting gently seemed wise. But any
resulting idea as to the establishment's sophistication
vanished when the young girl sitting alone at the table next
to me keeled over backwards and fell, unconscious, onto the
street. 'Leave it, Nicky, leave it alone,' the Glaswegian
manageress behind the bar squawked at her glass collector.
The girl just lay there until the drug dealers I'd turned down
ten minutes earlier took pity on her, heaved her up and
phoned an ambulance on their mobiles.

Feeling that this cast an unnecessary pall on my binge, I
swapped venues and slipped into Kiltie's Irish Bar, proud
owner of a banner proclaiming 'Who's your . . . who's your
. . . who's your fucking daddy?' Special offer that night was
a pint of vodka and Red Bull or a free shot on the side with any
drink ordered. I opted for a vodka freebie with my lager and
they sank it, depth-charge style, into my urine-yellow pint.
When I left Kiltie's, the warm hit of alcohol roused my

tired veins. I looked around as if a mist had lifted from my eyes. It suddenly seemed to me that the West End wasn't just an endless orgy of alcohol, violence and lust. Glammed-up twentysomething Victoria Beckham lookalikes tottered past walking the model walk, one foot in front of the other, wobbling on the kind of heels that shouldn't be mixed with vodka. 'I've been drinking all day,' one laughing girl said into her mobile. Teenage boys looked about with joyful disbelief as the fleshpots stretched before them. They were young. They had money. They were away from home. It was warm, and the bars stayed open all night. This was a tiny slice of hedonist heaven for them; they were free from Mum and Dad, bad weather and a frowning society. My basic problem was simple: I was too old to be there. No matter how hard I pretended to be eighteen, I wouldn't be fooling anyone. This was no place for me.

Admitting defeat wasn't too hard. Fundamentally I had no desire for a Long Slow Orgasm Up Against the Wall. I wandered back towards my hotel, surprised at how swiftly the West End fell away and the streets became almost silent. The foyer of the Hotel Abrat was deserted, but I somehow weaved my way through it, then lay on my bed as the lager and the vodka fought in my stomach. I became conscious of a low throbbing filling the air. It came from the roof of the hotel and seemed to fill my entire body. It was impossible to sleep.

The following day, my friend Matt phoned me. He was holidaying on the island with his wife and child and they'd checked into a cute little rural hotel called Es Cucons just five minutes away from me over the hills. Why didn't I come to lunch? I drove over there feeling stretched and exhausted, took one look at the vision of paradise he had lucked into, turned right around, drove back to San An, picked up my bags and left the Hotal Abrat for ever. They owed me money for the rest of my four-night stay, but I didn't care. I just wanted out.

Es Cucons was owned by a young couple, María and Maime, her Scandinavian husband. It was a seventeenth-century *finca* converted into a small rural hotel with lush, farm-style grounds and stark white walls. My room was at the back of the farmhouse with a low wooden porch standing over a small pool hacked into the hard rock. 'The family used to light fires on the rock year after year to crack it so they could scrape fresh layers of stone away,' Maime told me as he unlocked the door. I turned and looked out across the valley. The fields throbbed in the dry heat. Over in the distance, a chainsaw was at work. There were olive groves to my right and tiny white houses dotting the hill opposite. Every now and then, I could hear a cock crow.

Maria joined me. 'Our neighbour' – she pointed out into the valley – 'he still uses a horse to plough his fields. We see him go past, riding on the wooden plough at the back.' We stared at his land. 'You know, there are some people in the nearest village, Santa Agnes, older people, who have never even been to Ibiza Town in their whole lives,' she added with a sort of hushed wonder in her voice. We contemplated this for a while until she turned to me and smiled. 'Why don't you come into the library? I have a book to show you.'

I followed her into reception and off to the left where a small room was filled with shelves of books. She pulled one out, leafed through it and stopped at a page with photos on the right and a long list in Catalan on the left. 'This book has something on every old house in Ibiza.' She pointed to the entry headed Es Cucons. 'It says the house was built in 1652. The pond outside your room gave it the name. It means a sort of natural – how would you say it? Reservoir? In 1785 it was owned by Costa Cocous. I think that family lost it through gambling in 1977. The bank took it. It was empty until we bought it in 1997.' She took me back into the reception area and pointed up at the roof. A huge stone arch stretched across the hall, maybe seventy feet across at its base. 'It's the largest on the island. When we were renovating the place, a man came to see us. He must have been in his late nineties. He told us his grandfather had helped to build that arch. All the village came to help.' We marvelled in silence at the size of the stonework constructed by a village of amateur masons, and at the continuity of generations – the old grandson knowing the jobs his grandfather had taken part in. 'People would come and say they had got married in this house or been to a party in this house in the old days,' María said, smiling. 'All the marriages were over land. A man would want his son to marry the girl with the big farm over the valley. Which must have led to a little bit of in-breeding.' Her laugh was infectious.

Ibiza's political establishment hopes that María is the future. After thirty years politicians on the left and the right are finally fed up with San An. It started a while ago – at the end of the 1980s, the island's bishops published a thoughtful tract entitled 'Ecology and Tourism in Our Islands' that raised concerns over the impact of unrestrained development – but it died away once the recession hit. In the early 1990s, Ibiza's reputation as a place of violence and rowdy behaviour coupled with the Gulf War, a continent-wide economic slump and the strength of the peseta led to extremely lean years. Families, in particular, stayed away, and some hotels remained closed for the whole of 1990. As a result, hotels came under extreme pressure to modernize and improve. A sweeping programme of investment coupled with a resurgence of interest in the island as a clubbing destination created the second boom, the *recuperación turística*, which began in 1994 when numbers returned to 1987 levels of around 1.1 million. This figure has grown steadily, passing the two million barrier in 1999 and reaching 2.2 million in 2002. But with this success, all the old worries have returned.

The day after I checked into Es Cucons, I went to meet Jorge Alfonso, the island's director of tourism. He was a tall, distinguished man with a slightly careworn look to his strong, chiselled features. He was having a tough summer, with a recession in Germany cutting the number of Teutonic tourists, who make up the island's second largest market after the Brits.

We settled into comfortable chairs and talked for an hour. Jorge spoke slowly and clearly, as if giving me dictation. Sometimes he would look out of the window of his first-floor office down into the street below. Sometimes he would look into my eyes as he spoke.

'We need new tourists,' he said, 'new kinds of tourists. We have built a new dock for cruise ships, so now the biggest in the world will be able to dock in Ibiza. These are good tourists for us. You see, after the civil war Ibiza was the poorest part of Spain; now we are one of the richest. But all this development is not positive. We have lost the tranquillity, and people mistake our tolerance for permissiveness.

'In the beginning of the 1960s, Ibiza had forty to forty-five thousand people. That's doubled now. We need to protect this small island, her beauty, all the aspects that motivate people to come here. It must be defended for our children and our residents, and our quality of life. Is there no limit to development? No, we must stop. We must avoid being destroyed. We don't want to be Malta; we need to preserve our countryside, our hills, our valleys, our way of life. We can't make our money in just three to four months of the year any more. It's impossible. We have to move the island upmarket, because we can't compete against the Dalmatian coast.

'In the countryside you can see people working as they did three hundred years ago. I think these people must be financed to maintain this way of life.' He paused, then sighed. 'You know, I think we are raising our children wrong. Today, Ibiza is a nice community, but our best children don't stay here. If you are a civil service worker or a tourist worker you can find work here easily, but if you are an architect or philosopher you have to go to the mainland. If you have been to university, you have a lot of difficulties finding work here. The best children of Ibiza do not stay in Ibiza.'

We finished our coffee and talked about his hopes that direct flights by national airlines would gradually replace charter flights, 'just like Palma', then I thanked him and stepped out of his office, walking across the crowded Marina out to the old lighthouse that overlooked the cruise-ship dock. A massive Scandinavian liner was just getting up steam and hooting its stern call to late shoppers and sightseers. I watched the passengers scurry along the dock and wondered what they thought of the place. What does Ibiza mean to those who come here? Why do they still come?

If Jorge was correct, the old Ibiza was dying. Perhaps what survives, what attracts the day trippers and charter flight travellers, is a dream of Ibiza, marketed across television, music, fashion, clubs and, of course, my little Seat runabout. This Ibiza holds echoes of the island's past and offers a twenty-first-century message that is vaguely spiritual, vaguely hedonistic, vaguely chilled. The perfect sanctuary in a vicious world.

This vision, this blend of hedonism, tolerance and pagan dreaming as a global brand, was created entirely by accident. Something happened that combined everything Ibicenco – the tolerance, the liberalism, the jet-setters, the pagan orgies, even Bes, the little god of dance and sanctuary – into one explosive moment. It all came together on the dance floor of a converted *finca* out near the village of San Rafael. After Amnesia, the world would never be quite the same again.

CHAPTER 13

The DJ

Ibiza's music scene began after the Second World War with one man, a dubious former GI by the name of Bad Jack Hand who ran the Jamboree Jazz Club, a sleazy booze 'n' tunes dive in Barcelona. With brother Philly and wife Peggy, Bad Jack tramped it over to Tangier from New York on a beaten-up Yugoslav freighter for $110 of the funds he had left over from his GI pension. The three of them wound up serving hooch and jazz to disaffected Yanks beached on mainland Europe when the tide of war ebbed away.

Bad Jack probably headed out to Ibiza to avoid some heat in Barcelona; certainly he wound up back in Barcelona's prison doing life for murder by the end of the 1950s. His partner Philly was already locked up in a nice warm cell by the time the key turned on Bad Jack, and no-one is quite sure what happened to Peggy. During his brief stay on the White Island, however, Bad Jack booked American jazz musicians into local cafés and bars and threw open-air jams and parties on the beach near Figueretes, a tiny village with a wide, sandy beach. Chief among his acts was saxophonist Pony Poindexter from New Orleans, who played on the island with the likes of Billy Eckstine, Jon Hendricks and the young Norwegian guitarist and singer Magni Wentzel. With whip-thin bassist Titi, who once posed for Salvador Dali, and the painter Jesse Richardson, this crew came to be known as the Black Panthers of Figueretes. They'd jam on houses overlooking the beach with a flautist on the roof, a sax player on one balcony and a bassist on another.

At first, Bad Jack's clientele were the scores of dubious US ex-servicemen drifting around Europe at the end of the Second World War – men who didn't want to or couldn't go home. Gradually they were joined by the beatniks, and the beatniks led to the hippies, and the hippies founded Amnesia and Pacha, and then Space came along. Which is where I found myself standing one bright and sunny Sunday morning.

It takes a certain kind of person to leave his hotel room at seven a.m. on a Sunday with a few handfuls of fruit in his stomach, make for a vast concrete amphitheatre lined with towering speaker stacks and launch straight into debauched bedlam alongside people who still haven't gone to bed. For that kind of person, Space was invented. Hosted in a bunker near Playa d'en Bossa, Space opens at eight a.m. to huge queues of people either still up from the previous night or just out of bed, all of them ready to push through to Monday morning. The inside of the club looks like an air-raid shelter, but most people go for the terrace. This is an open-air football stadium affair dotted with huge, whirring fans where the main DJs play until noise restrictions at midnight force everyone inside. Where they carry on for another six hours.

The place used to be an exclusive conference venue. The plan was to host events such as 'The Future of Mechanized

Tunnelling' or 'Whither Carpets?' But by 1987 everyone involved had given up the ghost and it was quietly flogged off to a man called Pepe Roselló, who set it up as an after-party party. Clubbing legend has it that a DJ called Alex P was the first man to see the potential of the outdoor terrace when in the early 1990s he grabbed his decks and moved them out into the sunshine, but plenty of other platter spinners have also claimed that honour. Whoever it was, he made Space into a religious experience, a Sunday-morning ritual that claims back sinners from the Church with greedy glee. For those who head out to Ibiza for nights of mayhem and days of snoozing, Space is a symbol of all that is good about the island. For those who don't, it can be a little bit unnerving. Sometimes, getting out of bed in the morning and joining a queue for a nightclub can just seem, I don't know, against God's plan?

I'd joined the queue to see Danny Rampling, the painter and decorator who came to Ibiza for a weekend and left to invent Acid House. Through him, and three of his friends, the island sent tentacles around the world, entwining a generation and drawing them into heathen bacchanals of stomping house music, all-night hedonism and powerful ecstatic visions. It was as if the goddess of love and war had been biding her time for two thousand years, hiding out on the island where they still danced her dances. All she needed were some high priests to get her back out into the world again.

She chose some unlikely priests. As well as Rampling there were his three mates: Nicky Holloway, a pub DJ; Paul Oakenfold, a chef who pushed hip-hop records on the side; and Johnny Walker, a thirtysomething club promoter. And these four chancers had their moment of divine revelation at the height of the summer of 1987.

Danny Rampling had just come back from a year in America. He'd grafted his way across the States working in restaurants and on building sites and had almost lost his life in a car crash. He returned home feeling reborn after his narrow escape but quickly found himself back in a rut in London, bored out of his mind. It was barely two months before Black Monday killed the decade of excessive consumption, and for a kid with little left in his pocket, London was an unwelcoming place. If you wanted a drink, there were only smoky pubs or overpriced champagne bars; nightclubs closed at two a.m. and every single one of them had bouncers who sneered at jeans and trainers. Some door staff would quiz punters about their music tastes before pulling back the rope. Rampling hated it.

By the end of August he had spent the last of his US money and was stony-broke. With his vague dream of becoming a DJ so far out of sight that *Voyager* would have had trouble passing it his future looked bleak. When Nicky Holloway asked him out to Ibiza, he glumly refused, not having the pennies to afford the fare. Holloway just paid for the tickets himself, and the twosome headed off to join Oakenfold and Walker in a villa they had hired to celebrate Paul's twenty-sixth birthday. The plan was simple: cruise the bars and clubs in San Antonio on a lager-and-sunshine holiday, like countless British blokes since the 1960s.

But the Ibiza they visited was at a critical point. The glamorous early 1980s nightclubs such as Ku and Amnesia, deep in the heart of the island, had just pulled through some very tough times. Both had almost closed. After terrific years in the late 1970s and early 1980s, the middle of the decade had seen revenue dipping sharply.

Ku opened in 1978 as the pet project of three Basque businessmen who owned a club of the same name in San Sebastián on the mainland. They bought a small bar called Club Rafael, invested heavily and built Ku into the largest club in the world – as attested by the *Guinness Book of Records* – with a capacity of up to eight thousand people. This vast temple of hedonism sported an open roof, terraces lined with pine and palm trees, a restaurant serving Basque cuisine, seven bars, a swimming pool in the middle of the dance floor, laser shows that were visible from the mainland, Brazilian carnival parties with dancers and musicians flown in from Rio, and more celebrities than you could shake a stick at.

The early 1980s were Ku's golden years. Freddie Mercury sang 'Barcelona' there with Montserrat Caballé; Boy George held a birthday party there; Grace Jones danced naked in the rain; and James Brown played live in the same season as 1980s heroes Spandau Ballet, Kid Creole and the Coconuts, Talk Talk and, er, Animal Nightlife. Tina Turner, George Michael, Andrew Ridgeley, Sting, Joni Mitchell, Bob Marley, Led Zeppelin and Pink Floyd had all passed through its doors by the decade's mid-point. Ibiza clubs were just like the island itself – gay and straight, black and white, men and women, all mixed happily alongside one another. The only people missing were the poor.

The problem was, the celebrities might have spent heavily at the thirty-five huge parties Ku threw during the summer, but on every other night the venue had to cope with enormous overheads. After all, the club had to be able to serve eight thousand people should they decide to drop in. In 1985 it was charging £15 admission to try to support these costs – an unheard-of sum in those days. Of course, the vast majority of tourists just weren't prepared to stump up that kind of cash.

Over the road at Amnesia they had a slightly more pressing concern because they didn't even have the showbiz elite. Amnesia had grown organically from an old *finca* used by the hippies as a bar and party space. As Ku's fame grew, Amnesia became a second-tier option. The management invested in an open-air dance floor and all the Ku trimmings, but the punters stayed away. Just as the missing-punters problem became acute, local residents started to complain about the noise levels from both venues. The *consell* began discussing legislation that would force open-air venues to build expensive roofs, which neither of the straitened clubs could afford. Suddenly, the future of clubbing on the island looked doubtful.

And then, in 1985, help arrived in the shape of a small white pill. Since 1981, samples of the psychedelic amphetamine MDMA had been trickling out of the Bagwan Rajneesh cult's workshops around San Juan and Santa Eulalia. In 1985, the cult closed down and the trickle became a flood as the stockpiles were released into Ibiza's flourishing dope, speed and acid market. There were even rumours that you could buy cocktails laced with Ecstasy at certain bars in Ku. Punters initially found that the dance-floor diet of 1980s white-boy funk mixed badly with the blissed-out euphoria MDMA produced. Often, users would retire to sofas or quiet palm-tree-lined corners and talk or watch the sunrise. It took an exiled Argentinian journalist and accidental DJ to get them up and dancing again.

Alfredo, real name Jaime Fiorito, was born in Argentina in 1953. After leaving college, he got a job on *La Capital*, a Buenos Aires newspaper, as a film and music critic. He spent much of his spare time promoting rock concerts, which proved his undoing. After Argentina's right-wing military coup in 1976, this sort of reckless and seditious behaviour was enough to have him jailed. On his release he decided to get out of the country, and he headed for Spain with his wife.

Once there, on advice from a friend, he took the ferry to Ibiza where he turned his hand to anything he could to make money – running a shop, waiting tables, working behind a bar. At the end of a series of low-paid jobs, he got lucky: a friend returned to South America and left his bar in Ibiza Town to Alfredo. The bar came equipped with a set of decks and a mixer, and Alfredo couldn't bear to see them lying fallow.

He found he loved DJing. It felt like a calling, and he decided to make it his living, if he could. It was an unlikely decision. For one thing, Alfredo didn't have many records. He did, however, have a child to support, so he went touting for work. The bars and clubs of the island didn't exactly fall over themselves to employ him, but the man who owned Amnesia gave him a shot in 1983. He lasted one night and was sacked for playing too many Culture Club records.

The following summer, he was back. The fact that he was given a second chance reflected the dire straits Amnesia was in. Alfredo found he was playing six-hour sets to almost deserted dance floors. One night he had a total of twenty people shuffling around while the queues outside Ku tailed back to the road. He was miserable but he plodded on, shutting up the club by himself at six a.m. and then waiting an hour for the manager to arrive with his £20 wage.

At the end of August 1984, his girlfriend suggested he spark up the decks and play a few tunes to pass the time between six a.m. and his pay-cheque. He did. People on their way home from other clubs heard the tunes and popped their heads round the door. They stayed. They danced. They told their friends. Within three days Alfredo was playing to a thousand people, but only from six a.m. Amnesia's owner was no idiot. He switched the club's hours, opening at five a.m. and making Amnesia the first after-party club on the island, possibly in the world.

When E hit in 1985, Amnesia exploded. Alfredo had wintered in New York and picked up some underground disco records as well as a few tunes from a scene bubbling up in Chicago based around a club called the House. With constant disco-style drum beats, light synthesizer twiddling and full, throaty vocals, it was named after its birthplace – house music. Alfredo started to play house tunes in his sets at Amnesia in the summer of 1985, mixing them up with Tears for Fears, Bob Marley, Donna Summer, British indie bands, Prince, synth pop, Italian disco – anything he could lay his hands on. These eclectic sets, mixed with MDMA and the dawn sunshine on Amnesia's open-air dance floor, started to attract clubbers from all over Europe who were fed up with snooty door policies and hipper-than-thou clientele. By the time Danny Rampling and co. landed in 1987, hearing Alfredo play at Amnesia, and dropping an E to go with it, had achieved the status of a pilgrimage for anyone interested in dance music. His sets had even earned a nick-name from the music press – the Balearic Beat.

Initially the four friends resisted. Nicky Holloway was anti-drugs and Johnny Walker was slightly apprehensive about anything stronger than speed. On their first night on the island they opted for a bar crawl in San An and headed for a reasonably hip British boozer called Nightlife. A dealer cruised them, and Paul and Danny decided to try this strange white capsule they'd heard so much about. Nicky and Johnny also purchased but hung back, letting the other two take theirs first. Finally, after watching Danny and Paul run around the bar, hugging each other and smiling, Johnny and Nicky gulped their Es and the foursome headed for Amnesia.

The music Alfredo played that night – a set with house, hip-hop, Cyndi Lauper, the Woodentops, Thrashing Doves, Prince and George Michael – and the huge international crowd of gay, straight, black and white clubbers from across the continent blew the young Londoners away. They danced all night and spent the next day floating in the pool at their villa, playing a tape of Alfredo's set taken from the mixing desk and holding hands as they floated in the sunshine. That evening they swore an oath that when they went back to London they would find the records Alfredo had played and recreate the entire experience for the city's jaded scene.

At first, Nicky Holloway, Paul Oakenfold and Johnny Walker worked their existing small-scale industry contacts with mixed success. Danny Rampling, on the other hand, was a complete outsider as far as London clubs were concerned. With his girlfriend Jenni he started looking for a place to execute his mission, but could only find a basement gym near Southwark Bridge on the deeply un-fashionable south side of the Thames. They booked it anyway.

Klub Shoom began very slowly, with barely 150 people at the first night, most of whom didn't really understand the music policy or the silly baggy clothes. Over the cold, stormy winter of 1987/88, however, the club grew in reputation. Danny started DJing, playing Balearic sets in the dark basement filled with dry ice and lit with throbbing strobes. People came with sullen disinterest and left as excited converts. Shoom's yellow smiley symbol became the badge for a movement, and Acid House was born.

The rest is history, albeit history written by some very muddled people. Parties around the M25, tabloid outrage, London clubs changing their opening hours to compete with East End warehouse parties, house music storming the charts, superclubs opening across Europe – the tastes, fashions and fortunes of 1990s pop culture were created on that one night in Ibiza in 1987.

Danny Rampling had played in Ibiza every year since then, but this was his first time at Space. A huge crowd had turned out to see how he fared, and it promised to be a big day out. But once I'd finally navigated the pythonesque queue (not the surreal and comic Python but the very long and snaky python; although, then again . . .) I somehow couldn't face throwing myself into the surging mob with a glad shout of abandon. I was alone, I was sober, and it was eleven o'clock in the morning. I felt I'd be betraying the devil-may-care spirit of the club if I sat in the chillout lounge nursing a cappuccino, but throwing stronger stuff down my neck didn't really appeal. Ultimately satisfying neither urge,

I chose instead to walk around the outskirts of the dance floor sipping alternately on a bottle of mineral water and a can of Red Bull, hoping inspiration and caffeine would strike.

I was still ambling about the crowded dive in a crisis of indecision several hours later when someone tapped me on the shoulder and asked to get by. I turned and saw a familiar pretty blonde girl smiling politely. I explained, as loudly and succinctly as I could, that it was very crowded and I was stuck myself, and I was about to throw in a couple of vaguely flirty jokes when an absolutely enormous man – a man who literally towered over me – just pushed me aside as if opening net curtains to wave at his neighbours. I was about to protest when I realized he was accompanied by five equally huge companions who appeared to move into a flying V wedge formation to protect this blonde girl and a familiar-looking black guy who was clearly her companion. They practically trampled over my feeble frame as they cleared the way, but one of them thrust a bundle of white cloth into my shaking hand as I was expelled from the phalanx of muscle. I clung to it like a life raft in a sea of pecs and abs.

After the dust had settled, I gazed at the slip of material in my hands and gradually realized what it was: a T-shirt sporting the image of hip-hop megastar P Diddy looking all mean and gangstery like the good Bronx rapper he was. Of course! The guy was P Diddy! That's where I'd seen him before. And then I remembered where I'd seen the girl. She was Lady Victoria Hervey, and I'd last seen her sitting on a sofa in her underwear in the pages of GQ.

I looked around the club. The DJ had been playing a constant series of identical house tracks that bleeped and twiddled with such monotony that he had managed to drive the dance floor into a state of dumb stupefaction. The serried ranks of the terrace were dotted with gently swaying zombie shufflers who barely looked up, content to step from foot to foot with every beat of the bass drum. At which point Danny Rampling stepped into the DJ booth. It was the musical equivalent of a stand-up comedian walking on to crack a few funnies after a fundraising appeal from a child with cancer.

Perhaps as a result, he began his set gently, almost nervously, playing very similar stuff to his predecessor. I sat down, feeling a little bored. This man was supposed to be an Ibiza legend. I was at the dark heart of the island's debauchery and, frankly, I was looking at my watch. And then something extraordinary happened. He played a song that by every rule in the DJ book shouldn't be played in a nightclub. It started with a strumming, jangling acoustic guitar and a plaintive vocal, like Joni Mitchell on powerful amphetamines, which went on far too long. You have to keep the beats going as a DJ, I thought to myself; you have to keep the crowd dancing. Big mistake, Danny, big mistake.

But around the club, the dancers froze like meerkats, upright, curious, their gazes fixed on the DJ booth. The melody drifted around the club, haunting and beautiful, and the tempo of the song began to build. I could see Danny Rampling's face and he seemed to be nursing a secret smile, as if he knew what was coming next and was looking forward to seeing it happen. Then the drum beat started, soft and insistent, way down below as the drummer sound-checked in the cellar. But the beat was getting louder and the dancers were craning their necks and a deep, echoing bassline started that followed the drummer as he marched upstairs, alive with menace and sex and ready to kick down the door just as his snare drum came in crackling with suppressed tension, ripping crisply through roll after roll after roll until, sweet Jesus, with a boom I could feel in my guts the whole place exploded.

The song crashed into a euphoric wall of noise; the lights flashed white and blinding, drowning out the sun with their brilliance; the dancers hurtled into a frenzy of cheering and dancing; and Danny Rampling laughed like a madman, hauling the crowd higher and higher as he pushed his palms upwards in a gesture of supplication and joy that seemed like an act of worship in itself.

I was sober. It was late afternoon. I'd been bored for a good three hours and suddenly I was dancing like a lunatic – albeit a lunatic who has no space in which to move as the entire population of the island rushed the dance floor at once. With bodies pressing into me from every direction it became clear that I wasn't dancing; I was simply moving with the crowd. We rose and fell together, bouncing and waving and cheering and clapping with such idiotic joy that I found I was grinning all over my stupid face.

Astonishingly, Rampling managed to take it upwards from there. His set lasted two solid hours and he seemed to turn up the dial with every new track until I really thought that if he built things any higher my head would detonate completely. As he came towards his peak, he seemed to drop us slightly with a strange, electronic bleeping track featuring robotic vocals that brought us all down. I could hear a tune in the background, a tune the squeaking synth line was trying to play. It sounded like 'I Can't Get No Satisfaction', with Keith Richards' guitar riff fizzing along like a brittle, home-keyboard version of a pop tune. Then the tune began to pull out of its mechanical abyss with another snare drum build, and I wondered how high this was going to go if it was supposed to top all the other tracks. I doubted it could. And then Rampling did something so bonkers, so clearly the wrong thing to do that it was an act of pure DJ genius: he cut right into the chorus of the Rolling Stones with Jagger snarling 'satisfaction' and managed to sync up the two tracks so we didn't miss a beat. The wave of elation that beat against my spine was almost palpable. Everyone threw their arms into the air and sang as lustily as a male-voice choir. He cut the volume like a bad wedding DJ, we gave full vent to our throaty roar – 'I! Can't! Get! No!' – and the guitar riff filled the gap – 'Satisfayction!!!' And we sang the riff as well.

He raised his arms to us and we raised ours to him again. Men ran forward, pushing through the crowd to shake his hand, reaching up like toddlers to Father Christmas and clasping his fingers like a brother. He made his way out of the booth with difficulty, everyone shouting and cheering as they would a soul diva who'd just poured her heart out in songs of beauty and pain. I staggered back to the wall, exhausted as if I'd danced all night and drunk a bottle of vodka down in one. I was drenched in sweat. My vision was blurred. I was, in the words of bad sex writers, spent.

Monday morning came too soon. I was due to meet the final players in the strange game that had occupied the island since Tanit: Mike and Claire and Andy and Dawn from Manumission. Their club had rescued the island from its mid-1990s slump. As clubbing spread across the planet like a virus, everyone forgot all about Ibiza. In the first part of the decade, people were having so much fun at home that they couldn't see a reason to visit the place where it had all begun. Tourist figures were down, clubber numbers dwindled, and in 1991 the Ku club fell silent as the cost of that long-feared roof crushed the resources of its owners. Then, in 1994, the foursome behind Manumission turned everything around.

Manumission – a word derived from the Latin meaning to give a slave freedom – began in January 1994 as a Friday night special at a now defunct club in Manchester's gay village called Equinox. Promoted by three students – brothers Andy and Mike McKay and Andy's girlfriend Dawn Hindle – it was designed as an open, friendly, mixed gay/straight night. Unfortunately for the brothers, it opened in Manchester just as the city began its slide into the violence and lawlessness that had some wits dubbing it Gunchester. With an artful eye on promotion that would have impressed P. T. Barnum, the McKay brothers launched the night by creating an imaginary backer called Roger More – a pun on having more sex – who had arrived to save the city from its crime-ridden depression. 'And on the 14th day, Roger More re-created Manchester' read the flyers, spoofing a popular T-shirt from the early 1990s, 'And on the 7th day, God created Manchester'.

To start with, the gay village protected Manumission from the warfare decimating Manchester nightlife. Few of the local gangsters were at home enough with their sexuality to venture into Canal Street. The brothers played on rampant homophobia, with posters warning that 'Manumission can seriously damage your reputation as a heterosexual male'.

Manumission was regularly voted best club in Britain by the dance music press until, after twelve weeks and following their original prank-laden plan, the team pushed the biblical theme to the limit by crucifying someone dressed as Roger More outside the venue.

For the rest of the weekend the brothers handed out flyers saying they were off to New York to run the infamous Tunnel Club. At the end of the week, however, they opened in Equinox as usual, announcing – with the logical conclusion to the biblical theme – a resurrection. On the face of it, this was a disaster. From locking out over five hundred people every night, the club suddenly found a total of 250 people shuffling uneasily around the dance floor. The following week, numbers barely doubled. But Manchester clubbers had been mourning its passing, so when it became clear that the night hadn't died at all, week three was swamped. The team locked out more people than they let in. Everything seemed to have gone according to plan.

The fame of the night soon spread outside the tight-knit world of clubland and gay Manchester. This fame killed the club, and very nearly took Andy with it in the process. By week four post-rebirth, word had spread to Moss Side. Very, very nasty men started trying to get in. Hardcore thugs would even snog each other outside to 'prove' they were gay. Fearing violence, Andy and Mike doubled security. Then, in week five, it happened.

A very large and aggressive man showed up in the middle of the evening and demanded access. Andy, who was on the door at the time, refused to let him in. He became abusive. The bouncers pushed him away. He strode off into the night threatening vengeance, and that, they assumed, was that.

Half an hour later he was back, with ten mates and a can of petrol. The bouncers tried to shut him out but the gang broke down the doors and started spreading petrol on the stairs. Andy rushed up to try and negotiate, but they grabbed him, soaked him, threw him downstairs – dislocating his fingers in the process – and started looking for a lighter.

The gods often smile on the innocent. By a stroke of incredible good fortune, none of the thugs had thought to bring a light. While they searched in vain, Andy fled and managed to hide in the DJ booth. After breaking a few chairs and threatening a few clubbers, the gang left. The first man was arrested a couple of weeks later for stabbing someone in a different club. For Andy and Mike, however, it was the end. They cleared the club and, knowing that this incident would keep their gay clientele away, permanently changing the atmosphere, they closed Manumission down. With the final night's door takings, they paid for a holiday in Ibiza to get away and clear their heads.

They discovered an island living on its past reputation. Clubbing was uninspiring; young holidaymakers preferred backpacking across Thailand to two weeks on a beach in the Mediterranean. The Ku club had just reopened under new management as Privilege, but the owners were having trouble filling the place. An eight-thousand-capacity venue with a thousand people in it is basically an empty barn no matter how loud the music is. Andy and Mike weren't looking to set anything up, but they went to Privilege, had a chat and ended up taking over a bar at the edge of the dance floor called Coco Loco, on Monday nights. Coco Loco was pretty much a small nightclub in its own right, glued to the side of Privilege like an afterthought, and the brothers set about creating something using the theatre of their Manchester night. Free drinks, strange dancers, men sitting on toilets, outrageous drag acts – all sorts of nonsense went on. The island responded. Within weeks they had taken over the main club and were pulling in six-thousand-plus punters on a weekly basis. Then Mike met Claire.

Initially a propper for the club, Claire's astonishing prowess in attracting the punters rapidly came to Mike and Andy's attention. As did the funny little squiggles she put on the back of her flyers. Mike decided to meet her. Then decided to meet her again. Before you could say Summer of Love, they were an item. The following year, 1995, they began the sex shows described earlier. By the end of the summer, Manumission was possibly the most famous club night on the planet.

The sex shows stopped in 1998, but their reputation still echoes around Europe. I wanted to ask Mike and Claire if they had consciously been recreating Phoenician ceremonies when they stood up on that stage, with thousands of ecstatic worshippers yelling them on. We arranged to meet, all five of us, at a café on Ibiza Town's Botafoc Marina. It was a little slice of Monte Carlo, lined with million-dollar yachts and speedboats all clinking away as the steel hawsers blew against the masts. You could smell money. So, of course, the café was obscenely expensive, even by Ibiza's ludicrous prices.

When they arrived, I was a bit taken aback. I'm not sure what I'd expected, but they weren't it. They seemed . . . well, they seemed so normal. It was like meeting two couples from anywhere for a Monday-morning coffee. Which I have to admit slightly disappointed me. I wanted the portrait of Dorian Gray.

We sipped and chatted for quite a long time before I plucked up the nerve to ask about the sex shows. In fact, they were on the verge of leaving. Convinced my face was as red as a Scotsman who's fallen asleep on the beach, I hummed and hawed through the question: 'Did you . . . I mean, I know you must have had this asked so many times, but I've been reading up a bit about the island's history and there was this goddess, and the ceremonies, funnily enough . . . the priest and priestess used to actually have, erm, kind of on stage, you know, like, shows? And I wondered if you knew this when you did the shows?'

'Do you mean the sex shows?' Mike seemed puzzled.

'Er, yes.'

'I didn't,' said Andy, interested.

'Well, I knew a lot about the history of the island,' Mike came in. 'I mean, it just seemed that the energy was right, you know, for the island. It seemed to fit on the island. Plus, the club needed a boost and it just felt the right thing to do.'

I blushed again, and changed the subject to DJs, saying how good Danny Rampling had been and wondering who they had playing for them.

'We don't use big-name DJs,' Andy said. 'Although we do use Alfredo.'

Alfredo. I hadn't been sure he still lived on the island. There were rumours that he'd taken the success of his disciples badly. Some people said he was annoyed that Paul Oakenfold earned hundreds of dollars an hour playing in Las Vegas while he remained on Ibiza, unrecognized by the industry he had created. There was talk that young DJs found the buttons on the mixer all out of whack when they took over from Alfredo, so that their first record bombed and they had to work to bring the crowd back. And since I'd arrived, people had been telling me they hadn't seen him around this summer. It seemed to some that he'd disappeared. I begged Andy for Alfredo's number and, pausing only to ask for free entry to the club that night, ran for the phone and called him.

Although his voice sounded faint, he was very calm and polite, as if hysterical men calling him on his mobile were the commonest thing in the world. We arranged to meet that afternoon. He lived in the old town, he told me, right in the heart of the old hippy quarter, near the Placa des Parc – the square I'd stayed in on my first night in Ibiza.

I set out early and arrived outside his house about three quarters of an hour before our appointment. As I tried to work out what to do for the next forty-five minutes, Alfredo rang, trying to rearrange.

'I'm having a bit of a stressful time in my life,' he said, awkwardly.

'Oh,' I said, rather glum. 'But I'm just outside.'

There was a long pause.

'OK, we do it now.' He sounded tired. 'You know the market square? I'll meet you there in five minutes, Café Tomate.'

The 'market square' is the Placa de sa Constitucio, a peaceful square of elegant whitewashed and ochre-painted old merchants' houses that surrounds a pillared neo-classical roofed market where fruit and vegetables have been traded since 1873. Most Ibicencos, displaying, as always, their eminently pragmatic approach to life, now shop at supermarkets with air-conditioning, or at the far larger market in the New Town. A handful of stall holders still do a desultory trade with the odd local, however, and there's plenty of walk-through tourist business as the placa leads to the main ramped entrance to Dalt Vila.

Café Tomate was a small, sophisticated espresso bar offering the usual medley of coffee options as well as an incomprehensible list of hand-squeezed juices. By the time Alfredo arrived I'd tussled with various mistranslations of Spanish words for watermelon, given up and ordered the standard-issue *café con leche* and *agua con gas*. Alfredo lurched towards me at the helm of a vast dog that looked barely two evolutionary steps away from a killer wolf. I have already explained that I'm a fairly tall character – indeed, I'm usually the first to know it's raining – and this beast came up to my waist.

Alfredo ordered a water and turned to face me. I'm not sure what I was expecting him to look like – some mighty ego-driven, cocaine-fuelled club god in a leather jacket perhaps – but it wasn't this. His frame was slight and wiry, and his face carried the ghost of a tan; set deep into it were two pale blue eyes that seemed to carry a sheen as if he was barely a step away from tears. He spoke so quietly that I had to lean forward to catch what he was saying, and every now and then he would be drowned out altogether as his hound raised its muzzle and howled at the sky.

He started by asking me to switch off my tape recorder and put down my notebook. He just wanted to talk, he said; he didn't want to give an interview. He was having a tough time, his spirits were very low, and he didn't want this on the record at all. We spoke about lots of things: his love life, his depression, his regrets about the past and why he still stayed on the island; we talked about reggae, his favourite music, and his trips to play in smaller clubs around the world. 'People book me all over the world.' His voice was almost a whisper. 'I still love to play, but sometimes I wonder if I did the right thing. I am grateful to Manumission for giving me the work they do, but sometimes it's hard to put the head-phones on.' He paused and stared at the table, then looked up towards the walls of Dalt Vila. For a second I wondered if he knew I was there. Then he spoke again, but I wasn't sure I understood him. 'You know, this island is like a boat,' he said. 'People get on, people get off, but while they're here they have to get along.'

He turned to me, smiled, and said he had to get ready. I told him I was coming to see him play that night and he smiled again. We shook hands softly and he wandered out of the square, occasionally battling to keep his huge dog under control.

It made me wonder about the life of a DJ. Nightclubs are unreal places, intense and shallow at the same time, filled with instant satisfaction but ultimately only rewarding in the short term. Living your life in them, playing records every night to crowds of drunk or drugged young people, watching them stay the same age as you grow ever older – it must be like spending a lifetime eating chocolate eclairs in a student cafeteria, watching your soul drip like cream onto the plate.

That night, I took advantage of Andy's proffered guest-list place and clothed myself as best I could given a spartan wardrobe. As soon as I walked in, I felt underdressed. It was like a waiting room in heaven. Slim, tanned and beautiful young people drifted past, chatting to their friends, dancing to the driving beats and gazing up at an almost constant stage show that blended Keystone Kops slapstick chases with erotic bumping and grinding in a *mélange* I had not thought possible.

The club itself seemed infinite. Every time I turned a corner another bar appeared, or a small garden with sub-tropical flora, or a restaurant, or a new dance floor playing seventies funk, or – but of course – a merchandise shop. Every now and then the crowd would grab me in an undertow and I would be propelled through doors or down stairs like a twig bobbing along in rapids. Always I would return to the huge dome, high above my head like the observation tower of a space station on some Martian moon. Through it, the sky seemed dusted with more stars than I'd ever seen in London, and the moon seemed larger, as it does in corny rom-coms when he says he loves her at the climax of the feature.

Buffeted back into the main room, I looked around me at the dance floor, at the bodies writhing, at the performers prancing, at the DJ mixing and the dealers dealing. They might have stopped the live sex shows, but this was still a temple to a love goddess. Or it represented the worst indulgences of Nero's Rome, depending on your point of view. And then a dealer came by and offered me an E for a miserly price. I stared at him for a little too long; just as he started to get annoyed, I thrust my hand into my pocket and handed over some grubby notes. He slipped a tiny pill into my sweaty palm and melted into the crowd.

I moved off to the side of the dance floor, leaned against a pillar and thought about it for a while. I hadn't taken Ecstasy for a long time. For a while, in the mid-1990s, I'd taken a lot of it. It had become a prop, a happiness substitute during a very dark time. I was directionless, lonely and shy; taking the drug made me happy, filled me with a certain aimless form of confidence and offered me large enough weekends to forget about my direction entirely. Suddenly, however, a whole new truckload of dark times arrived and I suspected the drugs had a big part to play. I cut down, then stopped, then crashed as my brain tried to balance out all the chemicals surging around inside. It took me a good couple of years to sleep well again, although the depression lasted only a couple of months.

Lost in thought, I suddenly saw Andy walking towards me. He smiled and stood next to me with the air of a man who really needed to keep walking.

'Looks pretty full.' I nodded towards the crowd.

'Yeah,' he agreed carefully, 'but we're working very hard this year. I think this could be our best year yet, but it's very hard work.'

I asked him why.

'Well, we're in at the death of club culture.' He spread his hands out in front of him. 'I mean, it's had a bloody good run. What other music has dominated the planet for fifteen years? But Ibiza's going to have to get used to the decline of that British clubbing crowd. They've got other countries to rely on, but they can't bank on the clubbers any more. I think that's good though. Three years ago, every DJ had to play exactly the same records or people would walk off the dance floor. Now it's time for Ibiza to get creative again.'

He pushed on past me with a smile, a man with things to do. I considered the surging crowd and made my decision. It might not have been the right one, but at least it was a decision. I walked out of the guest-list entrance, climbed into my car and drove down the winding car-park exit slip onto the main San An–Ibiza Town road. Queues of cars snaked beside me, all of them packed with people, all of them heading in the opposite direction – towards the club, not home to bed.

Just before I turned onto the wide tarmac, I pulled in and stared down towards the walls of Dalt Vila, a city as old as Rome and thriving almost a thousand years before London's foundations were laid. I wound down the window and the warm night air flooded in, overpowering my feeble air-conditioning. I could hear the cicadas chirping and the throb of the bass drum from Privilege's glass-domed roof. I felt the hard nub of the pill in my jeans pocket, pulled it out and held it up to my eye in the dim light, then heaved it out onto the main road. It rolled off into the night and I watched it go for a second, then looked back at Ibiza Town and drew a deep breath.

'All right,' I said, out loud. 'What's next?'

CHAPTER 14

The End

In September I flew back to the island for the Closing Weekend, the official end of the clubbing season. Most of the clubs have their farewell parties around the middle of September, but Space throws a final, outlandish beano on the last weekend of the month. Some people take a plane out on Friday night, stay up all the way through and crash out on the late-night Sunday return before walking into the office on Monday morning.

I am made of softer stuff, so I resolved to steer clear of Space, at least until the sun went down. To pass the time, I made my way to La Marina, sat at the Café Mar Y Sol and flicked through my notebooks from the whole of the summer. I could see the names of all my vanished boys and girls: Raoul Hausmann, Tony Pike, Nico, Colin Casbolt, Elliot Paul, Erwin Broner, Marina Nixon, Stephen Seley, Laurie Lee, Sue Bennison, Freddie Mercury, Denholm Elliott, Alfredo, the Manumission crew, Mad Mike, Elmyr de Hory, Walter Benjamin, Brendan Behan – the list seemed almost endless. People fleeing hatred and violence, or a society of square pegs that couldn't find a hole to slot themselves into. Heading out to somewhere so they could vanish – to dream, forget and love.

Of course, it didn't always work. Sometimes their past caught up with them. Sometimes they inadvertently brought their past along with them. Sometimes an island paradise where everyone loved them and the good times were easily to be had was just a bit too much and they buckled under the pleasure of it all. But sometimes the island gave them what they wanted, becoming a place of sanctuary and joy, guarded and blessed by the benevolent pot-bellied dancing god.

And what about the rest of us? Older and wiser civilizations have always known that people need to let off steam. Whether you call it carnival or bacchanal, there has to be some time or place when the rules break down and you can do what you want, if only for a day. There's no space for that within today's cold, conformist culture. Absolute pleasure is vaguely sinful while pain, denial and sacrifice make you deserving – of respect, of admiration, of charity and of a place in heaven.

Recently I heard a radio programme in which a former MP discussed his attempt to live on unemployment benefit for a week. He struggled and failed with surprising good grace. Afterwards, though, he expressed horror that the people he met would cut corners and set aside cash to buy a pint and a packet of fags. It seemed utterly wrong to him that a brief moment of pleasure should be seen as one of the essentials of the human condition.

It reminded me of a flatmate of mine, a well-educated bloke who liked to talk about the ancient Greek philosopher Epicurus. Epicurus, Richard would explain earnestly, thought our life was simply this life on earth. No heaven, no hell, and above us only sky. There was this life, this universe, and its beauty and terror were ours. He believed we were in control of our own future and could decide on our course through life using reason rather than religious fear. But, above all, he believed in pleasure.

These days we think that by pleasure Epicurus meant the fine things in life – yachts, expensive wine, rich food and first-class air tickets. In fact, he saw pleasure as the absence of pain. For Epicurus, that meant having enough food and clothes and shelter to keep you from hunger and cold; it meant having good friends to talk to; it meant being free from control, from your employer or political master telling you what to do; and it meant freedom from fear. He bought a garden, grew his own food, and moved all his friends in. They spent their time discussing all their fears and worries until they were able to dismiss them and live in perfect happiness.

At the beginning of the twentieth century, Ibiza was a tiny island, largely ignored by the rest of the world. It struggled with famine and a medieval infrastructure for fifty years so that in 1950 it was still one of the poorest regions in Europe. Then they started selling moments in that garden – an Epicurean instant of pleasure when you push back from the table, sip your drink and look round at the people you're with, the people you love. Or maybe that moment is Saturday night after a week on the beach building up a celebrity tan to cover the pallor of another year in a grey stone city under the neon light of a soulless workplace, that moment when you step up to the podium and become a dancing god. Or maybe it's just that you don't have to answer the phone for one whole week, and the people in the street smile as you pass by. On an island where no-one minds who you are, you can finally be yourself.

There is supposed to be a Nostradamus quote – 'Ibiza will be the Earth's final refuge' – which refers to a myth that the island stands at a confluence of winds that will somehow keep it safe come a nuclear apocalypse. In fact, the quote is made up. Believe me, I read every single one of his nonsense quatrains and even got an expert to confirm the glaring absence. But, in a way, it's a little bit true. On a grim planet of war, disaster, lies and death, we all need somewhere we believe we can hide.

Just before I went to Space, I drove back to Sa Torre, Pedro's hotel outside San Antonio, to watch the sunset one last time. Pedro welcomed me with a hug and told me he was now a father. I bought him a drink. He bought me one right back. Then he stood to his decks and I wandered out to the patio to watch the day drift to a close. By the time the sun touched the sea, there were maybe twenty or thirty people sitting on the terrace, gazing out in rapt silence. Just as the disc lost its first, tiny sliver of light, Pedro switched the music from mellow, Latiny dance rhythms to an operatic air. As the woman's voice soared high I turned to look at the small group around me.

Over on the left there were dreadlocks, tattoos and piercings; right next to me a gang of German girls had their arms around one another, and just in front there were three sets of young lovers. I looked a little beyond them at the stairs leading to the sea. A few steps down sat a couple who must have been in their early fifties. As the opera singer's voice climbed still higher and the sun dipped further down, she rested her head on his shoulder and he wrapped his arm around her back. Their hair tangled together, both of them greying, both of them sporting the pink tan of the just-arrived holidaymaker. Maybe they were taking a break from the bustle of the family, maybe they had their child-rearing years behind them, but there they were, still sitting on a terrace to watch the sunset, still cuddling up together and still so clearly in love.

For some reason, as I watched them, I started feeling a fuzzy pricking at the edge of my eyes, the kind of feeling that ill behoves a hardened traveller and professional cynic. I blinked and looked away, then waved at the waiter to get me another beer. Maybe I'd looked into the sun for too long. That's probably it. Bright lights make you want to cry, don't they? Those Ibicenco sunsets can't be good for the eyes.

Picture Credits

View of Cala d'Hort and Es Vedra Islands. Robert Harding; statuette of Bes, Phoenicia, sixth-fifth century BC, Louvre, Paris. © RMN.

*Ibiza Bay from Dalt Vila, c. 1910. © collection Angela Sillars; Ibiza Bay, 2004. © Michael Stuart; Las Salinas. © Iain Stewart; *salt workers, 1950, by Frances Català-Roca. © Archivo Català-Roca; *traditional dance c. 1934. © Josep Planas y Montanyà; Clubbers, 1997. © Franck Sauvaire.

Still from *More* by Barbet Schroeder, 1969. BFI Stills, Posters and Designs; *Clifford Irving and Stephen Seley. © collection Martin Davies; *Bar Domino, 1961. © collection Jan Cremer; *street party, c. 1975 © Oriol Maspons; Day of the Drums, 1996. © Franck Sauvaire.

Drunken tourist, 1984. © Getty Images; Atlantis. © Iain Stewart; Freddie Mercury and Montserrat Caballé, 1984. © Richard Young/Rex Features; Manumission, 1984. © John Bryson/Rex Features.

Es Vedrà at sunset. © Iain Stewart; terracotta female bust, Ibiza, fifth century BC. Museo Arqueológico, Ibiza/Bridgeman Art Library.

*These photographs were originally published in *Eivissa-Ibiza: A Hundred Years of Light and Shade* (2000), edited by Martin Davies and Philippe Derville.

Index

NOTE: Names beginning with the prefix 'al-' are filed under A. Names of mythological/legendary people appear in *italics*.

absinthe 216, 221
Abu Ali Idris ibn al-Yaman (al-Yabisi) *see* al-Sabbini
Acid House 311
actors' holiday homes 257–9
agriculture 93, 95, 114
air travel 216–17, 287–8, 300
al-Himyari (Arabic author) 113
al-Kazwini (Arabic author) 113
al-Makkaari (Arab geographer) 112–13
al-Murtada 119
al-Sabbini 117–18, 243
al-Yabisi 117
Alfonso, Jorge 299–301
Alfredo (Jaime Fiorito) 308–10, 320–3
Algeria 144
Ali of Denia, king 117
almadraba fishing technique 94
Almohads 120
Almoravids 119–20
Alonso, Manuel 59
American War of Independence 142
Amnesia nightclub 242, 301, 305, 307, 308–10
Amsterdam artists in Ibiza 215

An Angel at My Table (film) 231
Anant (hippy-entrepreneur) 242
anarchism 174, 175
Anfora gay club 124–5
anti-Semitism 122–3
Apicius 74
Appert, Nicolas 77
Arberry, A. J. 118
archaeology 93
Arianism 114
Arias, Rodriguez 163
arson 65, 67, 318
art forgery 198–9, 201
    see also Hory, Elmyr de
artists 156–7, 215–18
Assyrians 36
Astarte (Phoenician goddess) 35, 39, 41–4
Atlantis 227, 230–1, 244–6

Baez, Joan 268
Bagwan Rajneesh cult 234–7, 307
Balearics
    and Almohads 120
    and Almoravids 119–20
    early mass tourism 290
    government 78–9
    origins 17–18

ball pagés 4
Banca Matutes 146–7
Bar Bahia 219
Bar Muralla 125
Bar Puerto 157
Barbarossa *see* Khizr
Barcelona 12–13, 111, 302
Barrau, Laureano 157
bars and clubs *see individual names*
Base Bar 25–6
Basque people 75–6
Bayo, Captain Alberto 179–80,
    181–2
beatniks 230–1, 303
Beevor, Anthony 186
Behan, Brendan 215–16
Bell, Andrew Napier 268
Benirras beach 152, 242
Benjamin, Walter 157, 282, 292–3
Bennison, Sue 30, 31–4
Beran, Bruno 157
Berbers 112, 119, 120
Berchtold, Erwin 215
Berlitz Spanish Phrase Book 25
Bes (god of safety, protection and
    dance) 9, 21–3
Bible 40–1
Birkett, Michael 292
Black Panthers of Figueretes 303
Blue Rose lap-dancing bar 107
Bolt Hole (Santa Eulalia) 190
Bonaparte *see* Joseph Bonaparte;
    Napoleon Bonaparte
Bonet, Rafael Costa 62–4, 85
bonfires 104–6
*The Book of the Banners of the
    Champions* 118
Botafoc Marina 319
Bradford, Ernle 42
brigantine 139
British expatriates 187–8, 193–4,
    253
British Museum 38
Broido-Cohn, Vera 158, 159, 161,
    185

Bromley (Kent) 59–60, 96–7
Broner, Erwin 123, 157, 163,
    214–15
Brown, Patricia 90–1
Buget, Narcis 156
building
    development 70–1
    finca architecture 161–2
    taxation 91
Byzantium 114–15, 134

Café del Mar 281–3
Café Tomate 322
Caja del Mediterráneo (CAM)
    147
Cala Conta 242
Cala de Sant Vincent 164, 167–8
Cala D'Hort 70–1, 79, 227, 246,
    248–50
Callow, Simon 262–3
Calvi, Giovanni Battista 76
Campbell, Lady Malcolm 203–4
Campion, Jane 230
Can Punta 242
Capella Sant Ciriac 92
Carbonell, Llorenc 159
Cardona, Bishop 181
Carthage 52–3, 55, 56–7
Carthaginians 4, 35–7, 50–1, 162
Casbolt, Colin 191, 192–3
Catalan language 63, 69, 86,
    110–12, 129
    distinct from Ibicenco dialect
    111
Catalans 5–6, 76
CEDA (Confederacion Española
    de Derechas Autonomas) 173
celebrities *see individual names
    and clubs*
Chamberlain, Jacques 204
Charles III, king 76
children attending festivals 100,
    102, 103
China and salt 72
Christianity 22, 39

Arianism 114
church attendance 174–5
and Reconquista 119–21
see also Roman Catholicism
Ciudad de Palma (ferryboat) 184
Civil War, Spanish 63, 123, 164,
170, 171
burning of churches 181
delayed revenge-taking 186–7
leaflet raid on island 179
Republican invasion 179–81
war readiness on Ibiza 176–7
see also Nationalists;
Republicans
cliff-jumping 242–3
'The Clomper' rucksack 30–1
Closing Weekend 327
Club 18-30 problem 291–2
Club Rafael 306
clubs
in London 310–11
see also individual names, e.g.
Amnesia; Space *etc.*
CNT (Confederacion Nacional del
Trabago) 173
cocaine 149–50
Coco Loco bar 318–19
College of Architects 78
Columbus, Christopher 128–30
communism 159, 173, 176, 185,
220
concentration camp (Formentera)
186
Conga club 65
Conillera 52
consell see politics, elections
Coogan, Michael David 40
Córdoba, Caliphate of 116–17
Cornelius family 98
Cornwall and tin 20, 21
Cornwallis, Lord 142
corsairs *see* pirates
Cosmi's Hotel (Santa Eulalia)
172–3, 188
costume, traditional 136–7

Cova des Cuieram 35, 46–50
cuisine *see* food
culture, Ibicenco 134

Dalt Vila 18–19, 27, 51, 92, 139
political affiliations 143–4, 175
dancing
flamenco 131–2, 133
hippies 238
Ibicenco 132–3, 160
Davies, Martin 107–10
Day of the Drums 152–6, 242
Diario de Ibiza 68–9, 182
Dido 36
Diodorus Siculus 50, 51
dogs *see* podenco hound
Domingo's bars (Clean and Dirty)
218–19
Domino's Café 24, 218
drag acts 60–1
'Dragons of Death' Italian platoon
184
Dragut (corsair leader) 137
dreams of paradise 193–4
driving on the island 276–8
drugs 149–51, 152, 191, 192–3,
265
in clubs 307–10
Ecstasy 30, 236, 307–8, 309
and hippies 234, 237
San Antonio bars 295–6
drumming *see* Day of the Drums
dye, purple 72–3

earthquake 66
Eco-Café (San Juan) 243
economy of island 20–1, 50–2, 286
1990s slump 298–9
post-Civil War 219–20, 222
VAT and Ecotax 291
see also salt flats/pans; tourism
Ecstasy *see* drugs, Ecstasy
education 175
Egg monument 128–9, 131
Egyptians, ancient 22

Eivissa (Ibiza) 64
Eivissa-Ibiza: A Hundred Years of Light and Shade (Davies and Derville) 108
El Divino club 66
El Gato festival 92, 175
El (Phoenician god) 38–40
Eleanor's Falcon 79
elephants 51, 54
Elliott, Denholm 18, 259–65
empire-building and salt 75–6
environmental problems 78–80
Epicurus 328–9
Equinox (Manchester gay village) 316, 317
Es Cucons hotel 296–8
Es Pins restaurant 251–2
Es Vedra rock 227, 246–50

Faber, Will 123, 157, 285
fake art 67
Falangists 173, 175, 184, 186
famine risk 217
Farragut, Mariano Juan 256
federation of Ibiza 94–5
Felicity (brigantine) 139–41
Fernand VII, king of Spain 143
Fernando, king of Castile 120–1
Ferrer, Juan Lluis 68–9
festivals 92–3
    see also free party movement;
        individual festivals
Figueretes 107, 302–3
Fina, Ramón 157
finca architecture 161–2
Fiorito, Jaime *see* Alfredo
fire-jumping ritual 104–6
firework display 1–2, 3
fish, salted 75–6
fishing 94
flamenco 131–2
Flood myths 16–17
Flynn, Errol 255–6
food, Ibicenco 253
    package hotels 279–80

football and politics 69
Formentera 18, 70, 96, 115, 122–4
    in Civil War 179–80, 185–6
    land ownership 174
    pig smuggling 145
    pirates and plague 136
    politics 176
    recolonization 138
Frame, Janet 230–1
France and Peninsular War 142
Franco, General Francisco 63, 110, 176, 178, 185
    and mass tourism 287, 290
    post-Civil War 217–18
free party movement 242–3
'Frenchman' *see* Villain, Raoul
Friends of the Earth 78

Gaetulicus, Caius Julius Tiron 97
Gaius Marius 95
galleons 135
galleys 21, 23, 136
Garbi Disco (Figueretes) 60–1
garum sauce 73–4, 93
gay community and visitors 124–7
GEN (Grupo de Estudios de la Naturaleza) 78–9
Genoa 75, 129–30
Gestapo in Ibiza Town 123
Gibraltar 139, 178
Goded, General 176
gods and goddesses 38–44
    see also *individual names*
gold trade 51
golf course construction 79
Green movement 78–9
Grunwald, Rabbi Moritz 123
Guardia Civil 239–41
La Guerra Civil a Eivissa I Formentera (Parrón) 185
Gulf Wars (1991, 2003) 152–3

Haedo, Diego de 135–6
Hamilcar Barca 52
Hand, Bad Jack 302–3

Hand, Philly and Peggy 302
Hannibal 52–6
happiness 8–9
Hasdrubal 53
Hausmann, Raoul 123, 157–61, 162–3
hedonism 7–8, 9–10, 43, 45, 93, 301
    final reflections 328–30
Heraclius, emperor 115
Hervey, Lady Victoria 312
Hindle, Dawn 316
hippies 26, 152–3, 227, 230–4, 303
    American draft dodgers 231
    Bagwan Rajneesh cult base 234–7
    European 232
    and Guardia Civil 239–41
    legacy 241–2, 243–4
    relationship with Ibicencos 238
Hispanic Society of America 148
History Buff's Guide to Ibiza (Kaufman) 108
history of Ibiza 3, 5–6, 9–10, 11, 36–7
    after fall of Rome 74–6
    Byzantines 115
    Civil War 171
    Fernando and Isabel of Castile 120–2
    Islamic rule 117
    its downfall 52, 53–4, 57, 74
    persecution of Jews 121–3
    Roman occupation 93–6, 97–8
    Visigoths and Vandals 113–14
    War of Spanish Succession 76
    see also Civil War, Spanish; *individual names and events, e.g.* Hannibal; pirates; salt flats/pans
Hoedown Barbecue *see* La Diosa restaurant
Holloway, Nicky 304, 305, 310
Homer 247–8

Honorius, emperor 113
hooligans, British 291–2
Hory, Elmyr de 201–14
Hostal Parque 25, 26
Hotel Abrat (San Antonio) 279–81
Hotel Augusta 147–8
Hotel de Portmany (San Antonio) 285, 293–4
Hotel El Corsario 215
Hotel Montesol 259, 294
Hotel Ses Figueres 89
hotels 287–8, 290–1
    see also individual names
house register 298
    see also building
Hughes, Dr Bart 237
Hughes, Howard 212
Huneric (Vandal ruler) 114

Ibiza Now magazine 87–8
Ibiza Town 3, 23, 50–1
    Anfora gay club 124–5
    artists' communities 215–18
    bars and restaurants 24–5, 218–19
    Carrer de la Verge 126
    compared with early London 51–2
    dockside 24–5, 51–2
    La Marina area 27–8, 51, 143, 175
    pirate attacks 136
    Placa de sa Constitucio 321–2
    Placa del Parque 26–7
    Renaissance walls 76
    Roman attack (217 BC) 55
    shopping 27
    in Spanish Civil War 182–4, 217
    see also Dalt Vila area *and individual bars, cafés, hotels*
Ibiza Uncovered documentaries 284, 292
Ibn Ganiya 120

Ibn Sa'id al-Magribi 118
Ignacio, Don (of Santa Eulalia)
181
Illa des Penjats 145
Illa des Porcs 145
Imilce (wife of Hannibal) 53
inheritance rules 45–6
Inquisition, Spanish 121–2
InterSun holiday company 32
Irving, Clifford 212, 213–14, 223
Isabel Matutes (schooner) 184
Isabel, queen of Castile 120–1, 128
Ishaq (son of Ibn Ganiya) 120
Islam 116–20
    see also Moors
Italy and Spanish Civil War
182–3, 184

Jagger, Jade 105
Jaime I (steamship) 216
Jamboree Jazz Club (Barcelona)
302
Jaume I (Catalan ruler) 5
Jaurès, Jean 168–9
Jews 118–19, 121–3, 214
Jones, Ernest 72
Jones, Grace 269, 306
Joseph Bonaparte 142
Juan, Captain 175
Julius Caesar 73
Justinian, emperor 114–15

Kaufman, Arlene 233
Kaufman, Emily 107–10, 131
Khizr/Barbarossa (pirate captain)
134, 135, 136, 137
Klub Shoom (London) 311
The Knight Has Died
(Nooteboom) 19
Kothuys, Anton 215
Ku nightclub (later named
Privilege) 305–7, 318

La Diosa restaurant 197, 199–201
La Tierra bar 233

Lake Trasimene 54
land customs and reform 45–6,
173–4, 298
language and dialect 63–4, 80, 86
    Arabic 112
    hierarchy and dispute 110–12
    social registers 252–3
    whistling language 137
Ledesma, Rafael Garcia 176, 181
Lee, Laurie 217, 291
Legros, Fernand 206–7, 208–9,
210–11, 213
Leonard, Vitol 157
Lessard, Real 206–7, 208, 209–11
Life and Death of a Spanish Town
(Paul) 147, 171
Livy 55
Llibreria international bookshop
87
Locomotives agency 30, 33
London clubs 310–11
Luis Salvador of Habsburg, Prinz
123

M&M's Bar (Santa Eulalia) 189
Macabich, Isidor 139, 175, 182
McCarthy, Joseph 220–1
McKay, Andy and Mike 316–18,
320
    and Claire 319
    see also Manumission club
'Mad Mike' 188–9, 194–6
Magon (Carthaginian admiral)
55–6
Mallorca 54, 113, 121, 176
    in Civil War 176, 179, 182
Malocello (Italian destroyer) 184
Man Ray 158
Mana coffee shop 65–6
Manchester clubs 316–18
Manumission club 44–5, 315–16,
319–20
    author's visit 324–6
Mar Y Sol Café 30, 183, 327
marble trade 51

Marga (in local newspaper) 69
Maria and Maime (owners of Es
    Cucons) 297–9
Marina (friend of Sue Bennison)
    34, 58–9, 64–5, 67, 83–6, 197,
    198
Marroig (Formentera) 122–3
marsh birds 77
Matt (friend of author) 296–7
Matutes family (Don Pedro and
    sons) 145–8, 183
Mayans, Mari 183
MDMA *see* drugs, Ecstasy
Meadows, Allgur Hurtle 208–10
Menorca 184
Mercury, Freddie 264–5, 269
Mestre, Juli 176–7, 177–8, 181
Michael, George 268
Michael (Mana coffee shop
    owner) 66–7
Miguel (La Diosa restaurant) 200
Minogue, Kylie 268–9
Moors 112–13, 116, 121, 135
    see also Islam
motorists *see* driving on the island
Movimiento Nacional 186
Muhammad, Prophet 115–16
Murex brandaris 72–3
music
    in clubs 302–3, 309–15
    DJ work 308, 313–15, 323
    in festivals 100–1
    see also Day of the Drums
Mussolini, Benito 182–3
My Disembarkation in Mallorca
    (Bayo) 180

Napoleon Bonaparte 142
Nationalists 176, 181, 182–3, 184
    pattern of violence 186
Nazis sheltered on Ibiza 214
Nico (Velvet Underground singer)
    243
Nieto, Miguel 157
nightclubs 30, 148

see also individual names
Nightlife club 310
Nixon, Marina 34, 58–9, 64–5, 67,
    83–6, 197, 198
Nooteboom, Cees 19
North Africa and Ibiza 112, 138
Nostradamus 330
Novelli, Michele 139, 141
Nuit de San Juan 91, 93, 99–106

Oakenfold, Paul 304, 305, 310,
    320
The Odyssey (Homer) 247–8
olive oil 93, 95–6
Olympia Press (Paris) 221
Onley, John 239–41
orchids, rare 79
Ortiz, Carmen 183
Ottoman Empire 134

P Diddy 312
Pablo (Hotel Ses Figueres) 89–91,
    106
Pacha nightclub 27, 67, 242, 272
PACTE Progresista 63, 70, 79–80,
    110
Padilla, José 281–2
Palau I Quer, Francisco 246–7
Palk, Bo 268
Palma 111
Parrón, Artur 185
Partido Popular *see* PP
Pascal, Blaise 194
Paul, Elliot 18, 171, 180, 181, 183
Pedro (Sa Torre hotelier) 33, 34,
    330
Penelope's nightclub 66
perfume trade 51
Perls, Klaus 205
Persians 115, 115–16
Philip V, king of Spain 76
Phoenicians 17, 20–3, 35–6
    deities 38–43
        see also individual names
    salt legacy 72

Pike, Anthony Dale 270, 274
Pike, Dounia 269–70
Pike, Tony 266–70
Pike's Hotel 265–6, 267–8, 270–1
pine wood trade 146
pirates 134
    adaptation to attacks 136–7
    Barbary corsairs 122, 135–7
    British privateers 139
    local corsairs 138–9
    subdued by French 144–5
    see also Khizr/Barbarossa;
        Riquer, Antoni
Pitiuses 115, 123, 158, 171
Pla, Cecilio 157
plague 136
Pliny the Elder 23, 52, 282
Pliny the Younger 98
podenco hound 254
Poindexter, Pony 302
police 154–6, 274
politics 69–71, 174–6
    elections 58–9, 62–3, 70, 83–6,
        176
    post-Civil War 186
    see also Civil War, Spanish; indi-
        vidual parties
Pontypridd Observer 68
population 299–300
porfedi (local song) 112
Portmany Hotel (San Antonio)
    157
pottery trade 51, 93
Pou des Lleo 180
PP (Partido Popular) 59, 64,
    69–70, 86–8, 176
    and Matutes family 147
Pratt, Sandy 251–2, 254–5, 257,
    258
PREF Party 58–9, 62–3, 69, 80
privateers see pirates
Privilege (formerly Ku club) 44,
    318
processions, late-night 28–9, 102
protest marches and rallies 70–1,

78, 79, 152–3
PSOE (Partido Socialista Obrero
    Español) 69–70, 173
Publius Cornelius Scipio 54, 55
pubs, British 187
Puig des Molins 50
Punic Wars 52, 53, 94

Quintus Fabius Maximus 54–5
Quintus Sertorius 94–5

Rampling, Danny 33, 304, 305,
    310–11, 313–14, 320
Reconquista 118–20, 134
Red House gallery (San Carlos)
    263
religion see Christianity; Islam;
    Jews; Roman Catholicism; syn-
    cretism
Renovación Española 173
Republicans 177–82, 184–5
    pattern of violence 186
Ribas, Antoni 159, 160–1, 176,
    185
Riego, Colonel Rafael de 143–4
Riquer, Antoni 138–41, 143–4
Riquer, Ignacio 172
road signs 63–4
roads, Roman 93
Robinson, Susan 260–1, 262,
    263–4, 265
Roca, Amadeo 157
rock stars influx 234
Rogers, Derek 178
Rolling Stones 314–15
Roman, Carlos 172
Roman Catholicism 98, 114, 122,
    173–5
    anti-clericalism in Spain 174–5
Romans in Ibiza, ancient 4, 23, 55,
    73–4
    author's early admiration 96–7
    federation 94–5
    fishing techniques 94
    golden age 93–4

relationship with island 95–6
  technology 93–4
Rome and Hannibal 55
Royal Navy 139
Royalty Hotel (Santa Eulalia) 172,
  188

Sa Caleta 23
Sa Torre hotel 33–5, 330
Sackler, Howard 256–7
Sainz, Rafael 166
Salinas *see* salt flats/pans
salt flats/pans 71–2, 74, 81–3
  Catalan generosity 75
  curing techniques 75, 82
  eighteenth century decline
    76–7
  export of salt 75, 82
  method of extraction 77
  modern development 77–9,
    147
  Muslim modernization 74–5
  plague effect 136
  War of the Spanish Succession
    76
  see also dye, purple; garum
Salt (Kurlansky) 72
Salvador, Cosmi 172–3
Salvador, General Julio 147–8
Salzano, Giuseppe 198–9
San Antonio 128–9, 275–6, 281,
  284
  Kiltie's Irish Bar 295–6
  mass tourism problems 291–3
  Scottish Pub 295
  West End 291–2
San Augusti 92, 242
San Carlos 180–1
San Jordi 83
San José 158
San Juan 93
  see also Nuit de San Juan
San Miguel (village) 186
Sandy's Bar 251, 258
Sant Raphael 197–8

Santa Eulalia 72, 124, 137, 187–9
  in Civil War 171–3, 174–5,
    177–80, 181
Santa Maria de las Neus cathedral
  3
S'Argenta iron mines 181
Satgunto 53
Scholem, Gershom 282
Schoulten, Adolf 158
Schroeder, Berbet 237
Scott, John 219
Seley, Rebecca 223–4
Seley, Stephen 220–6
Seltz, Jean 123
Senecio, Lucius Sempronius
  97–8
Serra, Juan Mari 85, 86–7
Sert, José Luis 163
shipbuilding 146
ships 51, 75–6, 113, 130
  author's ferry trip 11–12,
    13–17, 18–19, 23–4
  Barcelona–Ibiza steamers
    285–6, 287
  in Civil War 184
  cruise ships 299, 300
  European and American
    immigrants 216, 218
  refugee boats 184
  see also galleons; galleys; Royal
    Navy; triremes
Shulgin, Alexander 236
Sicily 21
silver trade 41
Skorenzy, Otto 214
Sleutelaar, Hans 282
slingshot fighters 54
smuggling 145–9
soil magic 23
Soler, Rigoberto 156
Sorolla, Joaquin 148–9
South Pacific (film) 248
Southern Ferries 14
soy sauce 74
Space club 303–4, 311–15, 327

Spain
    anti-clericalism 174–5
    civil war (1813) 143, 173
    class divisions 173
    land reform 173–4
    Napoleonic wars 142
    under Islamic rule 116–20
    see also Civil War, Spanish
Sperber, Josef 157
stalactites and stalagmites 48
Stamp, Terence 234–5
Stonewall riots (London) 126
street stalls in festivals 99
syncretism 99

Talamanca 89
Tanit (goddess of sexuality and
    death) 3–5, 35, 37–8
    and club culture 45–6
    Cova des Cuieram 35, 46–50,
        57
    worship changed to Juno 57
Tarragona 111
Theodosius I, emperor 22, 113
Thomas Cook travel agency 286
Thomas, Terry 233
tin trade 20–1, 51, 53
tobacco smuggling 145, 148–9
tolerance and lack of prejudice
    123–4, 301
tomato ketchup 74
Toonder, Jan Gerhard 222–3
Torre des Savinar 228
Torres, Father 172
Torres, Joán Serra I 177
tourism 70–1, 90, 147
    Club 18-30 problem 291–2
    early 285–7
    and Franco 287
    history of mass influx 284–92
    local problems 289–92
    need to go upmarket 299–300
    number of tourists 290, 299
    recuperación turística (1994)
        299

tolerance of local people 123–4,
    301
trade 51
trade unions 175
Trafalgar, Battle of 141, 142
Trafalgar Square potential 92
Trajan, emperor 98
trepanning cult 237
triremes 51
Tubbs, Jonathan 38
Tunnel Club (New York) 317
Tyre 35

UFOs 248, 250
Unsworth, Peter 252, 253–4
Uribarry, Manuel 179, 181
Urquhart, Babs 252

van Pallandt, Nina 212
Vandals 113–14
Vanishing Boy story 6–7, 10
Venice 75
Vespasian, emperor 57
Vietnam War 188–9, 216, 231
Villain, Raoul ('Frenchman' in
    Civil War) 164–71, 180
Villedieu, Daniel 126–7
Visigoths 113
Vives (pirate ship) 138, 140

Walker, Johnny 304, 305, 310
War of Spanish Succession (1702)
    76
water supply problem 87
watermelon fight 92, 93
Welles, Orson 213
West End, San Antonio 291–2
wheat-snatching from ship 138
Whittle, Danny 272, 273–4
writers, American 216

Yague, Juan 182, 183
Yahweh 40
Yebisah see history of Ibiza
Yern, Joán Riera 177